# ARGUMENTATION, COMMUNICATION, AND FALLACIES

## A Pragma-Dialectical Perspective

# ARGUMENTATION, COMMUNICATION, AND FALLACIES

## A Pragma-Dialectical Perspective

Frans H. van Eemeren
Rob Grootendorst
*University of Amsterdam*

LONDON AND NEW YORK

First Published by

Lawrence Erlbaum Associates, Inc., Publishers
365 Broadway
Hillsdale, New Jersey 07642

Transferred to Digital Printing 2009 by Routledge
270 Madison Ave, New York NY 10016
2 Park Square, Milton Park, Abingdon, Oxon, OX14 4RN



**Library of Congress Cataloging-in-Publication Data**

Eemeren, F. H. van.
Argumentation, communication, and fallacies : a pragma-dialectical perspective / Frans H. van Eemeren, Rob Grootendorst.
p. cm.
Includes bibliographical references and index.
ISBN 0-8058-1069-2 (C)
1. Persuasion (Rhetoric) 2. Fallacies (Logic) 3. Speech acts (Linguistics) 4. Communication—Philosophy. I. Grootendorst, Rob. II. Title.
P301.5.P47E33 1992
401'.41—dc20 91-40241
CIP

**Publisher's Note**
The publisher has gone to great lengths to ensure the quality of this reprint but points out that some imperfections in the original may be apparent.

He thought he saw an Argument
That proved he was the Pope:
He looked again, and found it was
A Bar of Mottled Soap.
"A fact so dread," he faintly said,
"Extinguishes all hope!"

From *Sylvie and Bruno* by Lewis Carroll

# Contents

# Preface

We could not agree more with Gilbert Harman (1986) that there is a difference in category between "rules of inference" and "rules of implication." Reasoned change in view should not be conflated with logical proof of a conclusion. In our opinion, the dissociation from logic should even be carried one step further. If it is argumentative inference that we are interested in, reasoned change is to be put in the context of communication where one party attempts to convince the other party of the acceptability of a standpoint. This does not mean that logic has no part to play in the study of argumentation. A difference of opinion can only be resolved if the argumentative discourse complies with a variety of norms for critical discussion. Logical validity has its own proper place among the multifarious norms incorporated in the "rules for critical discussion."

In *Argumentation, Communication, and Fallacies*, a critical discussion is conceived of as an interactional procedure aimed at resolving a difference of opinion through a regular exchange of speech acts. The book provides an outlook on a theoretical framework for analyzing and evaluating argumentative discourse as a critical discussion. Particular attention is paid to the things that can go wrong in the various stages of the critical discussion. It is shown that the verbal moves that are traditionally known as fallacies can be regarded as specific violations of the rules for critical discussion.

Our general aim in this book is to elucidate, on behalf of colleagues and interested students, our own pragma-dialectical perspective on the analysis and evaluation of argumentative discourse, which brings together pragmatic insight concerning speech acts and dialectical insight concerning critical discussion. Although we frequently refer to the literature, at this stage, we refrain from making detailed comparisons with other approaches. Such contrasting reviews simply have to wait. The same goes for expounding on further elaborations and applications of our approach. We trust that those who care about method will appreciate that we have set these limits to our ambitions.

## ACKNOWLEDGMENTS

First, we would like to acknowledge that a substantial part of this book is based on work we have done with Tjark Kruiger at the University of Amsterdam. By their valuable and detailed comments on earlier versions of the manuscript, Trudy Govier and John Woods helped us further in focusing the book. We wish to thank them for the stimulating discussions we had with them during their stay in our department in 1987 and 1988. We are also grateful to Maurice Finocchiaro and Charles Willard for giving their careful attention to the manuscript and to Anthony Blair for his thoughtful reactions to some of our contentions.

The work on this book was supported by our fellowships at the Netherlands Institute for Advanced Study in the Humanities and Social Sciences (NIAS). We are greatly indebted to the Royal Netherlands Academy of Arts and Science for giving us the opportunity to set up a Nucleus Group on "Fallacies as violations of rules for argumentative discourse" and to spend the academic year 1989–1990 in the company of argumentation experts at NIAS.

The members of the NIAS group, Douglas Walton, John Woods, Scott Jacobs, Sally Jackson, Agnes Haft-van Rees, Agnes Verbiest, and Charles Willard, encouraged us to finish the book by making useful suggestions to that intent. We hope that they will find that the final result testifies to our ability to make good use of their sometimes radical and undermining remarks.

Eveline Feteris, Fellow of the Royal Netherlands Academy of Arts and Science, and our research assistants Rinke Berkenbosch, Susanne Gerritsen, Peter Houtlosser, Willem Koetsenruijter, Pauline Slot, Francisca Snoeck Henkemans, and Erik Viskil helped us in completing the notes and the bibliography. Thanks are also due to the anonymous referees of Lawrence Erlbaum Associates.

*Frans H. van Eemeren*
*Rob Grootendorst*

PART I

# ARGUMENTATION AND COMMUNICATION

CHAPTER 1

# The Pragma-Dialectical Approach

## STUDIES OF ARGUMENTATION

In the past decade, the study of argumentation has developed into a field of study in its own right.[1] This evolution is achieved by an interdisciplinary venture of philosophers, formal and informal logicians, discourse and conversation analysts, communication scholars, and representatives of still other disciplines. Depending on the perspective on argumentative discourse that is taken as a starting point, different outlines of paradigms have been articulated. Basically, Chaim Perelman and Lucie Olbrechts-Tyteca's new rhetoric, Stephen Toulmin's analytic framework, Michel Meyer's problematology, Charles Willard's social epistemics, Anthony Blair and Ralph Johnson's informal logic, John Woods and Douglas Walton's post-standard approach to fallacies, Jean-Blaise Grize's natural logic, Else Barth and Erik Krabbe's formal dialectics, and several other theoretical contributions already constitute more or less worked-out frameworks for the study of argumentation.[2]

In North America as well as in Europe the study of argumentation has for a long time been dominated by the works of Toulmin and Perelman. Both Toulmin

[1]Nowadays, the study of argumentation has its own scholarly infrastructure of journals (*Argumentation*, *Argumentation and Advocacy*, *Informal Logic*), book series (*Studies of Argumentation in Pragmatics and Discourse Analysis*, Foris Publications/Mouton de Gruyter), societies (American Forensic Association, Association for Informal Logic and Critical Thinking, International Society for the Study of Argumentation), and conferences (AFA/SCA at Alta, USA; Informal Logic at Windsor, Canada; ISSA at Amsterdam, The Netherlands).

[2]Cf. Perelman and Olbrechts-Tyteca (1958/1969), Toulmin (1958), Meyer (1986a), Willard (1989), Blair and Johnson (1980), Woods and Walton (1982a, 1989), Grize (1982), Barth and Krabbe (1982).

and Perelman tried to present an alternative to formal logic that is better suited to analyzing everyday argumentation. Both did so by taking the rational procedures of legal reasoning as a model to start from. In our opinion, however, the result is in neither case quite satisfactory. This is at least partly due to their ill-considered prejudice that for the analysis of argumentation logic has nothing to offer. Without paying any attention to modern developments, formal logic is equated with classical syllogistic logic or, just like that, declared inapplicable to ordinary arguments.

More importantly, for their parts, Toulmin's and Perelman's alternatives just as much fail to recognize argumentation as a phenomenon of ordinary language use that should be treated as such. By dealing with isolated arguments, and neglecting the pragmatic aspects of the verbal and nonverbal context of the speech event in which they occur, as for an alternative to formal logic Toulmin and Perelman have less to offer for the study of argumentation than they claim.

In *The Uses of Argument*, Toulmin (1958) provides a model that is supposed to reflect the structure of arguments. His model constitutes a description of the procedural form of arguments. According to Toulmin, this procedural form is "field-independent," that is, independent of the nature of the issues to which the argumentation refers. The soundness of argument is, in his view, not primarily determined by its procedural form, but depends on the extent to which the backing renders the warrant acceptable. As the content of a backing—as opposed to its form—is related to the nature of the issue to which the argument pertains, Toulmin concluded that the criteria used in assessing the soundness of arguments must be field-dependent.

Apart from some major theoretical objections to Toulmin's ideas, it is worth pointing out that it is difficult to apply his model to real-life argumentative discourse. For one thing, the crucial distinction between data and warrants is only really clear in certain well-chosen examples. In ordinary practice, if one tries to apply his definitions, the two types of statement are indistinguishable. This effectively reduces the model to a variant of the syllogism—or enthymeme, if the warrant remains implicit.[3]

In *La Nouvelle Rhétorique*, Perelman and Olbrechts-Tyteca (1958/1969) give a description of existing argumentation techniques. They reckoned argumentation to be sound if the intended effect ensues, that is agreement or more agreement with the proposed statements. Soundness, therefore, is here tantamount to effectiveness with the "target group." In their publishing practice, Perelman and Olbrechts-Tyteca's theory boils down to a stocktaking of types of elements that can serve as "points of departure" or as "argumentation schemes" in persuading the audience, which can be a "particular" audience or the "universal" audience. As a criticism, it should be pointed out that the categories in Perelman and

[3]For a more extensive evaluation of the theoretical and practical merits and demerits of Toulmin's contribution to the study of argumentation, see van Eemeren, Grootendorst, and Kruiger (1987).

Olbrechts-Tyteca's catalog are not well-defined and not mutually exclusive. In addition, there are many other infirmities that prevent its unequivocal application in argumentation analysis.[4]

In the same way that Perelman and Olbrechts-Tyteca used rhetorical tradition as a basis for the development of a "new rhetoric," protagonists of a "new dialectic," such as Barth and Krabbe, set dialectic rules for arguing parties who wish to resolve their dispute by means of a critical dialogue.[5] The methods used here that give shape to such a dialectic include those by Paul Lorenzen, Kuno Lorenz, and other members of the Erlangen School; ideas of argumentation theorists such as Rupert Crawshay-Williams and Arne Naess are also incorporated. The nomenclature of this argumentation theory is derived from Charles Hamblin (1970): "Dialectic" is interpreted as critical discussion aimed at concluding a dispute, and "formal" as strictly regulated.

## COMPONENTS OF A RESEARCH PROGRAM

Scholars of argumentation are interested in how argumentative discourse can be used to justify or refute a standpoint in a rational way. In our opinion, argumentative discourse should therefore be studied as a specimen of normal verbal communication and interaction and it should, at the same time, be measured against a certain standard of reasonableness. If pragmatics is taken to be the study of language use, the need for this convergence of normative idealization and empirical description can be acknowledged by construing the study of argumentation as part of "normative pragmatics."

A perspective on argumentative discourse is required that overcomes both the limitations of the exclusively normative approach exemplified in modern logic and the limitations of the exclusively descriptive approach exemplified in contemporary linguistics. Most modern logicians restrict themselves to nonempirical regimentation; most contemporary linguists, particularly discourse and conversation analysts, limit themselves to pure and "unbiased" observation. The study of argumentation, however, can neither be based, unilaterally, on experience nor

[4]For a more extensive evaluation of the theoretical and practical merits and demerits of Perelman and Olbrechts-Tyteca's contribution to the study of argumentation, see van Eemeren, Grootendorst, and Kruiger (1987).

[5]The meaning of the terms "rhetoric" and "dialectic" can be stretched to such an extent that they become virtually interchangeable. We think it important however not to obscure the basic distinction that rhetoric refers to the art of influencing an audience by effective speech and dialectic to the art of resolving differences by means of regulated disputation (cf. Finocchiaro, 1987b). Seen in a rhetorical perspective, it is, ultimately, always the audience that decides what is acceptable, whereas in a dialectical perspective the acceptability of a move also depends on whether it is indeed a constructive contribution to the resolution of the difference. One could, of course, put such external restraints on rhetorical acceptability that it is, in fact, identical to dialectical acceptability. Then the remaining differences between rhetoric and dialectic would mainly be a matter of procedure and emphasis. Cf. also Rescher (1977).

on mere intellectual construction, but these two approaches must be closely interwoven in an integrating research program. This research program is to create a line of communication—a *trait d'union*—between the normative and the descriptive.[6]

In our view, scholars of argumentation should make it their business to clarify how the gap between normative and descriptive insight can be bridged. The complex problems that are at stake here can only be solved in an adequate way with the help of a comprehensive research program. As we envision it, this program includes a philosophical, a theoretical, an analytical, an empirical, and a practical component.[7]

On the one hand, a philosophical ideal of reasonableness is needed and, starting from this ideal, a theoretical model for acceptable argumentation must be developed. On the other hand, argumentative reality must be investigated empirically and it must be determined where, in practice, problems do occur. Then, the normative and the descriptive dimensions must be systematically linked together by developing analytical instruments that make it possible to view argumentative reality in the light of the favored ideal of reasonableness.

On the philosophical level, the question of argumentation and reasonableness is at stake. By taking up the issue of what it means to be reasonable, scholars of argumentation must reflect on the fundamentals of the study of argumentation. As it happens, the conceptions of reasonableness entertained by argumentation scholars diverge from the outset, so that quite different outlooks emerge on what is considered to be an acceptable argument.[8]

Rhetoricians favoring an anthropological outlook equate reasonableness with the standards prevailing in a certain community and consider an argument acceptable if it meets with the approval of the audience. If the ideal of reasonableness is linked to a particular group of people at a certain place and time, the rhetorical approach can be characterized as *anthropo-relativistic*.

For dialecticians who maintain a critical outlook, reasonableness is not solely determined by the norm of intersubjective agreement but also depends on the "external" norm that this agreement should be reached in a valid manner. As they

---

[6]Among the protagonists of a purely normative approach to the study of argumentation are Biro and Siegel (1991), who reject all descriptive approaches as leading to relativism. For a critique of contemporary epistemological relativism, see Siegel (1987). Biro and Siegel want to apply only objective normative standards to arguments. A purely descriptive approach to the study of argumentation is advocated by Willard (1983, 1989). He rejected all normative approaches: "The field must not ally itself with any particular 'rationality' or play at rank ordering 'rationalities' [. . .]. The better program is to study 'rationality's' myriad manifestations and to analyze its various uses" (1989, p. 167). A case for the relativity of standards (and the autonomy of fields) is made in Willard (1983).

[7]Cf. van Eemeren (1987).

[8]Following Toulmin (1976), one could roughly distinguish between (formal) "geometrical," (empirical) "anthropological," and (transcendental) "critical" perspectives on reasonableness, roughly underlying logical, rhetorical, and dialectical approaches to argumentation, respectively.

regard all argumentation as part of a critical discussion between two parties who are trying to resolve a difference of opinion, their extra criterion for reasonableness is whether an argumentative procedure is adequate for achieving this goal. Because of this linking of the ideal of reasonableness to the methodic conduct of a critical discussion, the dialectical approach can be characterized as *critical-rationalist*.

On the theoretical level, scholars of argumentation give shape to their ideals of reasonableness by presenting a particular model of what is involved in acting reasonably in argumentative discourse. An ideal model aims at providing an adequate grasp of argumentative discourse by specifying which modes of arguing are acceptable to a rational judge in view of a certain philosophical conception of reasonableness. Thus, a theoretical framework is created that, if things work out well, can fulfill heuristic, analytical, and critical functions in dealing with argumentative discourse.

In a rhetorical model, the argumentation techniques that are thought to be effective in view of the knowledge and beliefs of a certain audience are listed. As the acceptability of argumentation is thus linked to the specific epistemic background of an audience, this approach can be called *epistemo-rhetorical*.[9]

On account of dialecticians regarding every argument to be part of a critical discussion, whether explicit or implicit, their model provides rules that specify which moves, in the various stages of such a discussion, can contribute to resolving a difference of opinion. If this methodical verbal exchange is seen, pragmatically, as an interaction of speech acts, this approach, which is advocated by us, can be called *pragma-dialectical*.

Whether a rhetorical model is used or a dialectical model, in both cases argumentative discourse as it actually emerges has to undergo some analytic interpretation before insight provided in the theoretical model can be brought to bear in practical situations. In their analytic endeavors, scholars of argumentation, in a similar fashion as Freudian analysts, systematically aim to link the exterior appearance of practice with their ideal model. On the analytic level, the central question is how argumentative discourse can be reconstructed in such a way that all those, and only those, aspects are highlighted which are relevant in view of the ideal model that determines the focus of attention.

In a rhetorical analysis, by reconstructing argumentative discourse, insight is provided in those aspects of the discourse that have a persuasive effect on the audience. Due to its emphasis on the effectiveness of argumentative patterns with respect to the people who have to be won over, a rhetorical reconstruction can be characterized as *audience-oriented*.

In a dialectical analysis, by reconstructing argumentative discourse, insight

[9]Willard's theory of argumentation provides a good example of an epistemo-rhetorical approach: "rhetoric as epistemic" (1989). Linking together argument and knowledge is a strategy that has been part of Willard's rhetorical approach to rationality ever since *Argumentation and the Social Grounds of Knowledge* (1983).

is provided in the aspects of the discourse which are relevant to the resolution of the dispute. Because of its emphasis on the function of argumentation in bringing differences of opinion to an adequate conclusion, a dialectical reconstruction can be characterized as *resolution-oriented*.

In order to determine whether a particular reconstruction motivated by a theoretical model is indeed justified, one needs to have an insight into the particulars of argumentative practice. This kind of insight is to be gained from empirical research. On the empirical level, scholars of argumentation describe the actual processes of producing, identifying, and evaluating pieces of argumentative discourse and the factors that influence their outcome. Such empirical research may vary from quantitative measuring to qualitative studies.

In a rhetorical perspective, the emphasis is on explaining the effectiveness of a variety of argumentative patterns with different kinds of audiences. It is being examined in which way stylistic and other phenomena, in a certain context, contribute to people changing their minds. The interest of the empirical research centers then around factors affecting the *persuasiveness* of argumentative discourse ("persuasives").[10]

In a dialectical perspective, the emphasis is on explaining the ways in which various argumentative moves contribute to resolving a difference of opinion. Which linguistic and nonlinguistic elements play a part in the process of rationally accepting or rejecting a point of view is being examined. Then, the interest of the empirical research centers around factors affecting the *cogency* of argumentative discourse ("operatives").[11]

Argumentative competence is a complex disposition whose mastery is gradual and relative to a specific communicative setting. This means that the degrees of argumentative skill can only be adequately measured by standards relating to the objectives inherent in the context of communication. In order to improve argumentative practice, by way of education or otherwise, argumentation should, therefore, be studied in its diverse institutionalized and noninstitutionalized contexts, ranging from the formal context of law in an address to the court to the informal context of an ordinary conversation at home.

On the practical level, scholars of argumentation put their philosophical, theoretical, analytical, and empirical insights to good use in developing methods for improving argumentative practice while systematically taking account of the

[10]In the literature on persuasion, the role of argumentation is valued in different ways. In their Elaboration Likelihood Model, Petty and Cacioppo (1981, 1986) make a distinction between the peripheral route to attitude change where argumentation does not play a role and the central route where it does: Persuasive outcomes are influenced by factors that vary with variations in the degree that receivers engage in "elaboration" of information relevant to the persuasive issue (cf. O'Keefe, 1990).

[11]An interesting empirical approach to the cogency of argumentative discourse can be found in the work of cognitive psychologists such as Evans (1982) and Johnson-Laird (1983), but they tend to restrict their experiments to deductive reasoning. For cogency-centered research into factors affecting the identification of argumentation, see, for example, van Eemeren, Grootendorst, and Meuffels (1989).

diversity of communicative settings. They examine how one can methodically increase people's argumentative skills and abilities in the production of argumentative discourse as well as in its analysis and evaluation.

In a rhetorical approach, these practical exertions amount, first and foremost, to giving people directions for arguing successfully. By sampling shining examples, and enforcing imitative training, students are taught how to persuade an audience. Due to its tendency to aim for providing cut-and-dried drills for handling argumentative discourse, the rhetorical approach to practical problems can be characterized as *prescription-minded*.

In a dialectical approach, argumentative practice is improved by furthering a discussion-minded attitude and, starting from an increased awareness of the obstacles, promoting insight into the procedural prerequisites for resolving conflicts. By treating their students as active discussion partners who can respond critically, dialecticians try to bring about in them a better understanding of the problems involved in producing, analyzing, and evaluating argumentative discourse. Through its emphasis on stimulating independent thinking about argumentative discourse, the dialectical approach to practical problems can be characterized as *reflection-minded*.

## PRAGMA-DIALECTICAL STARTING POINTS

Although argumentation is a phenomenon of language use, it is clear that argumentative discourse, unlike conversation analysts seem to think, cannot be adequately dealt with by linguistics alone, certainly not as long as linguistics perseveres in its current descriptive preoccupation. Then, all normative aspects of reasoning would not be taken into consideration, so that an argumentation theory would arise that does not enable a critical assessment of the acceptability of arguments. On the other hand, unlike many writers of logical textbooks seem to suggest, argumentation can also not be dealt with adequately by normative logic alone, certainly not as long as logic maintains its current neglect of empirical linguistic data. Then, not all relevant aspects of argumentation as it occurs in everyday discourse would be taken into account and, as a consequence, it is not clear whether an argumentation theory thus developed relates in any descriptive way to reality.

We propose an approach to argumentation in which the descriptive and the normative aspects are systematically combined. Linguistics, notably pragmalinguistics, can be instrumental in doing justice to the descriptive aspect; the development of the necessary insights can be based on the speech act theory inspired by ordinary language philosophers such as Austin (1962) and Searle (1969, 1979). By incorporating logical, especially "new dialectic," insights concerning validity, consistency, and other determinants of rationality, the normative aspect can also be given its due. In so trying to bring about a convergence of different angles, we would, in a certain sense, stimulate an integrating return to the classical

roots of the study of argumentation as exemplified in Aristotelean Analytic, Dialectic, and Rhetoric.

This is exactly what we aim to achieve in the approach to argumentation we present when we explain our pragma-dialectical theoretical viewpoints against the background of critical rationalist philosophy. Thus, we give shape to the ideal of reasonableness in critical discussion. The dialectical aspect consists of two parties who attempt to resolve a difference of opinion by means of a methodical exchange of moves in a discussion. The pragmatic aspect is represented by the description of the moves in the discussion as speech acts.

In our pragma-dialectical theory of argumentation, we describe argumentation as a complex speech act, the purpose of which is to contribute to the resolution of a difference of opinion, or dispute. It is characteristic of this approach that we aim at externalizing, functionalizing, socializing, and dialectifying the subject matter of the study of argumentation.[12]

Externalization is achieved by starting from what people have expressed, implicitly or explicitly, instead of speculating about what they think or believe. Internal states of mind are not accessible, or at least not directly accessible, to outside inspection. Furthermore, they cannot always be controlled so that it is not clear to what extent people can be held accountable. In externalizing argumentation, unnecessary guesswork about motives is avoided, whereas all available indications of the speaker or writer entering into obligations are exploited. Insofar as implicit elements can be made explicit in an adequate reconstruction, they can also be used, so that everything that creates a commitment for the language users is taken into account.

Functionalization is achieved by treating pieces of argumentative discourse as being instrumental elements in conducting real-life speech events, instead of treating them as being isolated logical inferences. It is only possible to acknowledge the precise role of certain verbal expressions if they are looked on as speech acts that are an integral part of the context of the speech event in which they occur. In a speech event, logical inferences need not always have the argumentative function of convincing another language user; they may also be part of an explanation or other complex speech act. Besides, speech acts in which no logical inference is drawn may also play a constitutive part.

Socialization is achieved by regarding argumentation as part of an interactional process between two or more language users instead of a reasoning product of just one language user. If argumentation is treated virtually as a monologue, no justice is done to the fact that it always aims at bringing about the effect that another language user accept a certain standpoint.

Dialectification is achieved by treating argumentation as a rational means to convince a critical opponent and not as mere persuasion. The dispute should not

[12]Cf. for the principles of externalization, functionalization, socialization, and dialectification, van Eemeren and Grootendorst (1984).

TABLE 1.1
Dialectical Versus Hypothesized Rhetorical Version of Research Program

| *Rhetorical Program* | *Dialectical Program* |
|---|---|
| Anthropo-relativistic philosophy | Critical-rationalist philosophy |
| Epistemo-rhetorical theory | Pragma-dialectical theory |
| Audience-oriented reconstruction | Resolution-oriented reconstruction |
| Persuasiveness-centered description | Cogency-centered description |
| Prescription-minded practice | Reflection-minded practice |

just be terminated, no matter how, but resolved by methodically overcoming the doubts of a rational judge in a well-regulated critical discussion.

Before going further into the starting points of our own dialectical approach, let us summarize our conception of the constitutive components of a coherent research program for the study of argumentation. For the sake of clarity, we do so by contrasting our dialectical version with the hypothesized rhetorical version (see Table 1.1).

## OVERVIEW OF THE BOOK

In *Argumentation, Communication, and Fallacies*, a theoretical account is given of how argumentative discourse can be analyzed and evaluated. For that purpose, argumentation is first put in a communicative perspective (Part I), then the fallacies are discussed that occur when certain rules of communication are violated (Part II). In so doing, a pragma-dialectic alternative is offered to both a linguistically inspired descriptive and a logically inspired normative approach to argumentation.

Part I of the book, "Argumentation and Communication," provides a theoretical framework for dealing with argumentative discourse. We discuss the speech acts that play a part in a critical discussion aimed at resolving a difference of opinion. The various stages of a critical discussion are distinguished and the communicative and interactional aspects are considered of the speech acts that are performed in resolving simple or more complex disputes. Argumentation is characterized as a complex speech act in the argumentation stage. In order to make up for the seemingly unworldly ideal of critical discussion, special attention is paid to various real-life complications in dealing with argumentative discourse. Some guidelines are formulated for analyzing indirect speech acts and unexpressed premises and the structural differences are discussed between single, multiple, co-ordinatively compound, and subordinatively compound argumentation.

After having dealt with these crucial aspects of analysis, Part II, "Communication and Fallacies," links the evaluation of argumentative discourse to its analysis and concentrates on the obstacles to achieving a resolution of a dispute. Making use of the theoretical framework outlined in Part I, we present 10 basic rules for critical discussion. For each of the various stages of the discussion we explain the kinds of fallacies that can occur in a critical discussion: with regard to advancing standpoints and doubt in the confrontation stage; with regard to the distribution of discussion roles and the point of departure of the discussion in the opening stage; with regard to the means of defense (involving unexpressed premises, starting points, argumentation schemes or logical argument forms) in the argumentation stage; and with regard to establishing the result of the discussion in the concluding stage. Fallacies in usage, which may occur in all stages, are discussed separately.

CHAPTER 2

# Standpoints and Differences of Opinion

## RESOLVING DIFFERENCES OF OPINION

The pragma-dialectical approach centers around resolving differences of opinion by means of argumentative discourse. To be able to explain what resolving a difference of opinion entails, we must first explain what we mean by argumentative discourse, or rather by a *discursive text*, as we call that part of the argumentative discourse where a resolution for a difference is concretely pursued. In this book, a discursive text is the fully fledged constellation of utterances (which may be either written or spoken) that have been advanced in defense of a standpoint.

A standpoint only requires defense if not everybody fully agrees with it. It may have become clear that this lack of agreement is the case, but it is also sufficient if there is a suspicion that this might be the case. In principle, a discursive text can always be regarded as part of a discussion, real or imagined by the arguer, in which the arguer reacts to criticism that has been or might be leveled against his point of view.[1] It is characteristic of a discussion of this type that a difference of opinion is made the issue of a dispute and that the language users who are involved in resolving this dispute attempt to do so by means of argumentation.

The utterances advanced in the argumentation are reasons or, as we prefer to call them, *arguments* relating to a standpoint. It is their function that makes arguments and standpoints different from other utterances: Neither arguments

[1]In argumentative discourse there are, in principle, always two parties involved, but in a discursive text the contributions of one of the parties are, as a rule, only implicitly represented: the argumentative discourse, which is basically dialogical, then manifests itself monologically.

nor standpoints are primarily characterized by their form or content. In the communication between language users, with a standpoint, a point of view is expressed that entails a certain position in a dispute; with an argument, an effort is made to defend that position.

The same utterance can have different functions. For example, "Capitalism no longer has a future" may be an argument in a discursive text in which the standpoint being defended is that all business enterprises must be nationalized, but it may also function as a standpoint in a discursive text in which, say, the argument has been advanced that capitalism has proved incapable of preventing an economic crisis. In other contexts the same utterance might be intended as a gloomy prediction, a hopeful prophecy, or an urgent warning.

A standpoint can have any content because one can have a point of view with regard to every and any subject. Standpoints may express opinions concerning facts, ideas, actions, attitudes, or whatever. They can relate not only to relatively simple matters but also to matters of extreme complexity. We can take the view that Amsterdam is the dirtiest city in Europe, Baudelaire is the best French poet, dictators are always right-wing, it is bad manners to let an old lady stand when you are seated, shot-putters are usually thought heavier than they really are, but we can also adhere to the standpoint that altruism is cunningly disguised egoism, the teaching of grammar has a beneficial effect on the way schoolchildren use language, behaviorism is an outdated psychological theory, or that quantum theory is confirmed by relativity theory.

If a standpoint is being defended, this means that its *acceptability* is at issue. The arguer acts on the assumption that others either doubt or might doubt the acceptability of his standpoint, even if they need not regard it as totally unacceptable. Thus the purpose of his discourse is to convince someone else of the acceptability of his standpoint.

An arguer can only resolve a dispute concerning a standpoint in a rational manner if he succeeds in convincing his addressee by means of argumentation of the acceptability of his standpoint.[2] Argumentation comprises the whole constellation of utterances advanced in defense of a standpoint. The argumentation can be very brief and simple, consisting of only one argument, or elaborate and complex, consisting of many arguments.

A dispute can also be more or less complex. In the simplest case, in the discursive text only one standpoint is defended. If there are more standpoints being defended, they may all relate to the same subject but they may also relate to various subjects. In the latter case, there is effectively more than just one dispute. This is an example of a simple case:

---

[2]When talking in a general way about communicative and argumentative roles such as speaker, writer, listener, reader, arguer, protagonist, and antagonist we use the pronouns "he," "him," and "his" to refer to the actor. We are informed that some readers might be afraid that this implies sexism on our part. It does not. Gender only matters when it comes to concrete examples. In those cases we always indicate the speaker's sex.

1. *Mary:* "I don't think you should object to my smoking."
2. *John:* "I'm not so sure."
3. *Mary:* "After all, I don't object to your *not* smoking."

From (1) and (2) it is clear that Mary and John have a dispute. In (3) Mary advances argumentation to defend her standpoint, formulated in (1). If her attempt to convince John of the acceptability of this standpoint succeeds, their dispute will have been resolved. Incidentally, this does not seem all that likely, because however simple Mary's argumentation may be, there appears to be at least one dubious premise that has been left unexpressed but which is, in fact, indispensable: Nonsmoking can be just as objectionable as smoking.

## POSITIVE AND NEGATIVE STANDPOINTS

Suppose three people are attending a lecture and hear the speaker express the opinion that behaviorism is an outdated psychological theory. It may be that one of the three agrees with this view, that a second disagrees with it, and that the third is not sure what to think. They might express this as follows:

1. "It is true that behaviorism is an outdated psychological theory."
2. "It is not true that behaviorism is an outdated psychological theory."
3. "I don't know if it is true or not that behaviorism is an outdated psychological theory."

These three reactions represent the basic positions that can be taken to the proposition "Behaviorism is an outdated psychological theory."[3] The feature common to (1)-(3) is that they all contain the proposition *behaviorism is an outdated psychological theory*, with respect to which the differing standpoints are adopted.

In (1) it is affirmed that behaviorism is an outdated psychological theory: A *positive* standpoint is expressed with respect to the proposition. In (2) it is denied that behaviorism is an outdated psychological theory: A *negative* standpoint is expressed with respect to the same proposition. In (3), finally, there is neither an affirmation nor a negation that behaviorism is an outdated psychological theory: *Neither a positive nor a negative standpoint* is expressed.

It might be said that (3) is a case of *no* standpoint or, to put it another way, a zero standpoint being adopted. This is what happens if, for example, a person does not wish to tie himself down to any particular standpoint or really has no

[3]Strictly speaking, there is still another possibility: (4) "It is true and it is not true that behaviorism is an outdated psychological theory," but in classical logic (4) is not possible (*tertium non datur*).

idea what to think of something. That person may even believe that it is unwise to tie oneself down on any standpoint about behaviorism because there is not enough evidence available. In this case, the speaker does, in fact, have a standpoint but it pertains to a *different* proposition ("It is true that it is not possible to decide whether behaviorism is an outdated theory").

A standpoint can be expressed in all sorts of ways, varying from the explicit and forceful "My standpoint is quite simply that behaviorism is an outdated psychological theory" to the more cautious and less forceful "I think that behaviorism is an outdated psychological theory." The proposition to which the standpoint relates may also be more or less far-reaching, varying from "My standpoint is that behaviorism is an outdated psychological theory" to "My standpoint is that some aspects of behaviorism are outdated."

We represent the three possible types of standpoint as follows:[4]

1. $+/p$ *positive* standpoint with respect to proposition *p*
2. $-/p$ *negative* standpoint with respect to proposition *p*
3. $\emptyset/p$ *zero* standpoint with respect to proposition *p*

Someone who has advanced a positive standpoint is thereafter *positively committed* to the proposition to which the standpoint refers and someone who has advanced a negative standpoint is *negatively committed* to the proposition. The pragmatic consequence is in both cases that he is obliged to defend that (positive or negative) standpoint if it is attacked, that is, if its acceptability is called into question. This obligation continues to exist as long as the standpoint is not retracted. Someone who has advanced a zero standpoint is *neither positively nor negatively committed* to the proposition. Strictly speaking, indeed, there is no standpoint at all. Consequently, there is no obligation to defend. Of course, the person who adopts a zero standpoint may well be attacked precisely for not adopting a standpoint, yet this is quite a different matter.

## SIMPLE AND COMPLEX DISPUTES

For a dispute to arise at all it is necessary that there be *doubt* concerning a standpoint in the sense that its acceptability is not taken for granted. Someone doubts a standpoint when he has not yet accepted it and wonders whether or not he should accept it. Expressing doubt amounts to challenging the proponent of the standpoint to defend it; it does not automatically mean committing oneself to accepting the opposite standpoint.

[4]The terminological and conceptual distinctions that are made in chapters 2-7 are indispensable for a correct understanding of Part II of this book; the notational representations are helpful to an unequivocal description of argumentative discourse.

Although, in practice, this is very often the case, it is not necessary that there be two opposing standpoints in order for a dispute to arise. The simplest kind of dispute means no more than that someone has advanced a standpoint and then meets with doubt. How strong the doubt is, and exactly how it is expressed, is not pertinent. Quite often the dispute has already been resolved before it is really noticed as such by those involved. It should be noted that a dispute is not necessarily a squabble, quarrel, or "argument" in the everyday sense.

Expressions of doubt can vary from "But isn't that complete rubbish?" and "I don't think so" to "I have my doubts about that" or "I'm not so sure." There are also cases in which doubt is not so clearly expressed, but in which it must be supposed that there is doubt. Disputes where this is the case can be termed *implicit disputes*.

Complex disputes can be analyzed by breaking them down into a number of less complex disputes. Their complexity can vary in several ways. In the first place we must distinguish between *single* and *multiple* disputes. In a single dispute a standpoint is questioned that relates to only one proposition, whereas in a multiple dispute a standpoint relating to two or more propositions is questioned. The negative standpoint "It is not true that women are better cooks than men" might, for example, give rise to a single dispute. A multiple dispute arises, for example, when someone produces the negative standpoint "It is neither true that women are better cooks than men nor that they are better drivers than men."

In the second place, we must distinguish between *nonmixed* and *mixed* disputes. In a nonmixed dispute either a positive or a negative standpoint with respect to a proposition is questioned, whereas in a mixed dispute both a positive and a negative standpoint regarding the same proposition are being questioned. If only the positive standpoint "It is unquestionably true that women are better drivers than men" is questioned, without the negative standpoint "It is not true at all that women are better drivers than men" being put forward in opposition to it, the dispute is nonmixed. It is nonmixed if the only reaction to the original standpoint was "I wouldn't know." If the positive standpoint had been countered with the negative standpoint, then the dispute would have been mixed.

In a mixed dispute not only mutual denial of the opposing standpoints is at stake, but also mutual doubt is assumed with respect to the acceptability of these opposing standpoints. There is no point in putting forward an opposing standpoint if there is no doubt about the original standpoint and without doubt about the second standpoint the dispute would no longer exist, because the first standpoint would have been given up in favor of the second (e.g., because the second standpoint comes from a real expert). Granting that there are two opposing standpoints without assuming mutual doubt, would mean allowing for the possibility of accepting contradictory standpoints. Then, talking about disputes loses its point.

A simple dispute that is both single and nonmixed represents the most uncomplicated or *elementary* form of a dispute.[5] Multiple disputes and mixed disputes are more complex. Even more complex disputes arise when multiplicity and mixedness are combined. For example:

Ann: "It is not true that women are better cooks than men, but it is true that they are better drivers."

Bob: "I disagree. In my opinion it is exactly the reverse: Women are better cooks but certainly not better drivers than men."

The possibilities that we have distinguished as regards to the complexity of disputes constitute four standard types:

1. single nonmixed disputes (elementary form)
2. single mixed disputes
3. multiple nonmixed disputes
4. multiple mixed disputes

Because the standpoint adopted in a dispute with respect to a proposition can be positive or negative, there are two variants of the elementary dispute. Referring to the persons involved in a dispute as *Language User 1* ($LU_1$) and *Language User 2* ($LU_2$), and indicating an expression of doubt by a question mark, we can represent the two variants of the elementary dispute as follows:

*The two variants of the elementary form of dispute*

1a. $LU_1$: $+/p$     1b. $LU_1$: $-/p$
$LU_2$: $?/(+/p)$     $LU_2$: $?/(-/p)$

Using the same abbreviations, symbols, and variables we can also characterize the other three standard types of dispute schematically:

*General form of a single mixed dispute*

2. $LU_1$: $+/p$ , $?/(-/p)$
$LU_2$: $?/(+/p)$, $-/p$

*General form of a multiple nonmixed dispute*

3. $LU_1$: $+/p_1$ ; $+/p_2$ ; . . . ; $+/p_n$
$LU_2$: $?/(+/p_1)$; $?/(+/p_2)$; . . . ; $?/(+/p_n)$

*General form of a multiple mixed dispute*

4. $LU_1$: $+/p_1$ , $?/(-/p_1)$; . . . ; $+/p_n$ , $?/(-/p_n)$
$LU_2$: $?/(+/p_1)$, $-/p_1$ ; . . . ; $?/(+/p_n)$, $-/p_n$

[5]As a dispute of the elementary form is the easiest to handle and a great many disputes in everyday life start off in this fashion, it seems sensible for didactic purposes to concentrate first on the problems of dealing with nonmixed single disputes. For such reasons, "academic debate" tournaments in The Netherlands have, in practice, been restricted to settling simple disputes.

The *p*'s in a multiple dispute are always indexed because such a dispute contains more than one proposition. A semicolon is used to indicate when a new proposition is considered, whereas parts of a mixed dispute that relate to the same proposition are separated by a comma only.

## Examples of the Four Standard Types of Dispute

1. *Single nonmixed dispute*

$LU_1$: This problem will be easy to solve.
$LU_2$: Will it?

a. $LU_1$: $+/p$
 $LU_2$: $?/(+/p)$

$LU_1$: This problem will not be easy to solve.
$LU_2$: Won't it?

b. $LU_1$: $-/p$
 $LU_2$: $?/(-/p)$

2. *Multiple nonmixed dispute*

$LU_1$: People marry too young nowadays, they get divorced too easily and they're terribly egoistic.
$LU_2$: Why too young? What do you mean, too easily? And I don't quite get the egoistic bit.

$LU_1$: $+/p_1$ ; $+/p_2$ ; $+/p_3$
$LU_2$: $?/(+/p_1)$; $?/(+/p_2)$; $?/(+/p_3)$

$LU_1$: Dutch men are not romantic . . .
$LU_2$: I'm not so sure about it.

$LU_1$: . . . And they're not spiritual either . . .
$LU_2$: Why not?

$LU_1$: . . . But at least you can depend on them . . .
$LU_2$: I wonder.

$LU_1$: $-/p_1$ ; $-/p_2$ ; $+/p_3$
$LU_2$: $?/(-/p_1)$; $?/(-/p_2)$; $?/(+/p_3)$

3. *Single mixed dispute*

$LU_1$: You should never take aspirin with milk.
$LU_2$: Sure you can!

$LU_1$: $-/p$ , $?/(+/p)$
$LU_2$: $?/(-/p)$, $+/p$

$LU_1$: You should always take aspirin with milk.
$LU_2$: No you shouldn't!

$LU_1$: $+/p$ , $?/(-/p)$
$LU_2$: $?/(+/p)$, $-/p$

4. *Multiple mixed dispute*

$LU_1$: People shouldn't protest so readily . . .
$LU_2$: I don't agree.

$LU_1$: . . . And they should leave each other alone as far as possible . . .
$LU_2$: I don't agree with that either.

$LU_1$: . . . And anyway all that protesting doesn't get anything done . . .
$LU_2$: Yes it does!

$LU_1$: . . . And decent people have got better things to do . . .
$LU_2$: What a bigoted point of view!

$LU_1$: $-/p_1$ , $?/(+/p_1)$; $+/p_2$ , $?/(-/p_2)$;
$LU_2$: $?/(-/p_1)$, $+/p_1$ ; $?/(+/p_2)$, $-/p_2$ ;

$LU_1$: $-/p_3$ , $?/(+/p_3)$; $+/p_4$ , $?/(-/p_4)$
$LU_2$: $?/(-/p_3)$, $+/p_3$ ; $?/(+/p_4)$, $-/p_4$

## Single Versus Multiple Disputes

In the utterance "It is true that a positive attitude toward the use of dialect often goes together with a declining mastery of a particular dialect" the standpoint refers to a proposition that is more complex than the proposition in the utterance "Saul Bellow is a writer." Besides such "qualitative" propositional complexity, there is also a form of complexity where the standpoint refers to a number of different propositions. This "quantitative" complexity occurs, for example, in the standpoint "The poor are getting poorer and pollution is getting worse." In a standpoint, even much more elaborate combinations of propositions may occur, as when the acceptability of an entire theory is at issue in the dispute.

In cases of quantitative complexity the multiple dispute can always be broken down into a number of single disputes. Then, each of the propositions can be individually checked to see whether the standpoint is defensible. In a dispute about the standpoint "Political scientists may know a lot about political science but they know very little about politics" it might, for instance, ironically emerge that it is very easy to prove that political scientists know very little about politics but not that they know a lot about political science.

It is in cases of propositional complexity not always immediately clear whether a dispute is single or multiple. Ultimately, even in cases of quantitative propositional complexity, it depends on the other party's reactions to a standpoint whether or not it is justified to regard the dispute as multiple. If more than one of the propositions leads to doubt or opposition, then the dispute is multiple. But it may also be that only one of the propositions gives rise to response. In that case the dispute is to be considered as single: The other propositions are not questioned.

## Nonmixed Versus Mixed Disputes

Because it is sometimes difficult to distinguish between doubt and a negative standpoint, differentiating between mixed and nonmixed disputes can also be a problem. In practice, for reasons of politeness or face-keeping, it is very common for someone who disagrees with a standpoint to cloak his criticism in an expression of doubt. If the reaction to a standpoint is, in fact, not just an expression of doubt but a negative standpoint, then the dispute becomes mixed. The crucial question that has to be answered here is whether or not a language user who expresses doubt in a standpoint in doing this also obtains a negative commitment to the proposition referred to in that standpoint. Only then a negative standpoint may be ascribed to him, so that the dispute must be regarded as mixed.

Someone who defends a particular standpoint will often act as if the person he is trying to convince has adopted the opposite standpoint, even if his opponent has not expressly said he has; the dispute is then treated by him as if it were a mixed dispute. At first sight it would appear that nonmixed disputes do not frequently occur in unadulterated form, but on closer inspection they are quite common in ordinary argumentative discourse: People often raise an eyebrow or resort to another token of uncertainty just to indicate that they have not yet fully taken the point.

Although the situation in legal contexts is slightly more complicated, criminal law proceedings in many European countries provide a nice example of a nonmixed dispute between the prosecutor and the judge. In criminal law, the prosecutor acts as the defender of a standpoint and the judge as a systematic doubter. The prosecutor asserts that the accused has committed some offense and the judge must investigate whether this assertion is correct. Here, in contrast to a civil process in which plaintiff and defendant often adopt opposing standpoints and the judge remains passive, there is no question of opposing standpoints.[6]

In connection with mixed and nonmixed disputes it may be useful to remind ourselves that the expression "to adopt an opposing standpoint" can give rise to misunderstanding, because contradictory and contrary relations are easily confused. For example, instead of the standpoint "It is not true that women are better drivers than men" ($-/p_1$), the standpoint "Women are worse drivers than men" ($+/p_2$) is often seen as the opposite of the standpoint "Women are better drivers than men" ($+/p_1$), whereas "Women are worse drivers than men" ($+/p_2$) does

[6]Cf. Feteris (1987, pp. 335-336).

exclude the possibility that they drive equally well and "It is not true that women are better drivers than men" ($-/p_1$) does not.

In the standpoint "It is not true that women are better drivers than men" ($-/p_1$) the standpoint "Women are better drivers than men" ($+/p_1$) is negated; in the standpoint "Women are worse drivers than men" ($+/p_2$), the propositional content of this standpoint is, as it were, reversed. As soon as someone opposes the standpoint "Women are better drivers than men" ($+/p_1$) with the standpoint "Men are better drivers than women" ($+/p_3$), the dispute should be treated as both multiple and mixed, because there are two different propositions at stake in which both parties are supposed to have opposing opinions:

$LU_1$: $+/p_1$; $?/(+/p_3)$
$LU_2$: $?/(+/p_1)$; $+/p_3)$

## THE VERBAL PRESENTATION OF STANDPOINTS AND DOUBT

In principle, it must always be assumed that the verbal presentation of his communication reflects the intentions of the speaker or writer. In practice, of course, there may well be something wrong with this presentation. However, unless we can ask for clarification, we must base our interpretation on the verbal presentation as has arisen, and try to find the interpretation of utterances that are obscure, opaque, or vague that fits best into the context.

Sometimes it is clear that the speaker or writer is unaware of the fact that he has said something other than what he meant. This might be a case of a slip of the tongue or pen, but it might also be a matter of incorrect usage, as when "on principle" is misused by a foreigner for "in principle": "On principle I don't drink, but I have absolutely no objection to a glass to keep someone else company." The discourse of certain individuals and groups may also display some special peculiarities that lead to them appearing to say different things from what they intend to say: "I would put a question mark against that one" meaning "I reject it", or "Personally, I have my doubts on that" meaning "I don't believe it."

In all these cases the interpretation has to take account of the intention the speaker or writer, in all fairness, can be presumed to have. Certainly this may mean that we are skating on thin ice. However, knowledge of the linguistic idiosyncrasies of particular persons or groups can be of help here. Suppose we realize that it is one of the features of the language of sportsmen that it is littered with "you know." It would then not be doing them justice to suppose that every time they said "you know" they were actually assuming that you did "know."

## The Verbal Expression of Standpoints

Usually, it is fairly clear which standpoint is discussed in a dispute. In ordinary discourse, even for a person who wants to express himself perfectly clear, there is no need to be wholly explicit for a standpoint to be recognizable as such. The context will, in most cases, make plain what he means. Furthermore, often there will be fairly unambiguous indications in the verbal presentation that we are dealing with a standpoint:

*In my opinion* children are the hope of the future.
*I think* children are the cruelest of people.
*If you ask me* there is no way of expressing the deepest essentials of things.
*My conclusion is* that people do crazy things out of boredom.
*That is why* it calms you down to categorize fear and anxiety.
*So* he can't have done it.
*Ergo:* The poor get poorer and the rich get richer.
*In short*, that is one thing we must never do.
*This is how I see it:* Even if it does no good, at least it will do no harm.
*The point is*, you see, that romantic love was only invented to enable women to be manipulated.
*Am I right in thinking* that Verner's law was the first law of phonetics?
*What we have to agree on is* that swimming on an outgoing tide is more dangerous than when the tide is coming in.
That assertion, *then*, is false.
He *erroneously asserts* that "nice" is an adverb.
*It is nonsense to say* that the onus of proof is on me.
*It would be a good idea* to call the meeting well in advance.
*Taking everything into consideration*, it can hardly be true.

There are also cases in which it would be an exaggeration to say that the verbal presentation indicates that a standpoint is being advanced, but where there is a pattern that often occurs where a standpoint is expressed, thus facilitating recognition:

*We must* give every man his due.
*You must* not let your food go cold.
Stupid people *should not be allowed* to have children.
The revolution *should* start with the individual.
*I'm just brainstorming, but* surely everybody's work is equally important.
*In other words:* People who go mad are too sensitive.
*That is* impossible.
Eating too much *is* criminal.

The final example ("Eating too much *is* criminal") is a good illustration of the fact that it is not enough to rely on the verbal presentation when making an interpretation. One should also use one's knowledge of the context, general background knowledge, and even any further specific knowledge one may have of the situation. After all, the utterance "Eating too much is criminal" may be a standpoint when uttered in a country, such as the United States, where food is overabundant, but when uttered in a famine-stricken region, such as the Sahel, it may be a statement of fact that causes no doubts whatever. As we have observed before, standpoints are functional categories that do not primarily depend on form or content.

In more lengthy discursive texts, the main standpoints are often repeated more than once. Because the formulations that are chosen are usually not exactly the same each time, there is danger of the dispute being wrongly thought to be multiple. The standpoint that is at the center of the dispute is not always stated once and for all at the beginning. For the sake of clarity, or because he thinks this to be more effective, a discourser may restate his standpoint halfway through his discourse or even at the very end.

Because standpoints can be expressed with more emphasis ("It is certainly true that . . .") and with less emphasis ("It is plausible that . . ."), and because they may refer to propositions of greater scope ("All great artists are homosexuals") or of lesser scope ("Some great artists are homosexuals), when repeating his standpoint, the speaker may avail himself of the opportunity to make it more or less emphatic, or more general or specific, than it originally was.

If the emphasis or scope of a standpoint changes substantially, it is, of course, no longer the same standpoint. If such a change occurs halfway through the argumentative discourse, a dispute that was initially a single dispute may expand into a multiple dispute, or an entirely new dispute may have replaced the original one. Very often, however, the purpose of repetition may be anything but the introduction of a new standpoint, let alone the elimination of the original one. When interpreting the discourse, bearing Occam's razor in mind, for the sake of economy, no more standpoints (and no more disputes) should be distinguished than are strictly necessary.

## The Verbal Expression of Doubt

If a standpoint is sometimes not immediately recognizable as such, the same applies, only more so, to doubt. Expressions that are more or less clear indications of doubt include the following:

*I am not at all sure* that she could not have done it.

*Might it not be* that swimming is no more dangerous on an outgoing tide than on a rising tide?

*Do you really think so?* I am not so sure that John is looking ill.

*I don't know* if children *really are* the hope of the future.

*Actually I still can't quite understand* why the revolution should start with the individual.

*Yes, it is a little difficult, but perhaps* it is not true that the poor are getting poorer and the rich are getting richer.

*I will have to think about whether I believe* that there is no way of expressing the deepest essentials of things.

Doubt often remains implicit. Even so, some form of doubt is always assumed by someone who defends a standpoint. Sometimes because he thinks he saw the other frowning, sometimes because he has tried to put himself in the other's shoes and believes that his standpoint might give rise to doubts in the other's mind.

Here, again, another complication must be mentioned, which might arise even if the doubt has been expressed explicitly: An expression of doubt is sometimes difficult to tell apart from a negative standpoint. This is especially true when a negative standpoint is put forward hesitantly or with some qualifications, then it might easily be confused with an expression of doubt.

CHAPTER 3

# Argumentation as a Complex Speech Act

## COMMUNICATIVE AND INTERACTIONAL ASPECTS

When a person speaks or writes, he uses words and expressions that perform certain functions when communicating and interacting with other people. Communicatively, his utterances can function as questions, promises, statements, and so forth; interactionally, they may, for instance, lead to an answer, a satisfied smile, or a request for further information. In so expressing his intentions, the speaker (or writer) performs various sorts of speech acts.[1]

Every speech act creates particular commitments for the person who has performed it. If he has asked a question, for example, he may legitimately be assumed to be interested in hearing the answer; if he makes a promise, he is supposed to carry out his promise; and if he makes a statement, he must be able to support it.

In a speech act, one or more propositions are expressed in which reference is made to something and a particular predicate is assigned to that referent. In the performance of the speech act the proposition is given a particular "illocutionary force," which provides the speech act with its communicative function. For example, if the speaker refers to the listener and assigns to him the predicate "has a feeling for logic," he can lend the proposition the communicative function of a question by saying "Do you have a feeling for logic?"

Speech acts are not fully understood by a listener (or reader) until he knows

[1]This approach to verbal communication and interaction is based on the amended version of the standard theory of speech acts expounded in van Eemeren and Grootendorst (1984). The standard theory was, of course, developed by Austin (1962) and Searle (1969, 1979). Cf. also Fogelin (1972).

both which propositions are expressed and which communicative function they have. Understanding a speech act is the *communicative effect* that is aimed at by the speaker. As a rule, the speaker will also hope to achieve an *interactional effect*: that the listener accept the speech act that is performed or respond in a certain way. The listener's accepting the speech act is an interactional effect aimed at in performing any speech act, regardless of other desired responses. It is this pursuit of acceptance that makes speech acts interactionally meaningful.

The communicative effect of understanding a speech act and the interactional effect of accepting it need not necessarily coincide. It is therefore necessary to make a theoretical distinction in the speech act between the aspect of achieving understanding and the aspect of achieving acceptance. In the first case, we refer to the speech act as a *communicative* act, and in the second as an *interactional* act.[2]

The extent to which a listener understands a speech act and the extent to which he accepts it need not, of course, be the same. Complete understanding may go together with complete acceptance but also with complete nonacceptance or partial acceptance, and all but complete understanding may not only go together with partial acceptance but also with complete acceptance or complete nonacceptance. To bring about any degree of acceptance, however, it will, in principle, be necessary to achieve at least some degree of understanding.

The communicative and the interactional aspects of speech acts are not entirely independent of one another. They are incorporated in the same utterance. Sometimes, there is even a more or less fixed association between the communicative and the interactional aspects of a speech act. In the absence of such a fixed association, there may be clues concerning their relation that are, intentionally or unintentionally, given by the speaker. Otherwise, their relation can only be recognized with the help of the context in which the speech act is performed.

## Identifying the Communicative and the Interactional Aspect

There is no unambiguous formal criterion for distinguishing between communicative and interactional aspects of speech acts. A simple trick for testing the presumed communicative status of a possible speech act denominator is the "hereby test":

> Take the first person singular of the simple present of the verb that best seems to indicate the communicative aspect involved, insert the word "hereby" between the personal pronoun "I" and the verb, and check whether this produces a normal utterance; if it does, the verb, indeed, identifies a communicative function.

For example: "I hereby *promise* I'll be on time tomorrow," "I hereby *confirm*

[2]In this way, we give a clearer and more specific meaning to Austin and Searle's rudimentary distinction between "illocutionary" and "perlocutionary" acts.

that you were on time." If the "hereby test" produces an odd, or even impossible, result, as in "I hereby *convince* you that I'm right" and "I hereby *walk* you home," the verb does not indicate a communicative function. Rather, the verb *convince* indicates the interactional aspect of a speech act, and *walk* does not indicate any speech act at all.

The "hereby test" produces constructions that actually do occur in real life, albeit mainly in formal contexts. A chairman can open a meeting with the words "I hereby declare the meeting open" and he can close it with the words "I hereby declare the meeting closed." Business letters, contracts, and similar agreements are full of such constructions: "We hereby inform you that . . . ," "You are hereby notified that . . . ," "I the undersigned do hereby certify that . . . ," "It is hereby resolved that . . . ," and so on.

Unfortunately, the "hereby test" cannot be used for identifying the communicative function of all speech acts. It sometimes produces results that sound rather artificial: "I hereby assume that . . . ," "I hereby argue that . . . ," "I hereby criticize . . . ," and so forth. However, starting from clear-cut cases, it is possible to determine, with a little pushing and squeezing, whether a certain nominal characterization of an utterance can be a designation of the communicative aspect of the speech act concerned.

In order to identify the interactional status of a speech act, the following "thereby test" can be useful:

> Let the original utterance be followed by the phrase "He thereby . . . me," the dots being replaced by the past tense of the verb that best describes the interactional aspect that one thinks to be at stake, and check whether this produces a normal utterance; if it does, the verb, indeed, identifies an interactional aspect.

For example: "He thereby *cheered* me *up*," "He thereby *convinced* me."

## ELEMENTARY AND COMPLEX SPEECH ACTS

There are important differences between the speech act of argumentation and speech acts such as asserting, requesting, promising, cancelling, announcing, advising, and predicting as discussed in the standard theory of speech acts.

First, unlike assertions, requests, promises, and so on which can consist of only a single sentence, argumentation, in principle, consists of more than one sentence: "She'd better not take driving lessons because she is already 61, she panics easily, and she will never be able to buy a car out of her pension." Sometimes an argument, at first sight, appears to consist of just one sentence and is still a complete defense of a standpoint, but on closer inspection, it will then always be found that part of the argumentation has been left unexpressed: "She'd better not take driving lessons because she panics easily" where "Panicky people shouldn't get a driver's license" is left unexpressed. "Tomorrow I'll knock down that wall for you," on the other hand, is a complete promise by itself, "It's stopped raining" a complete statement, and "The best thing you can do is go and lie down for a while" a complete piece of advice.

Second, without being indirect speech acts, the utterances that go to make up the argumentation all have two communicative functions at the same time.[3] Someone who defends the standpoint "She'd better not take driving lessons" by saying "She is already 61; she panics easily; she will never be able to buy a car out of her pension" has uttered three sentences that, together, constitute the argumentation. Taken together, these three utterances have the communicative function of argumentation, but each of the utterances individually has a different communicative function in addition: it is also an assertion, a statement, or whatever.

There are, of course, more speech acts with such a dual communicative function. For example, an explanation, an amplification, or an elucidation all consist of utterances that are, taken separately, assertions, statements, or whatever and serve as an explanation, an amplification, or an elucidation when taken together. Another, slightly different but nevertheless analogous case, are instructions that together constitute a recipe: "Wash the grapes, remove from bunch, cut open, remove pits. Fill the space with a little cream cheese with garlic and herbs. Allow to stiffen in the refrigerator." In any case, it is the dual function of argumentation that is one of the features that make it a more complex speech act than a request, a promise or a statement.

Third, the speech act constellation that constitutes the argumentation cannot stand by itself. It must be connected in a particular way to another speech act: the speech act in which the standpoint is expressed that is supported by the argumentation. Speech acts such as promises, statements, and requests need not be linked to another speech act in such a special way.

The differences between argumentation and these other speech acts can be better understood when it is seen that argumentation has not a communicative function at the sentence level but at some higher textual level. We call speech acts at the sentence level *elementary* speech acts and speech acts at the higher textual level *complex* speech acts. Argumentation belongs to the latter category.

Although argumentation is sometimes easily confused with other complex speech acts such as elucidating, amplifying, and explaining, there is an important difference. It is assumed that something that is elucidated, amplified, or explained has, in principle, already been accepted by the listener, whereas when argumentation is put forward, the acceptability is the very point at issue. In ordinary discourse, in order to persuade the listener, the speaker may once in a while present his argumentation as an amplification, an elucidation, or something of the kind. By thus talking about the standpoint as if it already had been accepted,

[3]In indirect speech acts the dual function hinges on the difference between the literal meaning of the utterance and a nonliteral meaning which determines its "primary," indirect function (cf. chapter 5).

he suggests that his standpoint has no need of argumentation and that its acceptability is beyond doubt.[4]

## IDENTITY AND CORRECTNESS CONDITIONS FOR ARGUMENTATION

The felicity or "happiness" conditions that the listener may regard as having been fulfilled when encountering argumentation consist of *identity* conditions and of *correctness* conditions.[5] The identity conditions have to be fulfilled for an utterance to count as a particular speech act and to be identifiable as such.[6] If these conditions have not been fulfilled, it is not possible for the listener to decide whether he is dealing with a promise, a request or a statement and what it entails. The correctness conditions have to be fulfilled for the utterance concerned to be an appropriate performance of a particular speech act.

Of course, with a speech act that meets the identity conditions all sorts of things may still be wrong. It may, for example, be obvious that a question is asked without the speaker being interested in the answer, that something is asserted that the speaker knows to be untrue, or that something is promised without the speaker having any intention of doing it.

It may be difficult for the listener to determine whether the correctness conditions have been fully met, but the speaker is always committed to what he has said and will be answerable for it: The listener is entitled to assume that a speaker who has asked a question is interested in the answer, that a speaker who has made an assertion is convinced that this assertion is true, that a speaker who has promised something really intends to do it, and so forth.

In formulating the identity and correctness conditions for argumentation, we shall assume that the speaker, apart from the argumentation, has performed another speech act in which a standpoint is advanced with respect to a proposition *p* and

[4]In particular, we think it necessary to make a sharp distinction between argumentation and explanation (cf. Govier, 1987, pp. 159-176). Of course, the adequacy of an explanation may also come under scrutiny but then it is the acceptability of the explanans that is at stake and not the acceptability of the explanandum.

[5]The notion of felicity conditions for the performance of speech acts stems from Austin (1962). The distinction between identity (or recognizability) conditions and correctness conditions is developed in van Eemeren and Grootendorst (1984). There, it is explained that the felicity conditions for the complex speech act of argumentation can be motivated by pointing out the diverse consequences of their violations.

[6]Therefore, they can also be regarded as recognizability conditions for a speech act. In Searle (1969), the preparatory conditions play a role in determining the identity of a particular speech act, whereas we regard them as correctness conditions instead of recognizability conditions: They refer to two different aspects of efficiency. The identity of a speech act is, in our view, determined by its essential and propositional content conditions. Although these recognizability conditions are preconditions for identifying a speech act, they do, of course, not indicate exactly which verbal or other communicative means make the speech act recognizable, that is, how, in practice, it can be recognized as such.

that he is now addressing the listener with utterances 1, 2, . . . , n. If these utterances are to be considered a performance of the complex speech act of argumentation, two sorts of identity conditions have to be met:

1. *Propositional content condition:* utterances 1, 2, . . . , n constitute the elementary speech acts 1, 2, . . . , n, in which a commitment is undertaken to the propositions expressed.
2. *Essential condition:* the performance of the constellation of speech acts that consists of the elementary speech acts 1, 2, . . . , n counts as an attempt by the speaker to justify *p*, that is to convince the listener of the acceptability of his standpoint with respect to *p*.

The wording of the essential condition suggests that argumentation is exclusively used to defend positive standpoints, but this is not so. Although this is not mentioned in the conditions, negative standpoints can also be defended by means of argumentation; then, in the essential condition, reference must be made to refuting the proposition ("contra-argumentation") instead of justifying it ("pro-argumentation").[7] In order to avoid confusion, one must bear in mind that the proposition to which the standpoint pertains may itself also contain negative elements ("I don't think that women have no logic of their own").

There are two sorts of correctness conditions:

3. *Preparatory conditions:*
   a. The speaker believes that the listener does not accept (or at least not automatically or wholly accept) his standpoint with respect to *p*.
   b. The speaker believes that the listener is prepared to accept the propositions expressed in the elementary speech acts 1, 2, . . . , n.
   c. The speaker believes that the listener is prepared to accept the constellation of elementary speech acts 1, 2, . . . , n as an acceptable justification of *p*.
4. *Responsibility conditions:*
   a. The speaker believes that his standpoint with respect to *p* is acceptable.
   b. The speaker believes that the propositions expressed in the elementary speech acts 1, 2, . . . , n are acceptable.
   c. The speaker believes that the constellation of the elementary speech acts 1, 2, . . . , n is an acceptable justification of *p*.

The wording of the second and third preparatory conditions states nothing about how strongly the speaker must believe that the listener is prepared to accept the

[7]Naess (1966), among others, used the term *contra-argumentation* exclusively to refer to argumentation advanced to counter the argumentation of the opponent. In our terms, this restriction would mean that contra-argumentation only occurs in discussions aimed at resolving a mixed dispute.

propositions and the justification. It leaves room for absolute certainty but also for a vague expectation or faint hope that acceptance will be gained. It rules out, however, that the speaker assumes from the outset that there is no chance of achieving acceptance. Anybody who undertakes a serious attempt to convince others should at the very least assume that he has *some* chance, however small, of success.

The wording of the first responsibility condition does not exclude cases such as hypothetical reasoning and *reductio ad absurdum*, where the arguer proceeds as if this correctness condition were fulfilled although he knows that, in fact, it is not. By using *reductio ad absurdum*, for example, the arguer eventually hopes to demonstrate that the standpoint which is disputed must be false. In initially complying with the first responsibility condition, he commits himself for the time being to the belief stated in this condition. He adopts this argumentative procedure precisely because he thinks it serves his purpose to undertake a temporary commitment which can be disposed of after his task is accomplished: Starting from such a temporary commitment will make it easier to demonstrate the falsehood of the standpoint. Rather than believing in the acceptability of the standpoint in any deeper psychological sense, he resorts, as it were, to purporting a professed belief for which he accepts responsibility for as long as he can use it, however disingenuous this belief *au fond* may be.

The wording of the second and third responsibility conditions appears to exclude the possibility that a speaker does not really believe that the propositions expressed in his argumentation are acceptable or that they justify the proposition expressed in his standpoint. Nevertheless, he can, of course, aim at convincing the listener while knowing, and exploiting this knowledge, that the listener, unlike himself, finds these propositions and this justification acceptable. This way of proceeding does not necessarily stem from the speaker's desire to achieve at all costs the effect that the audience adhere to his view; it can also arise from a genuine interest in getting to know what exactly the consequences are of putting forward certain arguments.[8]

It is important to realize that the responsibility conditions do not imply that the speaker need always be sincere: He may be lying and think something quite different from what he says, but even then he is committed to what he has said and, consequently, the listener can hold him to his word.[9] For example, if the

---

[8]In the former case the speaker's objective is rhetorical in the sense of the new rhetoric, in the latter dialectical in a new dialectical sense (cf. Perelman & Olbrechts-Tyteca, 1958. Barth & Krabbe, 1982). For a broader conception of rhetoric, which includes dialectic, see Wenzel (1980, 1987, 1990).

[9]If the responsibility conditions were really sincerity conditions requiring a certain state of mind, as in Searle (1969), common and useful argumentation techniques such as hypothetical reasoning and *reductio ad absurdum* would be ruled out. The major consequence of the responsibility conditions is that the speaker, because he is answerable for what he has said, may be deemed to act *as if he were sincere*—whether he actually is sincere or not. For our purposes, it is what the speaker can be held accountable to that counts, not what he privately thinks. Occasionally, to avoid artificial language, we nevertheless speak of his "sincerity" instead of "responsibility."

speaker casts doubt on a proposition that he himself has earlier used in his argumentation, the listener may accuse him of being inconsistent (see Table 3.1).

TABLE 3.1
The Conditions and Effects of the Complex Speech Act of Argumentation: An Example

| | | | |
|---|---|---|---|
| SENTENCE LEVEL | elementary speech acts | 1. She is already 61<br>2. She panics easily<br>3. She has no money for a car | She had better not take driving lessons |
| TEXTUAL LEVEL | complex speech acts | argumentation | standpoint |
| Propositional content condition | | (1)-(3) express a commitment to the acceptability of the propositions that:<br>1. she is 61,<br>2. she panics easily,<br>3. she has no money for a car | |
| Essential condition | | Performance of (1)-(3) counts as an attempt by the speaker S to convince the listener L of the acceptability of the standpoint that she had better not take driving lessons | |
| Preparatory conditions | | 1. S believes that L does not accept the standpoint "She had better not take driving lessons."<br>2. S believes that L will accept the propositions expressed in (1)-(3), that is that (1) she is 61, (2) she panics easily, and (3) she has no money for a car.<br>3. S believes that L will accept the constellation (1)-(3) as a justification of the proposition "She had better not take driving lessons." | |
| Responsibility conditions | | 1. S believes that the standpoint "She had better not take driving lessons" is acceptable.<br>2. S believes that the propositions expressed in (1)-(3) are acceptable.<br>3. S believes that the constellation (1)-(3) constitutes an acceptable justification of the proposition "She had better not take driving lessons." | |
| COMMUNICATIVE EFFECT (UNDERSTANDING) | | L understands that (1)-(3) counts as argumentation for the standpoint "She had better not take driving lessons." | |
| INTERACTIONAL EFFECT (ACCEPTANCE) | | L accepts (1)-(3) as a justification of the proposition "She had better not take driving lessons." | |

CHAPTER 4

# Speech Acts in a Critical Discussion

## STAGES IN THE RESOLUTION OF A DISPUTE

A dispute ceases to exist if there is no longer a difference of opinion. There are all sorts of ways in which a party can be persuaded to withdraw a standpoint or to retract his doubt about a standpoint, thus ending the dispute. In talking about ending a dispute from a pragma-dialectical viewpoint, it is important to make a clear distinction between *settling* and *resolving* it.

Settling a dispute means that the difference of opinion is simply set aside. This can be done in a more or less civilized way by tossing a coin; even more civilized is calling on an unbiased third party for arbitration: a referee, an ombudsman or a judge.[1] It can also be done in a less civilized way by going for one another's throats and fighting it out or, perhaps even worse, by getting one's own way via intimidation or blackmail.

A dispute is resolved only if somebody retracts his doubt because he has been convinced by the other party's argumentation or if he withdraws his standpoint because he has realized that his argumentation cannot stand up to the other party's criticism. Critical reactions and argumentation play a crucial role in the resolution of a dispute. To really resolve a dispute, the points that are being disputed have to be made the issue of a *critical discussion* that is aimed at reaching agreement about the acceptability or unacceptability of the standpoints at issue by finding out whether or not they can be adequately defended by means of argumentation against doubt or criticism.

[1]Another civilized way of ending a dispute is agreeing on a compromise that involves modifying the disputed standpoint rather than really resolving the original dispute. This is what one frequently resorts to in diplomacy, negotiations, and the like.

Ideally, the resolution of a dispute passes through four stages which correspond to four different phases in a critical discussion. For a critical discussion arising out of a simple dispute, this ideal model takes the following form:

1. *Confrontation stage*. At the confrontation stage, it is established that there is a dispute. A standpoint is advanced and questioned.

2. *Opening stage*. At the opening stage, the decision is taken to attempt to resolve the dispute by means of a regulated argumentative discussion. One party takes the role of *protagonist*, which means that he is prepared to defend his standpoint by means of argumentation; the other party takes the role of *antagonist*, which means that he is prepared to challenge the protagonist systematically to defend his standpoint. In a nonmixed dispute, the party acting as protagonist has no other task than to defend his standpoint and the party acting as antagonist has no other task than to criticize the protagonist's defense for his standpoint, without having to defend a standpoint of his own. Both parties have to agree on the starting points and the rules of discussion.

3. *Argumentation stage*. At the argumentation stage, the protagonist defends his standpoint and the antagonist elicits further argumentation from him if he has further doubts. Because of its crucial role in resolving the dispute, the argumentation stage is sometimes regarded as the "real" discussion. In a nonmixed dispute, there is only one protagonist who advances argumentation; in a mixed dispute, more protagonists should advance argumentation.

4. *Concluding stage*. At the concluding stage, it is established whether the dispute has been resolved on account of the standpoint or the doubt concerning the standpoint having been retracted. If the standpoint is withdrawn, the dispute has been resolved in favor of the antagonist; if the doubt is withdrawn, its resolution is in favor of the protagonist. In the case of the protagonist withdrawing his standpoint, the protagonist may adopt a standpoint that is the opposite of his original standpoint, but this is not necessarily so: He may also water down or alter his original standpoint or adopt a zero standpoint. In the case of the antagonist withdrawing his doubt, the antagonist must accept the protagonist's standpoint.

Having resolved the dispute, the discussants may always embark upon a new discussion, relating to an entirely different dispute or to a more or less altered version of the same dispute. In this new discussion, the discussants' roles may switch. In any case, then, the discussion has to start all over again.

It is only in the ideal model of a critical discussion that all these stages are passed through completely. To some degree, real-life argumentative discourse will always deviate from the ideal model.[2] The discussion stages are seldom all passed

[2]Some examples of such real-life deviations in ordinary conversation, mediation talks, and verbal exchanges between witnessing evangelists and hecklers are discussed in van Eemeren, Grootendorst, Jackson, and Jacobs (1992), where the ideal model is used both as a heuristic tool and as a critical standard.

through explicitly, let alone in the same order. Sometimes, one or more stages, or parts of them, remain implicit. Nevertheless, all argumentative discourse by which a dispute has been resolved can be reconstructed as a discussion which contains all the stages of the ideal model.[3] Therefore, the model provides a useful heuristic instrument for a dialectical analysis of argumentative discourse.[4]

As a heuristic instrument, the model constitutes a tool for arriving at a decision about the communicative function of speech acts when this function is not immediately clear. The model suggests which options, at the stage that the discussion has reached, are the most relevant with a view to the resolution of the dispute, so that the analyst has, at least, something to go by if he wants to give optimal credit to the discussants for being reasonable.

The ideal model also fulfills a critical function. It provides a standard to which a rational judge may orient himself if he wishes to determine to what extent an actual specimen of argumentative discourse departs from the abstract ideal. The model specifies which speech acts, at which stages in the discussion, do contribute to the resolution of the dispute. Thus, it enables the critic to establish which necessary speech acts are lacking in the discourse and which of the speech acts that do occur are superfluous or even disruptive.

In practice, argumentative discourse is not always properly analyzed if it is looked upon as entirely aimed at resolving a dispute. There usually is also another dimension in argumentative discourse that has to do with gaining the adherence of the audience to get things one's own way. In order to do justice to this persuasive aspect, a rhetorical analysis is more appropriate.[5]

In the classical tradition, rhetoric is the theory of good and successful public speaking.[6] What constitutes a good and successful discourse depends on the genre of text concerned: In a forensic discourse, a plea is successful if the judge makes a decision that is favorable to the defendant; in a deliberative discourse, a political plea is successful if the proposed course of action is indeed adopted; in an epideictic discourse, the praise or condemnation is successful if it is generally appreciated as appropriate to the occasion. A judge in a court of law must

---

[3]The normative reconstruction that is required for analyzing argumentative discourse pragma-dialectically, constitutes a problem in its own right. See for a discussion of this problem van Eemeren, Grootendorst, Jackson, and Jacobs (1992).

[4]There are some important similarities between our normative approach to the analysis of real-life discourse and the descriptive analysis of Edmondson (1981). In Edmondson's model, speech events are regarded as speech act sequences whose coherence depends on the interactional structure of the speech event. The moves that are the basic interactional units combine in the exchanges that are the minimal units of social interaction; the exchanges themselves combine in the phases, or stages, that make up an ordered speech event. In the speech event, rational conversationalists try to achieve certain interactional effects by performing certain communicative (illocutionary) acts.

[5]The term "rhetorical" is used here in its limited sense.

[6]For a discussion of classical rhetorical tradition, see Kennedy (1963, 1972, 1980). A short introduction to classical as well as modern rhetoric is given in van Eemeren, Grootendorst, and Kruiger (1987, cf. also Meyer, 1986b).

be approached differently from an audience that wants nothing but to hear something praised or condemned, and a parliamentary committee requires yet another approach.

All the various types of discourse distinguished by rhetoricians require the speaker to make more or less the same preparations, such as considering what he is going to talk about, in what order, and exactly what manner of presentation he is going to choose. Just as in dialectically relevant discourse, four stages can be distinguished. These rhetorical stages are: *exordium*, *narratio*, *argumentatio*, and *peroratio*.

The *exordium* is an introduction with which the speaker begins by turning the audience's sympathies in his favor and interesting them in his subject. In the *narratio* he goes on to set out his subject or the course of events about which he wishes to speak. This is the preparation for the *argumentatio*, which often consists of two parts: a part in which evidence is put forward for his own standpoint (*confirmatio*) and a part in which he tries to refute the opposite standpoint (*refutatio*). The *peroratio* contains a recapitulation and conclusion. Sometimes, the *argumentatio* is started or ended with a digression that serves as a transition (*digressio*).

In the dialectical and the rhetorical model, the argumentation stage is roughly the same. In fact, all the stages show some similarity. However, there are important differences too. In the rhetorical model, the listener merely plays a passive role and the speaker may try to achieve the desired effect on the audience by whatever means of persuasion. In practice, it is not always simple to establish to what extent a discourse requires a dialectical or a rhetorical analysis.

## DISTRIBUTION OF SPEECH ACTS OVER THE DIALECTICAL STAGES

The ideal model of a critical discussion only becomes practically meaningful if it is clear what speech acts, at the various stages, can contribute to the resolution of a dispute. This can be explained with the help of Searle's classification of speech acts.[7]

Although, in principle, all types of speech act may occur in argumentative discourse, only certain types can contribute directly to the resolution of a dispute.

[7]Searle's taxonomy (1979) is to a large extent based on Austin's classificatory remarks in *How to do Things With Words* (1962); it is in some important respect comparable to Bühler's classical division of functions of language (1934, cf. also Popper's extended version of this classification, 1974). Our main addition to Searle's taxonomy consists in the introduction of the usage declaratives. Just as Searle, we aim for an analytic classification. Such an approach is criticized, among others, by Kreckel (1981). Opting for an emic, or purely "internal" perspective, she started, instead, from the categorizations made by the language users themselves. For other criticisms of Searle's taxonomy, see, for example, Ballmer and Brennenstuhl (1981).

Other speech acts do not play a constructive role in this, or only contribute indirectly. For each type of speech act, it can be indicated which speech acts play a part in a critical discussion.

## Assertives

Assertive speech acts, such as assertions, statements, and suppositions, are communicative acts by means of which the speaker states how something that is expressed in the propositional content of the speech act is. He makes himself in a particular way responsible for the acceptability (or unacceptability) of the proposition: His commitment to the proposition is such that he is obliged to give evidence for its acceptability if this is questioned by the listener. According to the responsibility condition, the speaker may be deemed to believe that the proposition is accurate.

The prototype of an assertive is an assertion by which the speaker guarantees the truth of the proposition expressed. There are also assertives that are concerned with acceptability in a broader sense than truth. All assertive speech acts can play a part in a critical discussion. At the confrontation stage, they can express the standpoint at issue; at the argumentation stage, the argumentation in defense of that standpoint; at the concluding stage, the outcome of the discussion.

Although they are prototypically expressed by assertions, a standpoint or an argumentation can also be advanced by statements, claims, assurances, suppositions and so forth. Furthermore, it is worth noting that the belief in a proposition can be very strong, as in the case of a firm assertion or statement, but it may also be fairly weak, as in a supposition. Of course, the more forcefully a proposition is put forward in a standpoint, the more powerful its argumentative defense needs to be.

## Directives

Directive speech acts, such as requests, questions, orders, and recommendations are communicative acts by means of which the speaker tries to get the listener to do something that is expressed in the propositional content of the speech act (or to refrain from doing this). According to the responsibility condition, the speaker may be deemed to want the action concerned (not) to take place.

Only those directive speech acts play a part in a critical discussion that challenge the protagonist to defend his standpoint (confrontation stage) or to give argumentation in favor of his standpoint (argumentation stage). In the ideal model, the protagonist may not be challenged to do anything else than give argumentation for his standpoint, nor may he be urged to give up his standpoint just like that—for the sake of peace and quiet, as it were, or to avoid disagreeable consequences for himself or others.

## Commissives

Commissive speech acts, such as promises, acceptances, and agreements are communicative acts by means of which the speaker commits himself to do something that is expressed in the propositional content of the speech act (or to refrain from doing this). According to the responsibility condition, the speaker may be deemed to have the genuine intention to do what he has undertaken to do.

Commissive speech acts can fulfill several roles in a critical discussion. At the confrontation and in the concluding stage, they can be used for accepting or not accepting a standpoint; at the opening stage, for accepting the challenge to defend a standpoint, for deciding to start the discussion, for agreeing on the distribution of roles and the discussion rules, and for agreeing on how to close the discussion; at the argumentation stage, for accepting or not accepting argumentation; in the concluding stage, finally, they can be used for deciding to start a new discussion.

## Expressives

Expressive speech acts, such as congratulations, condolences, and expressions of joy, disappointment, anger, or regret, are communicative acts by means of which the speaker airs his feelings concerning a certain event or state of affairs. According to the preparatory condition, it is taken for granted that this state of affairs really exists or that the event actually took place. According to the responsibility condition, the speaker may be deemed to genuinely have the emotion expressed in the speech act.

Because expressive speech acts express feelings of the speaker and do not lead to any specific commitment that is relevant to resolving the dispute, they have no place in a critical discussion. Of course, this does not mean that they cannot affect the resolution process at all. A sigh of the antagonist that he is unhappy with the protagonist's arguments is an emotional comment that may distract attention from the arguments and from the fact that the protagonist actually observes all the commonly agreed discussion rules.[8] On the other hand, expressives can also encourage or stimulate a meaningful exchange of ideas.

## Declaratives

Declarative speech acts, such as opening a meeting, pronouncing a couple man and wife, and firing an employee are communicative acts by means of which the speaker creates the state of affairs that is expressed in the propositional content.

[8]Just like "non-allowed" directives and other speech acts that are not integral parts of a critical discussion, expressives may sometimes be indirect speech acts through which "primary" speech acts are conveyed that *do* play a part in a critical discussion. In such cases, they should, naturally, be taken into account in the dialectal analysis (cf. for indirect speech acts, chapter 5).

Usually, declaratives are performed in more or less institutionalized contexts such as court proceedings, meetings, and religious ceremonies, in all of which it is clear who is authorized to perform a particular declarative. An important exception, however, are *usage declaratives*, such as explications, elucidations, amplifications, and definitions: "The term *rhetorical* is used here in the sense of persuasive." Their purpose is to facilitate or increase the listener's comprehension of other speech acts by indicating how they should be interpreted. Basically, the performance of a usage declarative does not require some special authority.

Precisely because declaratives, with the exception of the usage declaratives, depend on the authority of the speaker in a certain institutionalized context, nonusage declaratives make no direct contribution to the resolution of the dispute. At best, they can lead to the settlement of a dispute, not to its resolution. They, therefore, do not play a part in a critical discussion.

Usage declaratives can fulfill a useful role in all stages of a critical discussion. At the confrontation stage, they can unmask spurious verbal disputes; at the opening stage, they can clarify confusion about the starting points or the discussion rules; at the argumentation stage, they can prevent premature acceptance or nonacceptance; and at the concluding stage, they can prevent ambiguous resolutions. Requests for providing usage declaratives such as specifications and amplifications can therefore also fulfill a very useful role in a critical discussion.

## ARGUMENTATIVE DISCOURSE AS CRITICAL DISCUSSION

Scientific discussions are perhaps the closest we ever come in approaching the ideal model of a critical discussion. In principle, their purpose is at least dialectical.[9] At any rate, in scientific discussions no standpoint is accepted without some testing and the argumentation that is put forward is checked for its soundness. Yet it would be premature to regard scientific discussions simply as realizations of the ideal model. Even here, practice differs often from (normative) theory. Scholars and scientists have their own unproven assumptions, prejudices, illogicalities, and so on. Occasionally, even in the most rigid scientific disciplines, pathos and other rhetorical devices are not shunned.

The ideal model of a critical discussion specifies which speech acts can contribute directly to the resolution of the dispute at the various stages of the discussion. It goes without saying that speech acts that are not included in the model, because they do not in a direct sense contribute to the resolution, can be of other importance, say for psychological reasons. For example, jokes, anecdotes, and

---

[9]Such a dialectical view of the scientific enterprise as critical discussion is, for instance, put forward in Albert (1967, 1975) and Popper (1972, 1974). Feyerabend (1970) and Kuhn (1970, 1974), among others, have also pointed out the irrational aspects of science.

other asides may well help to ensure the relaxed progress of the discussion, and in so doing play a psychological part that should not be underestimated. Although they are not themselves integral parts of the resolution process, they may help create the right atmosphere for resolving the dispute.

In practice, some of the speech acts listed in the model may have been performed, in some form or other, before people start a discussion. Agreements about the discussion rules are often made or presumed in advance, so that this part of the opening stage can be omitted. These rules may have been established in the community long before the discussants first met, possibly even when they did not yet have a say so that they learned about them at school. They may have accepted them tacitly and, consequently, there is no need for performing the speech act concerned. Other speech acts may also be accepted tacitly. It is, for instance, obvious from the fact that the protagonist advances argumentation immediately after an expression of doubt by the antagonist that he takes this reaction to be an occasion to defend his standpoint. Then, there is no need for him to state explicitly that he accepts the challenge to defend his standpoint.

As a rule, discussion stages are neither explicitly announced nor completely externalized. Implicitness, notwithstanding its normality, can make it more difficult to recognize the various stages. As has been explained, a stage that is quite often only partly present is the opening stage. Although it is sometimes evident what the starting points are, and which rules apply to the discussion, this is not always so. For reaching a resolution of the dispute it is often imperative to raise certain principles explicitly, so that it is clear what the terms of discussion are. Refraining from this may be a rhetorical device to make it appear as if the other party has already agreed on the rules and starting points that the speaker chooses to use, whereas these are in fact suspect. It stands to reason that people who are aware of the significance of such "parameters for healthy debate" will insist on a proper completion of the opening stage:

> Chris Ham's call for a public debate concerning health priorities is to be welcomed provided that such a discussion is not conducted within unnecessarily narrow parameters. Such a debate should include a critical review of such issues as clinical and administrative decision making.
> (Robert Page, Lecturer in Social Policy, Nottingham University, in a letter to *The Guardian*, February 16, 1991)

Some institutionalized speech events, have more or less formalized discussion procedures. This is particularly obvious in the proceedings at a court of law. When analyzing argumentative discourse that occurs in legal proceedings, scientific and scholarly dissertations, political debates, policy documents, and so on, knowledge of the conventions pertaining to such speech events can be very useful. On occasion, the verbal and nonverbal context indicates what can reasonably be expected to hold. When the speaker is reacting seriously to what someone else has brought forward, it may, for instance, be assumed that he will deal with the various points made by the other.

Having the knowledge that the discourse belongs to a particular genre of text can furnish the analyst with some insight into the types of speech act that may be expected: In a cross-examination, for instance, one sequence of speech acts will appear more natural than another. General and specific background knowledge may also help to excite particular reasoned conjectures. We may, for example, know that in a particular circle discussions are always conducted along the same lines or that a certain author always constructs his essays in accordance with the same plan.

Taken together, these different kinds of knowledge can build up a hypothetical pattern that can serve as a framework for interpretation and analysis: It is then assumed that the discourse will proceed in the usual manner and that the appropriate speech acts will be performed.

In real life, argumentative discourse often contains several discussions at the same time that may be intertwined. Even if the original dispute is simple, new disputes may come up and any number of subdisputes can still arise out of the argumentation advanced to resolve the original dispute. These can, in turn, also lead to discussion and hence to the advancing of new arguments. A dispute that originally was not mixed can easily lead to a mixed dispute or mixed subdispute and a single dispute can lead to a multiple dispute or subdispute. This does not make things any easier when it comes to distinguishing the speech acts that are relevant to the resolution of the principal dispute.

Moreover, very often the protagonist is not really trying to convince the professed antagonist but addresses, instead, over his head, a third party. In a political debate, the target group may, in fact, consist of the television viewers; in a letter to the editor, of the newspaper's readers. Then, there are actually two antagonists: the "official" antagonist and the people who are the real target group. A quasi-dialectical goal is then pursued with regard to the first antagonist, whereas the predominant goal with regard to the second is rhetorical.

Another complication may arise from the fact that many spoken and written texts are not themselves specimens of argumentative discourse but reports of such discourse. The person who is reporting is, for example, a news reporter who is only informing the reader about how other people have tried to sort out their differences and is not himself intent upon resolving the dispute by convincing an antagonist. In particular when no explicit thesis is formulated and no explicit conclusion is drawn, discursive texts and such reports are sometimes hard to tell apart, so that a report may be erroneously analyzed as if it were an implicit discursive text.

Argumentative discourse can, in principle, always be dialectically analyzed, even if it concerns a discursive text that, at first sight, appears to be a monologue. The monologue is then, at least partially, reconstructed as a critical discussion: The argumentative parts are identified as belonging to the argumentation stage and other parts as belonging to the confrontation, the opening or the concluding stage. Usually, this reconstruction is not so much of a problem as it may seem. A speaker or writer who wants to convince his audience should, after all, make it clear to the audience that there is, or may be, a difference of opinion, that he intends to offer a reasonable solution for this problem, that he will do so by putting forward arguments in favor of his standpoint that overcome all critical doubt, and that the difference of opinion has thus been terminated.

A speaker or writer who is intent on resolving a dispute will have to take just as much account of implicit doubt about his standpoint as of doubt that has been expressed explicitly. He may also deal with doubt that is purely imaginary. The presumed antagonist need not even exist, as when the speaker or writer imagines how his standpoint might be received by a skeptical listener or reader. Then he is anticipating possible doubt. His argumentative discourse is in all these cases, as it were, part of a real or imagined *implicit discussion*.

In such an implicit discussion, not all speech acts that are, according to the model, performed in a critical discussion will actually occur. Besides, certain speech acts that are in the model performed by the antagonist, are in monological argumentative discourse, where no antagonist plays an active role, just reacted to or anticipated by the protagonist. Although, ultimately, the speaker or writer can, of course, only speak for himself, they can in the dialectical analysis be represented in the form of references or quotations.

CHAPTER 5

# Implicit and Indirect Speech Acts

## IMPLICIT SPEECH ACTS IN ARGUMENTATIVE DISCOURSE

When analyzing argumentative discourse as a critical discussion, the problem is that the communicative function of speech acts often remains implicit. In practice, the explicit performance of a speech act is the exception rather than the rule. Explicitness is restricted to emphatic or formal usage and to situations in which the speaker wishes to exclude all possible misunderstanding. For some speech acts, an explicit formula is even not available:

*"I (hereby) amplify that . . ."
*"I (hereby) explain that . . ."
(* = not acceptable)

The complex speech act of argumentation, too, does not lend itself to performance by means of a standard formula:

*"I (hereby) argue that . . ."

Another way of indicating the communicative function of a speech act is to give an explicit characterization, preceding the speech act to which it refers ("The standpoint that I shall defend in this article is the following") or following it ("Good listening demands much more effort than good reading. That is the standpoint of which I hope to have convinced you by this lecture").

The argumentation for a standpoint can also be announced in advance or specified as such afterward:

> "My argument for this is that . . ."
>
> "This was my main argument. Another argument is . . ."

Sometimes, the analyst must hear the entire speech before he can establish that the speaker intends certain utterances to be particular speech acts.

This is not necessary if expressions are used as:

> "The reasons for this letter are . . ."
>
> "There are sufficient arguments to support the view that . . ."

There are also specific verbal indicators of the communicative function. Indicators for standpoints and argumentation are, for example: "for," "because," "since," "so," "hence," "after all," "therefore," "ergo," "in short," and "in other words." In "It's wise to emigrate to Australia, because this country's getting too full of people for my liking," "because" indicates both that what follows is argumentation and that what precedes is a standpoint.

Here, we have a "retrogressive" presentation, because the word "because" refers back to the standpoint on which the argumentation centres. In "This country's getting too full of people for my liking, so it's wise to emigrate to Australia," the presentation is "progressive." Unfortunately, the words and expressions that can serve as indicators of argumentation or a standpoint can also refer to other communicative functions: The word "so," for example, can be a filler with no special significance.

The less clear the verbal pointers are, the more it will be necessary to make use of clues from the further verbal and nonverbal context. Usually, some background knowledge, or general knowledge of the world, is also helpful. Without such knowledge, it would be difficult to tell that in "He should buy a Rolls; there is no better car" two assertives are performed of which the first represents a standpoint and the second an argument. Speech acts whose communicative function is not clearly indicated must be given a standard paraphrase by the analyst. In such a standard paraphrase their communicative function is expressed unambiguously: "Bob's standpoint is that I should buy a Rolls."

Often, the structure of the discourse will play a part in determining the communicative function of speech acts. As a rule, a paragraph in an argumentative text will, for example, constitute a unit in which the argumentation and the standpoint appear in a more or less logical order. The standpoint is more likely to be at the beginning or at the very end than in the middle; the argumentation usually precedes or follows the standpoint:

> "Women are better drivers than men. They pass their tests earlier. And they cause fewer accidents."

"Women pass their driving tests earlier than men. And they cause fewer accidents. They are better drivers."

It is often said that the argumentation always contains the more specific and factual information, but this is not true. Both "Women are better drivers than men" and "Women pass their tests earlier than men" are statements that, although factual, may constitute a standpoint. Anyway, it is sometimes difficult to decide which utterance is the more specific or the more factual. This is, for example, the case in:

"Eve picked the apple. She was hungry."

Without further information there is no way of knowing whether the correct interpretation is "Eve picked the apple *because* she was hungry" or "Eve picked the apple, *so* she was hungry." If it is clear that it is dubious who picked the apple, the first interpretation might be correct; if it is being discussed whether or not Eve was hungry, the second interpretation might be correct.

Sometimes, general or specific background knowledge can be of help in identifying standpoints and argumentation:

*Peter:* "Smoking is bad for you."
*Arnold:* "What do you mean?"
*Peter:* "Just look at Jack."

Without the background knowledge that Jack was known to be a heavy smoker and has recently succumbed to lung cancer, it is not clear that "Just look at Jack" is an argument for Peter's standpoint that smoking is bad for you, because it could also be a piece of advice urging Arnold to take a look at his young son Jack who despite being an inexperienced swimmer has ventured into the sea.

In principle, it is in the speaker's own interest to ensure that the communicative function of his speech acts is clear. When it comes to interpreting unclear implicit speech acts in argumentative discourse, the analyst must assume first of all that the speaker is attempting to contribute to the resolution of a dispute. All the same, there is always a risk that a role will be attributed to speech acts that is different from that intended by the speaker. In analyzing argumentative discourse, this risk is greatest in the case of assertives, which have a variety of roles in a critical discussion: They can serve to advance a standpoint, to retract or to sustain it, to put forward argumentation, to establish the outcome of the discussion or to define a term, explain a statement and so forth.

Argumentative discourse may contain implicit speech acts that are part of the argumentation for the standpoint that is defended but that, at first sight, do not appear to belong to the category of the assertives:

"Let's take an umbrella, or did you want to get wet?"

Taken literally, this is a proposal to the listener accompanied by a question (which may be rhetorical). It is clear, however, that this question must be interpreted as argumentation for the standpoint that the speaker and the listener should take an umbrella.

All the same, the question asked here cannot simply be equated with argumentation, nor the proposal with a standpoint. Otherwise, we should have to abandon the idea that argumentation and standpoints are always advanced by means of assertives and no account would be given of the specific commitments undertaken by these speech acts. But closer analysis reveals that these speech acts are, indirectly, used as assertives. Although "Let's take an umbrella" serves here as a standpoint, it is not a direct expression of a standpoint: It is impossible to cast doubt on this utterance or to reject it by means of expressions like "I do not agree with you." A similar problem arises when we try to paraphrase "Or did you want to get wet?" as an argumentation. This rhetorical question cannot be regarded directly as argumentation.

A correct analysis of such a speech act must show to what exactly the speaker is committed. In cases like the umbrella example, to be able to account for his commitments, the speaker's language use must be recognized as indirect. Here, he anticipates a dispute between himself and the listener about the question of whether his proposal that they take an umbrella is a good proposal, and he advances argumentation to defend his standpoint that this is the case.

The speaker's standpoint can be formulated as follows:

"It is advisable to take an umbrella,"

or, more fully reconstructed:

"My standpoint is that it is advisable to take an umbrella."

His argumentation for this standpoint can likewise be reconstructed:

"Otherwise we will get wet,"

or, more fully reconstructed:

"My argument for this is that we do not want to get wet."

A similar reconstruction can be made for cases like:

"I promise, because then at least you'll believe me."

"You can depend on it, for I promise."

"Congratulations, because I'm glad everything has come out all right in the end."

"The discussion is closed, for we're never going to agree."

"You're fired, because your work's no good."

So, there are no good grounds for abandoning the idea that standpoints and argumentations can always be analyzed as assertives. Incidentally, in practice, all speech acts that are crucial to a critical discussion can be indirectly performed by way of speech acts that, at first sight, do not express their primary function:[1]

*Indirect expressions of a standpoint*

1. What a lot we owe to communism! (*expressive*)
2. But don't you think the universities are full of arrogant bastards? (*directive*)
3. You can depend on it that this won't leak out. (*commissive*)

*Indirect expressions of argumentation*

4. . . ., or did you want to get wet? (*directive*)
5. . . ., because I personally guarantee it. (*commissive*)
6. . . ., because I feel awful. (*expressive*)

*Indirect expressions of doubt*

7. Do you really mean that? (*directive*)
8. That sounds dubious to me. (*assertive*)
9. How strange! (*expressive*)

*Indirect challenges*

10. You'll never be able to prove it. (*assertive*)
11. Would you be prepared to defend that standpoint? (*directive*)
12. I'd like to see you! (*expressive*)

*Indirect requests for usage declarative or argumentation*

13. I've no idea what that word means. (*assertive*)
14. I'd love to know what arguments you've got to support that. (*expressive*)
15. I assure you I'm interested to hear your argumentation. (*commissive*)

The failure to recognize argumentation is one of the most serious errors that can be made in analyzing argumentative discourse. Even though, at first sight, no assertive seems to have been performed, a discourse may contain argumentation and can be reconstructed in such a fashion. On the other hand, it should be kept in mind that not every assertive is part of an argumentation.

---

[1]Although she did not envision arguments and standpoints as basically assertive, Jackson (1985) also pointed out that argumentation can pertain to all types of speech act (cf. Jackson & Jacobs, 1980, 1981, 1982).

In analyzing argumentative discourse as a critical discussion, it is recommendable to opt for the argumentative interpretation if a speech act could just as well be considered to be argumentative as to be not argumentative. Implicit assertives that may be argumentative but that can also have some other communicative function are then interpreted as part of the argumentation. The same applies to implicit speech acts that, at first sight, appear to be commissives, directives, expressives, or declaratives but that only play a constructive role if they are analyzed as assertives that are constitutive parts of an argumentation. The recommendation to opt for such a resolution-oriented decision procedure can be referred to as the strategy of *maximally argumentative interpretation*.

The recommendation applies, for example, to the following passage from an advertisement for trousers:

> *Supremely comfortable and yet always smart*. The material, a brand-quality jersey of 100% diolen/polyester, is elastic in both length and breadth and yet keeps its shape perfectly.
>
> *The finish leaves nothing to be desired*. It's just as impeccable as the cloth and moreover is subjected to very stringent quality control.

Here, the arguments intended to dispose the reader to buy the product are accompanied by amplifications that, presumably, are also meant to have an argumentative function, so that a maximally argumentative interpretation seems justified. The same holds true for Yoko Ono's teasing addition to her obliquely stated view that it is amazing that men can get serious at all:

> I wonder why men can get serious at all. They have this delicate long thing hanging outside their bodies which goes up and down by its own will [. . .]

Assuming that he is sincere in wishing to arrive at a resolution of the dispute, a maximally argumentative interpretation is in the interest of the speaker because, otherwise, strong points of his argumentation may go unnoticed. What is more, it is also in the interest of an adequate analysis because otherwise weak points of the speaker's argumentation may remain unnoticed. If a speaker who wants to convince his audience defaults by failing to provide sufficient clues for the communicative function of his most crucial speech acts, he can, in the context of a dialectical analysis, nevertheless be held to the results of a maximally argumentative interpretation.

## COMMUNICATION RULES AND INDIRECT SPEECH ACTS

Besides implicit speech acts, argumentative discourse may also contain indirect speech acts by which the speaker means more, or something else, than he actually says. In order to analyze indirect speech acts, which are usually also implicit, it is necessary to have insight into the rules of communication which speakers and listeners normally observe.[2]

People who are communicating with each another generally try to ensure that their communication goes as smoothly as possible. Accordingly, when they perform speech acts, they observe certain rules which further this purpose. Underlying these rules, are some rational standards that, taken together, constitute a general principle governing all verbal communication, the Principle of Communication:[3]

*Be clear, honest, efficient and to the point*

In practice, of course, it is not at all uncommon for one or more of the rules of communication to be broken, but this does not necessarily mean the Principle of Communication has been abandoned.[4] If it would be abandoned, then the person doing so is reneging on a basic convention of his communicative community.[5] In the absence of any evidence to the contrary, listeners may assume the speaker to comply with the Principle of Communication.

Breaking a rule of communication will, if it is noticed, have repercussions on the interaction. The implications of violating a particular rule depend on the conditions that have not been fulfilled in the performance of the speech act concerned.

The commandment "Be clear" refers to the identity conditions of the speech act concerned: The speaker has to formulate the speech act in such a way that the listener is able to identify its communicative function and the propositions that are expressed. This does not mean the speaker must be completely explicit but it does mean he must not make it impossible, or all but impossible, for the listener to arrive at the correct interpretation. If the identity conditions are not met, the speech act is incomprehensible. Therefore, the first rule of communication is: *Do not perform any incomprehensible speech acts.*

---

[2]Here, we present our integrated version of Searle's theory of indirect speech acts (1979) and Grice's exposition of conversational maxims (1975).

[3]The Principle of Communication fulfills a similar role in communication and has a similar epistemological status as Grice's Co-operative Principle. We agree with Kasher (1982) that observance of the standards which are inherent in the Gricean maxims stems from a more general "rationalization principle" that is based on the principle of effective means. The rationalization principle says that "[the speaker's] end and beliefs, in a context of utterance, should be assumed to supply a complete justification of his behaviour, unless there is evidence to the contrary" (1982, p. 33).

[4]In fact, in ordinary communication people often play with the rules in making jokes, amplifying a story, and so forth without having any intention to give up the Communication Principle. Of course, there is nothing wrong with such communicative behavior. In order to explain how it works, especially in argumentative discourse, we set out the rules which are then being utilized. Even if the rules are violated without any such communicative intent, as may also happen, there is usually no great harm done, but neither could one say that such moves are very helpful to resolving a difference of opinion in a critical discussion.

[5]Cf. Grice (1975, 1989).

The commandment "Be honest" refers to the responsibility condition that is part of the correctness conditions of the speech act: The speaker may have deemed to be in the frame of mind presupposed in the speech act. If he performs an assertive, he can be assumed to sincerely believe in the acceptability of the proposition expressed; if he performs a directive, to sincerely desire the performance by the listener of the action referred to, and so on. The second rule of communication is: *Do not perform any insincere speech acts.*[6]

The commandment "Be efficient" refers to the (compound) preparatory condition which is also part of the correctness conditions: The speech act should be neither needless or superfluous nor pointless or futile. For example, the performance of the complex speech act of argumentation is needless if the speaker knows the listener is already convinced of the acceptability of the standpoint being defended (violation of the first preparatory condition). And the performance is pointless if he knows in advance the listener will not, under any circumstances, be convinced by the argumentation (violation of the second and third preparatory conditions). In either case, performing the speech act of argumentation would be a waste of time and is therefore inefficient.

A superfluous assertive is to tell that John and Mary are back together again to a person who has known this for days. If someone who lacks all technical expertise tells someone who lacks all interest that he thinks that the machine is put to work by moving the left-hand pawl, he performs a futile assertive. A superfluous directive is performed if it is clear that the listener already intended to perform the action desired or if it has already been performed; and a futile directive, if the action cannot be performed. Superfluous or futile commissives can be characterized in similar ways, albeit that then the action is predicated of the speaker instead of the listener. An expressive is superfluous if it is already clear what the speaker feels; it is futile if the listener is not interested in what he feels. If a meeting has been going on for some time, "The meeting is now open" is a superfluous declarative; if the president of the football club in this capacity declares Parliament open, the declarative is futile.

Violations of the requirement of efficiency may not always have exactly the same implications for different types of speech acts, but aiming for efficiency amounts, in any case, to trying to avoid superfluity and futility. Because violating a preparatory condition always leads to a form of inefficiency which involves superfluity or futility, the third and fourth rule of communication are: *Do not perform any superfluous speech acts* and *Do not perform any futile speech acts.*

The commandment "Be to the point" does not refer to conditions for individual speech acts: It pertains to the relation between speech acts in a speech event. In order to fulfill this requirement, the performance of the speech act has to be

[6]As has been stressed in chapter 3, for our purposes, it does not really matter what the speaker privately thinks but what he can be held accountable to publicly. For the sake of convenience, the terms "responsibility" and "sincerity" are here used interchangeably.

a relevant addition to the speech acts already performed in the verbal and non-verbal context where it occurs. The requirement is fulfilled only if the sequencing of speech acts is appropriate in the discourse. Therefore, the fifth rule of communication is: *Do not perform any speech acts that do not appropriately connect to preceding speech acts.*

It is difficult to specify what an appropriate sequel or an appropriate reaction is. As every speech act seeks to achieve the communicative effect that the listener understands the speech act and the interactional effect that he accepts it, a speech act expressing that another speech act has been understood or accepted will always be relevant. The same applies, of course, to an expression of nonunderstanding or nonacceptance. Along the same lines, giving reasons for why something is or is not accepted will also be relevant. Incidentally, one important complication that should be borne in mind when determining the appropriateness of a certain continuation is that a relevant reaction need not necessarily be appropriate in the sense that it meets the speaker's wishes or expectations most closely: Turning down a request may be as relevant as accepting it.[7]

As a matter of fact, it is not always easy to say exactly when a rule of communication has been violated. In one case, the rules will have to be applied more stringently than in another. Some discussions, for example, are highly organized and subjected to a strict rule of order, in which case it will be easier to tell what is and what is not appropriate (Rule 5) than during a spontaneous conversation over a couple of beers. It will also be easier to determine the degree of efficiency (Rules 3 and 4) in formal discussions with strict time limits than in a free talk. And it is to be hoped that honesty (Rule 2) is more scrupulously lived up to in cabinet meetings than is usually the case in a bar.

In the context of a conversation about where to buy a toaster, "Woolworth's toasters are the best" can be an example of an indirect speech act. By performing a speech act with the communicative function of a statement (assertive), the speaker is indirectly performing a speech act with the communicative function of an advice (directive). Reactions like "Thanks for the hint" and "I'll make a note of it" show that the listener has understood the indirect speech act correctly.

There are various things about indirect speech acts that are striking. First, an indirect speech act has, simultaneously, two communicative functions: The toaster example, for instance, is both a statement and a piece of advice. In some cases, the speaker deliberately tries to leave it indeterminate whether his utterance also has an indirect function.

Second, the speech act that is performed literally remains the same in all

[7]For one part of the text to be relevant to another, a functional relation must exist between these two parts that is instrumental in light of a certain textual objective. In the literature, two different approaches to textual relevance can be distinguished: Dascal (1977), Sanders (1980), Tracy (1982), and other discourse analysts opt for an interpretative angle, whereas Johnson and Blair (1983), Govier (1985), and Iseminger (1986), and other (informal) logicians have taken a normative approach. (For a more comprehensive conception of relevance cf. Sperber & Wilson, 1986.)

contexts, whereas the speech act that is performed indirectly can vary according to context. If the statement about toasters is the answer to the question "Where can I get a new toaster?", then the indirect speech act is a piece of advice, but in another context it might be the conclusion of a comparative test. In other cases where the speaker leaves the exact function of his utterance indeterminate, the interpretation is not so clear. Then, the exact communicative function may even be subject to negotiation between the speaker and the listener.

Third, the speech act performed literally is, as a rule, implicit. Usually, the indirect meaning can be conveyed thanks to this implicitness. If, in the example, the speaker had said emphatically "I assert that Woolworth's toasters are the best," there would be little room for the indirect interpretation that it is a piece of advice to buy a toaster at Woolworth's. The very fact that the speaker emphasizes that his speech act is an assertion can even be taken to be an indication that he does *not* want to advise the listener.

Finally, the indirect meaning of the speech act is related to its literal meaning. Assuming that the stress on "Woolworth's" and "toasters" was not equal and that the reply was not intended to suggest that if Woolworth's toasters are good, their kettles may also be good, then answering the question "Where can I get a red kettle?" by saying "Woolworth's toasters are the best" is not an appropriate reaction and certainly not a piece of advice. And if the question "Where can I get a new toaster?" is not answered with the statement "Woolworth's toasters are the best" but with the counterquestion "Is your old one broken, then?", that might be an appropriate reaction but it is not a piece of advice.

Not every hypothetical speech act that comes out well in the context can simply be taken to be an indirect speech act performed in that context. Which indirect speech act is performed also depends on the literal speech act by means of which it is performed. In a given context, in order to be regarded as the indirect speech act, the speech act performed literally must be linked to this indirect speech act in a meaningful way. In natural discourse, this normally means that there must also be a relation either with the propositional content or the communicative function of a speech act performed earlier or with the nonverbal context.

In the Woolworth's example there is such a meaningful relation if the statement "Woolworth's toasters are the best" is regarded as a recommendation to go and buy a toaster at Woolworth's. Then, the assertion made in this utterance is linked to the preceding request for advice concerning the best place to buy a new toaster, since the assertion provides a reason why it is possible to recommend Woolworth's as a place to buy toasters, and thereby fulfills one of the preparatory conditions for a correct piece of advice.

In practice, listeners are almost always perfectly well able to establish, on the basis of what the speaker has said, which indirect speech act has been performed. If this were not the case, there would be no point in performing it.

However, unlike people communicating person to person, the analyst does not always have sufficient insight into all the contextual and other factors. He must be able to provide reasons in support of his analysis. When can the speaker be held to something? How exactly can an indirect speech act be inferred from the implicit speech act that is performed literally? In answering these crucial questions, the general rules of communication are indispensable.

With indirect speech acts, one of the implications of the literal interpretation is always that a rule of communication would have been violated. This violation may be remedied by interpreting the speech act as an indirect speech act. To the extent that we can put up a plausible argument that if we take the speaker's words literally we accuse him of not observing the principle of communication, when all the time it is also possible to attach to his words a nonliteral interpretation in which he does, and which also appears to be closer to what he could sensibly mean, a nonliteral interpretation must be chosen. Unless he ostentatiously prefers to be thought unreasonable—as people sometimes do—the speaker can also be held to this. Only in case of irony or sarcasm it is more often less clear to what exactly the speaker is committed.

The rules of communication make it possible both to establish that the literal interpretation of the speech act is not the right one and to find out how the correct interpretation can be inferred. To regard the utterance "Woolworth's toasters are the best" in the given context merely as an assertion is to ascribe a violation of Rule 5 to the speaker, because, in itself, the assertion is not an appropriate reaction to the request for advice on where to buy a new toaster. This violation can be made good by analyzing the utterance as meaning something like "I advise you to buy a toaster at Woolworth's." According to this analysis, the speaker has given a piece of advice, so that there is no need to ascribe a violation of Rule 5 to him. The relation between the indirect and the literal speech act is that the former links the latter, in an adequate way, to the question to which the speech act reacts.

In every case where an utterance is analyzed as an indirect speech act it must be possible to indicate which rule of communication would be broken if the speech act were to be analyzed literally. It must also be possible to make it clear that the violation concerned can be undone by analyzing the utterance as an indirect speech act.

Take "Can you get going?" Literally, this is a question about someone's physical abilities. In a situation in which the speaker and the listener know each other well and know that there is no reason to doubt the listener's physical abilities, the implication of a literal analysis is that it is assumed that Rule 3 has been violated: The speaker has asked a question to which he already knows the answer. If that is true, then his speech act would be superfluous.

If the utterance is interpreted as a request to get going, the violation of Rule 3 is undone. Here, against this background, Rule 4 enables us to link the literal speech act to the indirect speech act. A preparatory condition for a request is that the speaker must assume the listener to be in a position to accede to the request. If he knew in advance that this is not the case, he would be performing a futile speech act, thereby violating Rule 4. By asking "Can you get going?" he ensures that he will not be violating Rule 4.

In many cases, indirectness may be motivated by the wish to remain polite. Instead of giving straightforward, and possibly face-threatening orders, the boss can then take refuge in asking a polite question. In cases like "Miss Finch, can you help at desk four for a moment?", this endeavor to create a semblance of politeness is very clear.

The general inference schemes for analyzing direct and indirect speech acts run as follows.

1.
The speaker/writer S has uttered *U*.

2.
If *U* is taken literally,
S has performed speech act 1,
with communicative function 1
and propositional content 1.

| DIRECT SPEECH ACTS | INDIRECT SPEECH ACTS |
|---|---|
| 3a.<br>In context C, speech act 1 observes the rules of communication. | 3b.<br>In context C, speech act 1 is a violation of communication rule *i*. |
| 4a.<br>*Therefore*: Speech act 1 is a correct interpretation of *U*. | 4b.<br>In context C, speech act 2 observes rule *i* and all other communication rules. |
| | 5.<br>Speech act 1, speech act 2 and the context C can be linked by means of rule *j*. |
| | 6.<br>*Therefore*: Speech act 2 is a correct interpretation of *U*. |

## CONVENTIONALIZATION OF INDIRECT SPEECH ACTS

In indirect speech acts, the context plays an important role. Although in some special cases the inferences can take place without referring to the context, in most cases it cannot.[8] The role of the context can be illustrated by reference to two examples discussed earlier.

1. Speaker 1: "Where can I get a new toaster?"
   Speaker 2: "Woolworth's toasters are the best."
2. Speaker: "Can you get going?"

In Example 1, Speaker 2's utterance is a response to Speaker 1's question. It cannot simply be interpreted as an assertion but must be analyzed as a piece of advice. This analysis will also hold in other specific contexts where the assertion is a reaction to a request for advice. However, "Woolworth's toasters are the best" can only be analyzed as a piece of advice in a context where such advice is called for; in other contexts, the same utterance may be an assertive which functions as a standpoint or simply as a statement of fact. Only in a specific and well-defined context is it justified to analyze this utterance as a piece of advice.[9]

In Example 2, on the other hand, "Can you get going?" is understood to be a request, unless it is uttered in a specific context where it is clear that a direct answer to the literal question is called for. Such a specific context occurs, for instance, when the listener has only just recovered from a broken leg. If there is no special context like this, the utterance is more likely to be interpreted as an indirect request than as a question designed to elicit information about the physical capabilities of the addressee.

It is not difficult to find other examples of utterances which, when interpreted literally, merely ask for information concerning the listener's capacity to carry out a particular action but which, normally, must be interpreted as indirect directives: "Can you turn the radio down a little?", "Can you pass the mayonnaise?", "Can you give me that bikini back?", "Can you take your fingers out of your nose?", "Can you just mow the lawn this afternoon?" The same holds for utterances that, when interpreted literally, ask whether the listener is willing to perform a particular

[8]In the course of a conversation (or any other form of discourse) the context is constantly developing: it "takes into itself" from what is said and what is happening all that is relevant to the production and understanding of further utterances. Most utterances depend for their understanding upon the information contained in previous utterances. According to Lyons, cases of "restricted contexts" in which the participants in a conversation do not draw upon their previous knowledge of one another or the "information" communicated in earlier utterances, but where they only share the more general beliefs, conventions and presuppositions governing the particular "universe of discourse" in the society to which they belong are comparatively rare (1971).

[9]It is worth noting that the term "context" is used here in a similar broad sense as in Crawshay-Williams (1957), where it pertains to the purpose of utterances in a speech event.

action: "Will you settle up?", "Will you help me put my curlers in on Tuesday?", "Will you shut up for a moment?", "Will you turn the radio down a bit?", "Will you pass the mayonnaise?"

As is clear from these examples, some indirect speech acts performed by means of fixed modes of expression ("Can you," "Will you") do not require a well-defined context for their interpretation.[10] Such indirect speech acts are strongly conventionalized: The expressions used in presenting the speech acts concerned are conventionally used to perform these speech acts. The convention may even be so strong that it seems as if the speech act is not indirect at all but direct.[11]

Nevertheless, it is not difficult to think of examples of cases in which speech acts of the "Can you" type are performed without being indirect requests: "Can you play the piano?", "Can you juggle with three balls?" Even with questions that are meant as requests it is always possible to react to the question as literally worded: "I can, but I shan't," "No I can't, my foot's gone to sleep," "No I won't; do it yourself." So it is not the case that the indirect meaning has become the only meaning.

Indirect speech acts may vary from weakly conventionalized (requiring a well-defined context) to strongly conventionalized (not requiring a well-defined context), but, of course, in practice, there are many cases which lie between these extremes.[12] In all cases, the indirectness may affect the propositional content as well as the communicative function:

| | *literal interpretation* | *indirect interpretation* |
|---|---|---|
| 1. | (I assert) Woolworth's toasters are the best. | I advise you to buy a toaster from Woolworth's. |
| 2. | (I ask you) are you able to get going? | I request you to get going. |

There are examples of indirect speech acts in which the propositional content remains the same and only the communicative function changes. There are also examples in which it is the communicative function that remains the same and the propositional content that changes. "He's a real Dutchman" may be an example

[10]In such cases, the blank context that Lyons calls "restricted" would suffice (1971, p. 419).

[11]This explains why some authors are inclined to consider such cases to be abbreviated forms (Levinson, 1983) or part of the literal meaning (Sadock, 1974) instead of considering them as indirect speech acts. Ultimately, it depends of course on the basic assumptions of one's theory of meaning whether such expressions are considered as direct or indirect.

[12]Because of its usage-dependent and context-dependent relativity, indirectness is, in our opinion, hard to classify into a limited number of well-delineated and homogeneous types. In Jacobs and Jackson's (1983) middle course between Searle (1979) and Levinson (1983), indirectness is, just like in our approach, a matter of degree. From an analytical perspective, the degree of indirectness corresponds to the extent that the speaker strategically keeps his distance from the communicative meaning he tries to convey.

of the latter, if this assertion in a well-defined context indirectly means "He wants everybody to pay for themselves." An example of a change that is limited to the communicative function, is the expressive "I would like you to do it at once," which in any context indirectly performs the request "I request you to do it at once" with the same propositional content (*you do it at once*).

With the help of the inference scheme for analyzing indirect speech acts it is possible to infer the indirect function or the indirect proposition from the utterance (see Tables 5.1 and 5.2).

TABLE 5.1
Weakly Conventionalized Indirect Speech Acts in a Well-Defined Context

| *Communicative Function* | *Propositional Content* |
|---|---|
| a. "I suppose the WC's downstairs." | b. "There's a fantastic film on at the Regal." |
| 1. S, who has come to see L's new house, has said (a) | By way of reaction to L's suggestion that they stay at home, S has said (b) |
| 2. Interpreted literally, (a) is an assertive (supposition) | Interpreted literally, (b) is an assertive (statement) with the propositional content that there's a fantastic film on at the Regal |
| 3. In this context, this literal speech act is superfluous because L surely knows where, in his own house, the WC is (violation of Rule 3) | In this context, this literal speech act is not to the point because it is not an appropriate reaction to L's suggestion (violation of Rule 5) |
| 4. In this context, the directive (question) "Where is the WC?" is not superfluous, because S is a stranger to L's new house | In this context, the directive (suggestion) "Let's go to the cinema" is to the point because it is a rejection of L's suggestion (violation undone) |
| 5. By supposing that the WC is downstairs, S indicates that he does not know the answer to the question of where the WC is: the question is not superfluous (linked through Rule 3) | To S, the fact that there is a fantastic film on at the Regal is a reason for rejecting L's suggestion and advancing his own proposal: (b) is an appropriate sequel to S's suggestion (link through rule 5) |
| 6. *Therefore:* The question "Where is the WC?" is a correct interpretation of (a) | *Therefore:* The suggestion "Let's go to the cinema" is a correct interpretation of (b) |

TABLE 5.2
Strongly Conventionalized Indirect Speech Acts Without a Well-Defined Context

| *Communicative Function* | *Propositional Content* |
|---|---|
| c. "I would like to know the time." | d. "The coast's clear." |
| 1. S has said (c) | S has said (d) |
| 2. Interpreted literally, (c) is an expressive (expression of a wish) | Interpreted literally, (d) is an assertive (statement) in which S informs L that there is nobody there |
| 3. In most contexts, this literal speech act is futile because L will not be interested in such a wish (violation of Rule 4) | In most contexts, this literal speech act is futile because L will not be interested in this information (violation of Rule 4) |
| 4. In most contexts, the directive (request) "Please tell me the time" is not a futile speech act, unless, for example, L is not wearing a watch (violation undone) | In most contexts, the directive (recommendation) "Go ahead" is not a futile speech act, unless, for example, L is not capable of moving (violation undone) |
| 5. By expressing the wish to know the time, S fulfills the responsibility condition for a sincere request (link through Rule 2) | The fact that there is nobody there may to L be a reason for implementing the recommendation that he go ahead: (d) is an appropriate sequel to S's recommendation (link through Rule 5) |
| 6. *Therefore:* The request "Please tell me the time" is a correct interpretation of (c) | *Therefore:* The recommendation "Go ahead" is a correct interpretation of (d) |

CHAPTER 6

# Unexpressed Premises in Argumentative Discourse

## ANALYSIS AT THE PRAGMATIC AND THE LOGICAL LEVEL

To establish precisely what someone who has advanced argumentation can be held to if the argumentative discourse is analyzed as a critical discussion, an analysis must be carried out both at a pragmatic and at a logical level. At the pragmatic level, the analysis is directed toward reconstructing the complex speech act performed in advancing the argumentation, while at the logical level, the reasoning underlying the argumentation is reconstructed. In practice, the logical analysis is instrumental for the pragmatic analysis.

If, in the argumentation, parts of the arguments are implicit, then a logical analysis is indispensable. There may be unexpressed premises but also unexpressed conclusions.[1] In both cases, the missing elements can only be properly identified by starting from the explicit elements and then reconstructing the argument so that it becomes logically valid.[2]

---

[1]Other authors sometimes talk about elements that are "hidden" or "suppressed" by the speaker. As we do not want to speculate about what the speaker "had in mind" when putting forward his argumentation, let alone about his rhetorical strategies, we prefer the neutral term "unexpressed." In our externalizing perspective, making unexpressed elements explicit amounts to reconstructing with the help of the rules of communication what can reasonably be deemed understood in the discourse. Unexpressed premises and conclusions are then specific implicit elements in the presentation of the argumentation.

[2]Although some commitment to a clear criterion of validity is here required, this does not necessarily imply a dogmatic commitment to deductivism. At this juncture, we do not want to take a specific and definitive stance on the question exactly what kind of logical validity criterion is to be preferred. Just for the sake of simplicity, we shall restrict ourselves in our present exposé on unexpressed premises

It is perfectly normal for argumentative discourse to contain elements that remain implicit or speech acts that are performed indirectly. From a pragmatic point of view this does not automatically mean that the discourse is defective.

Sometimes, in argumentation, the identification of implicit and indirect speech acts is quite simple. For example, a woman who argues (a) "All women are nosy" and (b) "Angie's certainly a real woman" can clearly also be held to the unexpressed standpoint (c) "Angie is nosy." By adding (c) as a conclusion to the argument whose premises are expressed in (a) and (b) we arrive at a logically valid argument. Although the speaker has said only (a) and (b), if it may be assumed that she is advancing argumentation and that in doing so she wishes to abide by the rules of communication, she can also be held to (c).

In many cases, however, it is not as easy as this to see exactly what needs to be added to an incomplete argument. This is particularly true if what is missing is not a conclusion but a premise, because then there usually are various possibilities.

To be able to establish which premise has been left unexpressed, an appeal must be made to the rules of communication and to the logical validity criterion. Leaving a premise unexpressed appears, at first sight, to be a violation of a rule of communication. However, this is only so if nothing more is taken into consideration than what is expressed explicitly and if this is interpreted literally. The violation can be made undone by treating the unexpressed premise as a special sort of indirect speech act which is conveyed implicitly by the argument.

An important difference between an unexpressed premise and other implicit speech acts is that in analyzing an unexpressed premise the logical validity criterion can be used, whereas in other cases there is no such tool available for the analysis. Taken literally, in an argumentation in which a premise has been left unexpressed, the argument concerned is invalid. If it is analyzed as conveying an indirect speech act, however, the missing premise can be added to the argument so that the invalidity is corrected.

A speaker who performs the complex speech act of argumentation does so in order to convince the listener that his standpoint is acceptable. Because of the responsibility condition, the listener is entitled to assume that the speaker himself believes that the argumentation is an acceptable defense of his standpoint; if the speaker does not believe this, he is guilty of manipulation or deceit. Because of the preparatory condition, the listener is also entitled to assume that the speaker believes that the listener will accept his argumentation: If the speaker does not believe this, the performance of the speech act is, seen from his angle, pointless.

---

to making use of the well-known and ready-made instruments of propositional logic and first-order predicate logic. This does not automatically mean that we agree with Rescher's view of an "inductive inference" as *"an aspiring but failed deductive inference"* (1980, p. 10). For a discussion of some alleged disadvantages of dogmatic deductivism, see Govier (1987).

If the speaker is sincere and does not believe that his argumentation is futile, this also means that he assumes that the listener will be inclined to apply the same criteria of acceptability as himself. These criteria will include the criterion of logical validity: Because of the responsibility condition the speaker may be assumed to believe that the argument underlying his argumentation is valid, and because of the preparatory condition he may be assumed to believe that the listener will believe this too.

If a literal interpretation of the argumentation produces an invalid argument, the speaker appears to have performed a futile speech act, thus having violated the fourth rule of communication. He may also appear to have been insincere, thus having violated the second rule of communication. However, argumentative discourse must be analyzed on the basis that the speaker observes the principle of communication and wishes, in principle, to abide by all the rules of communication. Therefore, the analyst must examine whether it is possible to complement the invalid argument in such a way that it becomes valid.

If it is indeed possible to add a proposition to the invalid argument which validates it, the violation of the second and fourth rule is undone. Assuming that contextual and other situational factors are duly taken into account, the added premise may then be regarded as the unexpressed premise of the argumentation. Here is an example:

1. Angie is a real woman
2. Therefore, Angie is nosy

In the form in which it is proffered, the argument "(1) therefore, (2)" is invalid and the fourth rule of communication, and possibly also the second, has been broken. The argument can be rendered valid by adding the proposition (1a) "All real women are nosy," thus undoing the violation of Rule 4 (and 2). In principle, (1a) could therefore be regarded as an unexpressed premise in the argumentation.

If, in this example, the speaker is acting on the generally understood assumption that real women are, indeed, nosy, then the performance of the speech act "All real women are nosy" is superfluous. If made, the utterance would be an infringement of the third rule of communication. By apparently breaking Rule 4, the speaker avoids a real violation of Rule 3. So, the rules of communication are not only tools for identifying unexpressed premises, but they make it also possible to explain why a premise could have been left unexpressed.

If an argumentation in which a premise has been left unexpressed can be reconstructed in such a way that a valid argument is produced, there need no longer be any question of any kind of shortcoming. Anybody who nevertheless, for this reason of incompleteness, considers the argumentation defective, erroneously takes the logical requirement of formal validity to be one of the felicity conditions for the performance of speech acts, thus confusing the logical and the pragmatic level of analysis.

## UNEXPRESSED PREMISES AS INDIRECT SPEECH ACTS

Unexpressed premises are a special sort of indirect speech acts. This can be illustrated by showing that the inference scheme for identifying unexpressed premises is, in fact, an amended version of the general inference scheme for analyzing indirect speech acts:

1.
The speaker/writer S has uttered utterance $U_1$
in defense of his standpoint *Stp*

2.
S has thereby performed a complex speech act
of argumentation that is directed toward
justifying *Stp*

3.
The argument expressed in "$U_1$, therefore *Stp*" (a)
is invalid;
the performance of the speech act of argumentation
is a violation of Rule 4 (and possibly Rule 2)

4.
Adding $U_2$ to argument (a) produces
a valid argument (b) "$U_1$ and $U_2$, therefore *Stp*";
the performance of the speech acts $U_1$ and $U_2$
constitutes an argumentation which conforms
to all the rules of communication

5.
*Therefore:*
$U_2$ is an unexpressed premise of S's argumentation

Of course, there are various ways of augmenting an incomplete argument to validate it. Theoretically, there are in fact too many logical possibilities. However, as stated in (4), an unexpressed premise is only pragmatically appropriate if the reconstruction conforms to *all* the rules of communication. So, it is not enough that the added premise renders the argument valid.[3]

When identifying an unexpressed premise, the question of how to choose from a variety of different candidates can be more easily answered if a distinction is

[3]This observation is made by many authors. Scriven (1976) proposed to single out the optimal assumption and Hitchcock (1987) to formulate the universal generalization of the associated conditional.

made between a "logical minimum" and a "pragmatic optimum." The logical minimum is the premise that consists of the "if . . . then . . ." sentence that has as its antecedent the explicit premise and as its consequent the conclusion of the explicit argument. The valid argument resulting from this addition has the form of *modus ponens*. So, the logical minimum amounts to connecting the pieces of information that are already there: All it does is to state explicitly that it is permitted to infer the given conclusion from the given premise.

Pragmatically, this is not enough. From the very fact that he advances this particular argumentation for his standpoint it is already clear that the speaker assumes that this conclusion follows from this premise. The logical minimum contributes nothing new and is, therefore, superfluous. Identifying this logical minimum as the unexpressed premise means that a violation of the third rule of communication is unnecessarily ascribed to the speaker.

The pragmatic optimum is the premise that makes the argument valid and also prevents a violation of Rule 3 and any other rule of communication. Predominantly, this is a matter of generalizing the logical minimum, making it as informative as possible without ascribing unwarranted commitments to the speaker and formulating it in a colloquial way that fits in with the rest of the argumentative discourse. In "Angie is a real woman, therefore, she is nosy," these requirements can be met by adding "Real women are nosy." Here, the logical minimum (2a) and the pragmatic optimum (2b) are:

1.
Angie is a real woman

2a.
[If Angie is a real woman,
then she is nosy]

2b.
[Real women are nosy]

3.
*Therefore:* Angie is nosy

## THE ROLE OF THE CONTEXT IN DETERMINING THE PRAGMATIC OPTIMUM

The question is: How far can the analyst go in "pragmatizing" the logical minimum? In our opinion, the decisive factor is that it should be reasonable to attribute the added premise to the speaker in the context in which the argumentation occurs.[4] If the speaker says in an ordinary conversation that Angie is a real

[4]Our use of the term *context* is in accord with the rhetorical tradition and includes the verbal as well as the situational context. The situational context may be determined by the circumstances in which the communication takes place and by the institutional framework of the speech event, that is a legal procedure in a court of law or a procedure of congressional decision-making.

woman and that she is, therefore, nosy, he has, at the same time, committed himself to the proposition that real women are nosy. To assert the first and deny the second would be a pragmatic inconsistency. There is always a danger, however, that the added premise goes too far and that more is attributed to the speaker than he can be held responsible for.

The analyst must determine what the speaker can be held to on the basis of what he has said. He must establish whether it is reasonable to assume that a would-be unexpressed premise actually belongs to the commitments of the speaker. Otherwise, it might even be the case that something is attributed to him of which it is clear that he regards it as false. Quite without reason, he is then blamed for violating the second rule of communication.

Even if all the communicative requirements are met, this does not automatically mean that the analyst has arrived at the one and only unexpressed premise. This can be illustrated with the help of an example:

1.
Maggie is a liberal

2a.
If Maggie is a liberal, she is progressive

2b.
Liberals are progressive

2c.
People with an interest in politics are progressive

2d.
All women are progressive

3.
*Therefore:* Maggie is progressive

In this example the speaker has said: "Maggie is a liberal, so she is progressive." (1) is the argumentation that he has advanced in defense of his standpoint (3). Literally, the argument "(1), therefore (3)" is invalid. This argument can be validated by adding the logical minimum (2a), which is, of course, part of the speaker's commitments. However, because it adds nothing new, it does not fulfill the nonsuperfluity rule. If (2b) refers to all liberals, it also validates the argument. Unlike (2a), (2b) does add a new element and this is unquestionably one of the speaker's commitments: If nothing specific is known about the context which explains otherwise, he can hardly maintain that he does not believe that liberals are progressive without being guilty of inconsistency. So, (2b) complies with all the rules of communication.

With some minor adjustments, (2c) and (2d) are also capable of rendering the argument valid. Unquestionably, they too contribute a new element, but with the contextual information so far available it is doubtful whether this new element is part of the speaker's commitments. If the context provides no further clues, commitments as implied in (2c) and (2d) can certainly not be inferred from the speaker's words. The danger would therefore be that he will be credited or blamed, as the case may be, for something he does not believe at all.

In some cases, the context will allow the analyst to attribute more detailed or more far-reaching commitments to the speaker such as implied in (2c) or (2d). At an earlier stage in the conversation, the speaker may, for example, have said that he equates being liberal with being interested in politics, or being liberal with being female. It may, of course, also happen that the speaker later on in the conversation takes responsibility for more than he is committed to on the grounds of what he has actually said, but such extra commitments can never be regarded as unexpressed premises in his argumentation as stated. In other words, unless a well-defined context clearly indicates otherwise, (2b) is the only serious candidate for the pragmatic optimum.

Unfortunately, the context does not always provide enough clarity to decide about the pragmatic optimum. Take the following text of a lecture entitled "The destruction of beauty as a means of pushing back the past":

> Running down the levels of heritage conservation is a short-sighted policy. It leads not only to a decline in people's memories of the past but also to an irrevocable impoverishment of the natural beauty of the countryside.

Here, it is not very informative to add "Reducing people's memories of the past is short-sighted" and "The irrevocable impoverishment of the natural beauty of the countryside is short-sighted" as unexpressed premises. Yet, in this case, it is difficult to find more informative candidates to which the speaker may be held committed. In cases like these, it is all too easy for a conflict to arise between the requirements of informativeness and commitment. So the analyst has to sail between the rocks of triviality and noncommitment. Sometimes, as in this example, he may even be forced to consider the logical minimum as the pragmatic optimum as well. As long as the context provides no clue at all as to what has been left unexpressed, a strategy of *minimal complementization* should be adopted that implies that an added premise is being chosen that is virtually identical to the logical minimum.

The general procedure to be followed by the analyst who wants to determine the pragmatic optimum can be summarized as follows:

1. Determine what the argumentation is in which a premise has been left unexpressed.
2. Determine how well-defined the context is in which the argumentation occurs.

3. Determine which added premises could validate the argument underlying the argumentation.
4. Determine which of these added premises may, in the context at hand, be considered to be part of the commitments of the speaker.
5. Determine which of the added premises to which the speaker is committed, is the most informative in the context at hand.

## Example of How an Unexpressed Premise can be Made Explicit

Father, mother, and daughter are finishing supper. The daughter is looking rather depressed.

Mother: "There's no sense in waiting for Mr. Right to come along, dear: *I* never did."

## Analysis

Standpoint: It makes no sense for you to wait for Mr. Right to come along.
Argumentation: I never waited for Mr. Right to come along.

## Reconstruction of the Argument: Logical Minimum (2a) and Pragmatic Optimum (2b)

Premise 1: I never waited for Mr. Right to come along.
Premise 2a: [If (1), then (3)]
Premise 2b: [As far as your love life is concerned, you should always behave like me]
Conclusion 3: It makes no sense for you to wait for Mr. Right to come along.

## Procedure for Inferring the Unexpressed Premise

a. To support her standpoint (3) that it makes no sense for her daughter to wait for Mr. Right to come along, the mother has argued (1) that she herself never waited for Mr. Right to come along.
b. The argumentation is put forward in the context of a conversation about the problem of finding a suitable husband between mother and daughter, who just had a disappointing experience.
c. The argument "I never waited for Mr. Right to come along (1), therefore,

it makes no sense for you to wait for Mr. Right to come along (3)" can, for example, be validated by adding the premise:

(2a) "(1), therefore (3)"

or (2b) "As far as your love life is concerned, you should always behave like me."

or (2c) "You should always behave like me."

or (2d) "I always do what makes sense."

or (2e) "One should always do what makes sense."

d. In this context, the speaker, Mother, is, at any rate, committed to (2a) and to (2b), but not to (2c), (2d) or (2e) because (2c) ignores that Mother may consider herself to be an expert only in love affairs, (2d) that she may know quite well that she makes lots of mistakes in other spheres of life, and (2e) that she may find that other people than her daughter are free to do foolish things, whether in their love life or in other matters.

e. In this context, (2b) is more informative than (2a), so, (2b) is the pragmatic optimum and must, therefore, be considered as the premise which has been left unexpressed in Mother's argumentation.

## THE ROLE OF LOGIC IN MAKING UNEXPRESSED PREMISES EXPLICIT

The starting point for making unexpressed premises explicit consists in reconstructing the reasoning underlying the argumentation as a logically valid argument, whose conclusion cannot be false if the premises are true. Often, it is easier to recognize that the argument is invalid in the form in which it is presented than to formulate the extra premise or premises that validate it. Moreover, it is not always clear whether the argument should indeed be validated. The speaker may, after all, well have argued in an invalid way.

The problem of validating an incomplete argument can be simplified by assuming that every argument, whether it is part of a chain of reasoning or not, consists of two premises and a conclusion. In reality, this need not necessarily be so, but there is little harm in starting from this assumption. For its logical reconstruction, an argumentation can then be split up into one or more separate arguments each of which consists of two premises and a conclusion. Usually, in the presentation of these arguments in the argumentation one of the two premises is left unexpressed.

One advantage of this simplification is that the analyst can work with small, manageable units. Following classical syllogistic logic for once in handling these units, he might take it that each of them is supposed to have a *major* premise (containing the *major* term) and a *minor* premise (containing the *minor* term). The subject part of the conclusion refers to the minor term (B) and the predicate part to the major term (A). Since the minor and the major premise also have a subject and a predicate part, there are four ways in which these parts can be distributed:

| a. 1. A is M | b. 1. A is M | c. 1. M is A | d. 1. M is A |
|---|---|---|---|
| 2. B is M | 2. M is B | 2. M is B | 2. B is M |
| /∴ 3. B is A | 3. B is A | 3. B is A | 3. B is A |

There is a common (subject or predicate) part in both premises: the *middle* term (M). If one of the premises is missing, it is in these cases easier to reconstruct it correctly, starting from the conclusion and from the premise that has been formulated. The number of possibilities has now, at least, been reduced to two: one with the middle term as subject and one with the middle term as predicate.

In some contexts, the major premise may be missing, in others the minor. In either case, it is pragmatic, not logical, factors that determine what a speaker leaves out (and *can* leave out without problems). An example may clarify the two possibilities:

1a. Charlie Parker was a great jazz musician
2a. [All great jazz musicians die young]
3. *Therefore:* Charlie Parker died young

1b. All great jazz musicians die young
2b. [Charlie Parker was a great jazz musician]
3. *Therefore:* Charlie Parker died young

Someone who defends (3) with (1a) assumes that the listener does not know who Charlie Parker was but *is* aware that great musicians always die young, whereas someone who defends the same standpoint with (1b) assumes that the listener knows that Charlie Parker was a great jazz musician. Although the argumentation in (1a) is different from that in (1b), in both cases the same logically valid reasoning is expressed.

Of course, although they may not be very common in practice, there are some arguments that neither have two premises nor can be easily reconstructed as arguments with two premises:

| | | |
|---|---|---|
| 1. | $p \vee q$ | Clothes either follow the fashion or go against it |
| 2. | $p \rightarrow r$ | If they follow the fashion, they are worn by the vain |
| 3. | $q \rightarrow s$ | If they go against the fashion, they are worn by stick-in-the-muds |
| /∴ 4. | $r \vee s$ | Clothes are worn either by the vain or by stick-in-the-muds |

The suggested procedure of simplification, furthermore, only works with "categorical" propositions of the following four types: "All S are P," "No S are P,"

"Some S are P," and "Some S are not P." In argumentative discourse, not all premises are of these types, although they can often be rewritten as such.

Apart from the valid argument forms of syllogistic logic, there are, of course, many other argument forms which are valid in other logical systems.[5] In classical propositional and predicate logic, which we have chosen as our practical starting point, well-known valid argument forms are, for example, *modus ponens* and *modus tollens*. With the help of these argument forms a proposition can be methodically justified or refuted:

1. If *p*, then *q*
2. *p*
3. Therefore: *q* (*modus ponens*)

If it is true that "If (proposition) *p*, then (proposition) *q*" and "(proposition) *p*," then it is also true that "(proposition) *q*":

1. When Jack goes dancing he puts on his black dancing shoes.
2. Jack is going dancing.
3. Therefore he is putting on his black dancing shoes.

Should the conclusion (3) prove to be false, then, because the argument is valid, either premise (1) or premise (2) is false, or both. If one or both of the premises are false, then there is no guarantee that the conclusion is true.

1. If *p*, then *q*
2. Not *q*
3. Therefore: not *p* (*modus tollens*)

For example:

1. When it thaws, the snow melts.
2. The snow is not melting.
3. Therefore it is not thawing.

In this argument, the proposition that it is thawing is refuted. If the refutation not only takes this logically valid argument form but it also happens to have premises that are true, then it is beyond question that the proposition "It is thawing" has been refuted. Should it emerge that the conclusion (3) is false, then, again, at least one if not both of the premises must also be false. If it *is* thawing, the snow, according to Premise (1), ought to be melting. According to Premise

[5]For a discussion of the variety in systems of logics, see Haack (1978). Barth and Krabbe (1982) illustrated the dimensions along which logics may differ.

(2) this is precisely what is not happening. In this case, Premise (1) and Premise (2) cannot both be true, so that either (1) or (2) must be false.

The logical knowledge to be used in the reconstruction of argumentation includes, among many other things, that, in classical propositional logic, a double negation of a proposition is equivalent to that proposition itself. Then, an argumentation that first seems nonsensical can sometimes be reconstructed as an argument of the *modus tollens* form. For example:

> Arnold's not going dancing, because when he goes dancing Bert doesn't. And Bert is!

This text can be abbreviated as follows:

1. not A

*because*

2. a. If A, then not B
   b. B

At first sight, the underlying argument is:

2. a. $A \rightarrow \neg B$
   b. $B$

---

/∴ 1. $\neg A$

This argument may at first sight seem invalid but because B is equivalent to $\neg\neg B$, it is, in fact, valid (*modus tollens*):

2. a. $A \rightarrow \neg B$
   b. $\neg\neg B$

---

/∴ 1. $\neg A$

If the analyst were to rely only on the literal verbal presentation of argumentation, he would find very few complete arguments in argumentative discourse, let alone valid ones. In argumentative discourse, usually, no two utterances are wholly identical. Suppose someone tells a story that can be analyzed as follows:

1. My standpoint is that Charlie is going dancing.
2. My argumentation for this is that
   a. Andrew is going dancing.
   b. Either the woman next door or Karen is going dancing.
   c. If Dory goes dancing, Eddie goes too.
   d. Either Fred or Germaine is going dancing and Harry is certainly going.
   e. If the man next door goes dancing, his sister doesn't.

f. If all his pals go dancing, my brother goes too.

This can be formalized as follows:

2. a. A
   b. W v K
   c. D → E
   d. (F v G) . H
   e. M → ¬S
   f. P → B

/∴ 1. C

No utterance or part of an utterance occurs more than once in the text. On the face of it, it would be difficult to say whether the argument is valid. This changes, however, when it is remembered that Charlie is the speaker's brother, Karen is the sister of his neighbor Andrew, Dory is the woman next door, and the pals of the speaker's brother are Andrew, Dory, Eddie, and Harry. Utterances that differ on the surface may express the same proposition (just as an utterance in English and an utterance in Dutch can express the same proposition). If full account is taken of this in an interpretation at the logical level, we arrive at the following (valid) chain of reasoning:

2. a. A
   b. D v K
   c. D → E
   d. (F v G) . H
   e. A → ¬K
   f. (A . D . E . H) → C

/∴ 1. C

It will be necessary to draw on pragmatic aids, for example, to interpret an argumentation like "If Dory goes dancing, Eddie goes too. And the woman next door, so she's just told me, is certainly going. So Eddie will be going dancing." The valid argument underlying this argumentation can only be reconstructed with the help of the prior knowledge that Dory is the speaker's next-door neighbor.

In order to be able to establish whether "It's already past ten and my train was supposed to leave at five to" leads to the (unexpressed) conclusion "I've missed my train" or to "My train's late," the analyst needs more information about the (nonverbal) context. Has the speaker been waiting on the platform for 20 minutes or is he running into the station from a taxi? Here, more detailed contextual information and specific background knowledge will be indispensable.

CHAPTER 7

# Complex Argumentation Structures

## MULTIPLE ARGUMENTATION

The argumentation put forward in favor of a particular point of view may have a structure that is to a greater or lesser extent complex.[1] Of course, the complexity of the argumentation structure depends not only on the complexity of the dispute the protagonist attempts to resolve, but also on how he thinks he should organize the defense of his standpoint. In principle, every single argumentative move serves to remove some form of doubt that the antagonist may have with regard to the standpoint. In the simplest case, a *single* argumentation, containing just one argument with, usually, one explicit and one unexpressed premise, will be deemed to suffice. In other cases, the protagonist may advance a combination of single argumentations.

Analytically, complex argumentation can always be broken down into single argumentations. Just as a multiple dispute can be analyzed as a combination of two or more simple disputes, so it is possible to analyze *multiple* argumentation as a combination of two or more single argumentations. In multiple argumentation, the constituent single argumentations are, in principle, alternative defenses of the same standpoint.

An example of multiple argumentation is:

> Postal deliveries in Holland are not perfect. You cannot be sure that a letter will be delivered the next day, that it will be delivered to the right address and that it will be delivered early in the morning.

[1]Other authors who pay attention to complex argumentation are Beardsley (1975), Scriven (1976), Finocchiaro (1980), Nolt (1984), Thomas (1986), Fisher (1988), and Freeman (1988).

Here, three independent argumentations support the standpoint that postal deliveries in Holland are not perfect:

1. Sending a letter sometimes takes longer than one day
2. Letters are not always delivered to the right address
3. Deliveries are not always early in the morning

Because each of these single argumentations is, in principle, in itself sufficient to defend the standpoint, one may wonder what is the point of advancing the other two. They seem superfluous. However, they need not be: It is possible that the speaker tries to cater for various kinds of doubt about his standpoint, pertaining to different aspects.[2]

Multiple argumentation can also be used for rhetorical reasons: The profusion of arguments makes the defense appear stronger. The speaker gives the impression of having taken account of every possible objection to his standpoint. He should bear in mind, though, that the abundance may also arouse suspicion: why the overkill? On the other hand, the speaker may realize that the listener need not find all the elements of the multiple argumentation equally compelling, and hope that the acceptance of the one argument will psychologically add to the acceptance of the other, unrelated as they may be. Because acceptance is liable to gradations, in producing a multiplicity of arguments the speaker may gradually overcome the last remaining morsel of doubt in the listener.

It may also simply be that after one argument the speaker advances another quite different sort of argument in the hope that it will be more successful:

> *Father:* "You don't want to vote tomorrow. Who are you going to vote *for*, anyway? All that fuss and bother . . . having to get out of bed . . . Isn't voting rather a right-wing activity, anyway? . . . You'd do better demonstrating if there's something you're not happy with. Why not just stay at home, son."
>
> *Son:* "Nice try, Pa."

Another nice manifestation of multiple argumentation can be found in Multatuli's *Max Havelaar*, a Dutch literary masterpiece:

> *Constable:* "My lord, this is the man who murdered Barbertje."
>
> *Judge:* "The man must hang. How did he do it?"
>
> *Constable:* "He cut her into small pieces, and salted her."
>
> *Judge:* "That was very wrong. He must hang."

---

[2]Then, the speaker assumes that the proposition which is at issue in the standpoint can be specified into various components which can be called into question separately.

*Lothario:* "Your honour, I didn't kill Barbertje! I fed her and clothed her and looked after her. There are witnesses who will testify that I am a good man, and not a murderer."

*Judge:* "Man, you must hang! You are compounding your crime with your conceit. It does not befit someone who has been accused of something, to consider himself a good human being."

*Lothario:* "But your honour, there are witnesses who will confirm it. And now that I am accused of murder . . ."

*Judge:* "You must hang. You cut Barbertje up into little pieces, you salted her away, and you are full of yourself . . . three capital crimes! Who are you, woman?"

*Woman:* "I am Barbertje."

*Lothario:* "Thank God! You see, your honour, that I did not murder her!"

*Judge:* "Hmm . . . yes . . . all right. But what about the salting?"

*Barbertje:* "No, your honour, he never salted me away. On the contrary, he has been very good to me. He is a noble human being!"

*Lothario:* "There you are, your honour, she says I'm a good man."

*Judge:* "Hmm . . . so the *third* count stands. Constable, take him away, he must hang. He is guilty of conceit. Clerk, in the premises, cite the jurisprudence of Lessing's patriarch."

In his concluding words, the judge refers to Lessing's play *Nathan der Weise*, in which the patriarch ignores all the evidence and sends a Jew to the stake.

It is not always so obvious that arguments are actually unconnected. Even if they are dealing with roughly the same thing, two or more separate arguments may also be intended as constituting multiple argumentation. What matters most is that the individual arguments should count as independent defenses of the same standpoint.

Certain words and phrases can, when they occur in argumentative discourse, serve as indicators of multiple argumentation. One complication is that they can all also be used in other ways. Examples of clear indicators are "by the way," "moreover" and "incidentally":

> Willem could never have written that letter. He knows absolutely nothing about economics. Incidentally, he's a real illiterate.

Among the words and phrases that are also employed to indicate multiple argumentation are such common expressions as "quite apart from," "and then I haven't even mentioned the fact that," and "needless to add that."

It is naturally just as well possible to state explicitly that one is about to embark on multiple argumentation: "I shall now give four arguments each of which you will find sufficient to prove that. . . ." And there are also expressions that clearly suggest that the argumentation is *not* multiple. For example, if a succession of arguments is followed by the expression "this proves that . . . ," it may be assumed that it refers to all the preceding arguments together rather than to each of them separately.

Multiple argumentation can be represented schematically as follows:

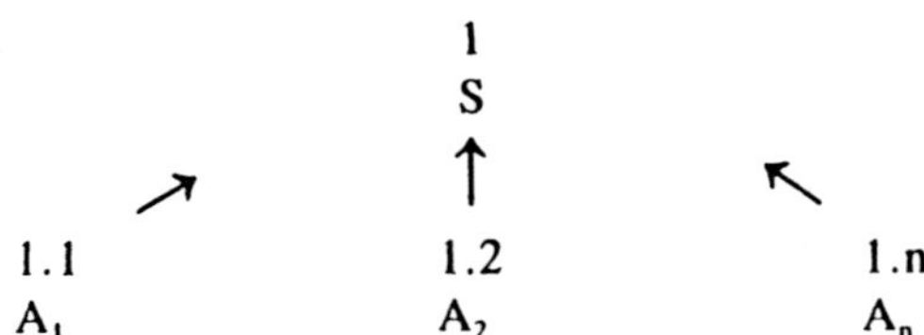


S is the standpoint, A is a single argumentation. Multiple argumentation consists minimally of two single argumentations, numbered sequentially A1, A2, and so on. To make clear that each single argumentation is, in principle, a separate and independent defense of S, each single argumentation is individually linked to S by an arrow.

With this notation it is possible to indicate the precise position of every constituent part of a multiple argumentation. For example:

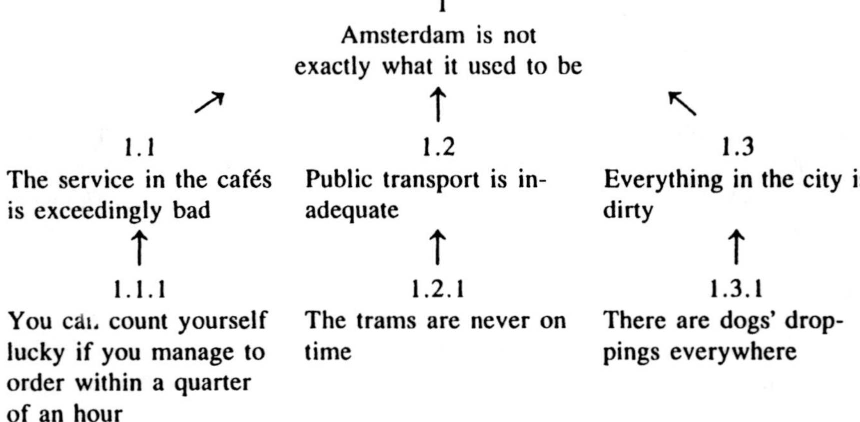


Here, there is multiple argumentation consisting of three single argumentations: 1.1, 1.2, and 1.3 (and three single subargumentations: 1.1.1, 1.2.1, and 1.3.1).

## COORDINATIVELY COMPOUND ARGUMENTATION

Compound argumentation consists of a combination of single argumentations that are, in contrast to multiple argumentation, presented collectively as a conclusive defense of a standpoint. In many cases, it is not possible to remove all the antagonist's doubts by means of one argument. When defending his standpoint, the protagonist then has to advance two or more connected arguments that, only when taken together, are supposed to constitute a well-rounded and conclusive defense.

There are two different ways in which single argumentations can be combined into a compound argumentation: by linking the argumentations coordinatively or subordinatively. In the first case, the result is *coordinatively compound* argumentation; in the second, *subordinatively compound* argumentation. In coordinatively compound argumentation, all the arguments relate directly to the standpoint; in subordinatively compound argumentation, the first argument relates directly to the standpoint, the second to the first argument, which now serves as a substandpoint, and so forth.

In coordinatively compound argumentation, unlike in multiple argumentation, all the component single argumentations are, in principle, necessary for a conclusive defense of the standpoint. For example:

> Postal deliveries in Holland are perfect. You can be sure that a letter will be delivered the next day, that it will be delivered to the right address, and that it will be delivered early in the morning.

Here, the three argumentations that support the standpoint that postal deliveries in Holland are perfect are interdependent: Only if they are taken together, they are deemed to provide sufficient grounds for accepting the standpoint. If either of the single argumentations proves to be unacceptable, the entire coordinatively compound argumentation falls apart.

In a coordinative argumentation, each argument individually is presented as being a partial support for the standpoint, but it is only in combination with the other arguments that it is presented as a conclusive defense. Although the term *coordinative* may suggest that the argumentation consists of a series of arguments that are equally important, this need not be so. It is, for instance, quite possible for one argument to account for, say, 60% of the cogency of the argumentation, the next for 10%, and the third for 20%.

Coordinative argumentation can be represented schematically as follows:

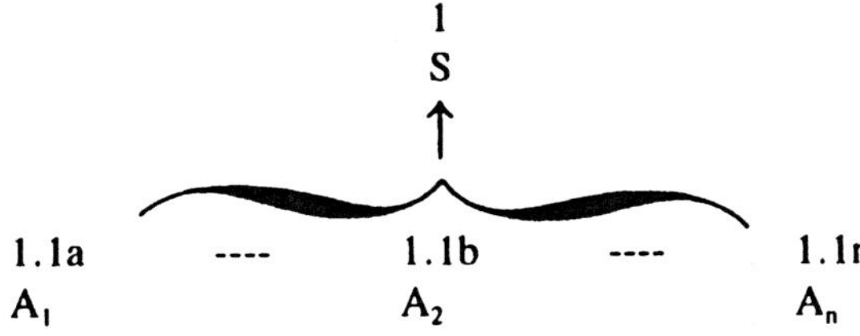


To make clear that the single argumentations only together purport to present a conclusive defense of the standpoint, they are grouped together by a brace and then jointly linked to the standpoint by a single arrow. To further emphasize their mutual linkage, a horizontal line is used and the single argumentations have the same number followed by a, b, and so forth.

For example:

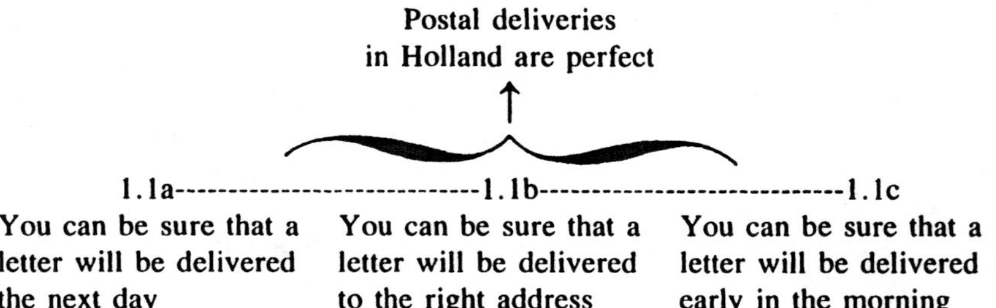
1
Postal deliveries
in Holland are perfect
1.1a
1.1b
1.1c
You can be sure that a letter will be delivered the next day
You can be sure that a letter will be delivered to the right address
You can be sure that a letter will be delivered early in the morning

A major problem when one is analyzing a complex argumentation structure is that it is often unclear whether one is dealing with multiple or with coordinative argumentation. If arguments are adduced each of which unquestionably can be regarded as an independent and conclusive defense of the standpoint that is disputed, then there is a strong case for regarding the argumentation structure as multiple. If, on the contrary, it is evident that the arguments advanced are meant to be a conclusive defense only if taken together, and certainly not individually, then the argumentation should rather be considered as coordinatively compound.[3] Although such clear cases are rather rare, they do occur:

> He's cheating me. He said he was ill but yesterday he was having a drink at a café on Rembrandt Square. He promised to tell his wife last month about us, and he still hasn't done so. He says he loves me, and behind my back he keeps telling nasty things about me.

This is multiple argumentation. A clear example of coordinative argumentation is:

> Rizla cigarette papers are the best. They roll better, they stick better, and they burn better than other cigarette papers.

In the first of these two examples it is clear that each of the facts adduced is by itself a conclusive argumentation for the standpoint being defended. True, one fact may weigh more heavily than another, and one piece of information may appeal to the listener more readily than another, but the arguments put forward

---

[3]For some authors, such as Finocchiaro (1980) and Govier (1988), dependency is the sole criterion for distinguishing between two kinds of horizontally linked arguments. Govier considered premises to be interdependent if each premise alone could not lend any support to the conclusion without the others. According to both Govier and Finocchiaro, reasons do not have to be individually sufficient in order to be independent as long as each reason does not depend on the others to support the conclusion.

are (if they are true) individually sufficient to defend the speaker's standpoint conclusively. It would be perfectly possible to leave one of them out without thereby undermining the argumentation.

In the second example, if one of the three supporting statements is left out because it is false, this does affect the acceptability of the standpoint. It is even more unlikely that the mere fact that Rizla cigarette papers stick better or that they burn better would in itself be suffient to call them the best. It is only in combination that the three arguments can constitute a convincing argumentation for the standpoint.

Here is an example of a text in which it is not so clear whether the argumentation is multiple or coordinative:

> Siamese cats are nicer than ordinary cats. They are more beautiful, they are better company, and they are more playful.

In this case, it is possible that the single argumentations individually should each be regarded as conclusive defenses of the speaker's standpoint, but it is equally possible that they are only meant to be conclusive if they are taken together. If the argumentation structure is analyzed as multiple, the outward appearance of a Siamese cat is apparently regarded as enough by itself to make one consider them nicer than ordinary cats; and the same applies to the other qualities that are mentioned. If the argumentation structure is analyzed as coordinative, no individual argument is considered to be conclusive by itself and dropping one of the arguments will damage the entire argumentation.

Explicit indications of the argumentation structure are generally fairly thin on the ground. Sometimes, the speaker will announce that he is going to produce two, three, or more arguments in favor of the standpoint and that these arguments collectively constitute a conclusive defense of his standpoint, but usually there are no such explicit pointers. In some cases, a "listing" tone of voice, or the typographical presentation (listing items point by point, paragraph divisions, and the like), may provide some grounds for attributing a coordinative or a multiple character to the argumentation. As a rule, the person doing the analyzing will have little more to fall back on than the connectives that are used in the text, such as "and" and "also."

The absence of explicit and unambiguous pointers in the text does not mean that the analyst can take whichever path he pleases. It also certainly does not mean that all analyses are equally valid. A reasoned choice will have to be made, taking into account, among other things, the type of text one is dealing with, and the intentions that on the basis of a careful interpretation of the text may be attributed to the speaker. The point is then which intentions may be rightfully ascribed to the speaker.

In any event, the argumentation structure needs to be established in a way that is independent of the analyst's personal judgements. Here, the trial of Barbertje's supposed murderer may serve as a warning. Initially, the argumentation advanced by the judge in support of his contention that Lothario must hang ("You cut Barbertje up into little pieces, you salted her away, and you are full of yourself") seems to be coordinative. Going by his own ideas about what would make sense, the analyst may be tempted to analyze it in such a way. But on closer inspection it proves to be multiple: In the judge's eyes the vanity on its own is enough to hang Lothario.

When allotting a particular argumentation structure, the analyst will have to rely on the clues contained in the verbal presentation and on common sense. Take the following example:

> This book has no literary qualities: the plot has little originality, the story is very shallow, the dialogues are stilted, and the style is wooden.

If the four arguments in this example are not presented with the pretense that each single argumentation individually constitutes a conclusive defense of the standpoint, the argumentation is coordinative. The speaker then takes account of the fact that it is perfectly possible that the story testifies to considerably psychological insight and is cleverly put together, but that the style is wooden, so that the listener is not convinced of the book's literary merit. Just as it is possible for the dialogues to be brilliant but for the idea and the plot to be unoriginal. For lack of any distinct verbal pointers, in view of how common sense has that literary qualities are to be judged, this analysis of the argumentation structure as coordinative seems preferable to an analysis as multiple.

There are certain words and phrases that can be indicators of coordinatively compound argumentation: "these two things combined lead to the conclusion that," "when it is also remembered that," and so on. Take, for example, this pompous editorial comment:

> The seat in the United Nations was taken by a representative of the bloodthirsty Khmer Rouge regime of Pol Pot, which liquidated a large part of the country's population. Voting in favor of accreditation for that genocidal regime was nonsensical. This becomes clear if one realizes that the Khmer Rouge had been driven out of Phnom Penh in 1979 and it is also remembered that actual power in Cambodia was wielded largely by the government of Heng Samrin that had been placed in the saddle by Hanoi.

Other indicators of coordinative argumentation are: "in addition to the fact" and "as well as the fact that." There are also words and phrases that are a little too grandiose to be used for concluding or rounding off a single argumentation and that certainly cannot refer to multiple argumentation, but that can refer to compound argumentation be it coordinative or subordinative: "in conclusion," "it follows from this that," "this follows from," "taking everything into consideration," "all things considered," "ergo," "all in all," and so on. Frequent words and phrases such as "also," "and also", and "further" may refer to coordinative but also to multiple argumentation.

Numbering of arguments ("first," "second," "third") may suggest that the argumentation is multiple, whereas on closer inspection it might be clear that this cannot be the case, and that the argumentation must be coordinatively compounded. Here is an example:

> You really must buy that TV coffeepot. For a start it'll be very convenient and secondly you can always exchange it.

As nobody in his right mind may be expected to buy a special TV coffeepot just for the fun of exchanging it, in spite of the "secondly," this argumentation can hardly be multiple.

In borderline cases, by the way, it is a good strategy to start by analyzing the argumentation as multiple if no good reason can be found to opt for coordinative. That way, at least there is a guarantee that the strength of each single argumentation will be duly examined. Because, in following this course of action, we attribute a maximum of argumentative force to each individual single argumentation, this recommended option is called the strategy of *maximally argumentative analysis*.

By way of this strategy, all single argumentations are being given the greatest possible credit. If every single argumentation individually proves, indeed, by itself conclusive, then it has become clear that the argumentative discourse contains two or more of these conclusive defenses. If, on the other hand, one of the single argumentations proves to be unacceptable, so that it drops out as a defense of the standpoint, this has no further effect on the argumentation: The other single argumentations still stand. In this sense, a maximally argumentative analysis is extremely charitable to the arguer.[4]

On the other hand, if the arguer (without making this clear) had in fact the intention of advancing an argumentation whose various arguments are only collectively meant to be conclusive, he suffers unjustly if the analyst chose a maximally argumentative analysis: In case of multiple argumentation, each individual single argumentation is judged for its conclusiveness so that in complying with the strategy of maximally argumentative analysis there is a danger that the whole argumentation will be rejected because none of the individual single argumentations proves to be conclusive by itself whereas taken together they would be conclusive. In this sense, a maximally argumentative analysis does not seem to be charitable to the arguer.

In conclusion, analyzing the structure of argumentation as multiple can, at the same time, be called more and less "charitable" than analyzing it as coordinative. It is more charitable, because in multiple argumentation each individual argument

[4]For a discussion of principles of charity, see Govier (1987).

is supposed to have its own, independent argumentative force and, in addition, dropping one unacceptable argument does not automatically undermine the whole argumentation. It is less charitable, because in multiple argumentation, in principle, all the individual arguments must be separately conclusive. More important than charity, however, is from a dialectical perspective that the quality of each and every individual argument shall be examined critically. In cases that cannot be decided on pragmatic grounds, opting for a maximally argumentative analysis is the best way of ensuring that this will indeed happen.

## SUBORDINATIVELY COMPOUND ARGUMENTATION

Subordinatively compound argumentation for a standpoint arises when the arguer assumes that a single argumentation will not at once be accepted because it is itself in need of defense. The defense of argumentation leads to a longer or shorter series of "vertically linked" single argumentations. Each of the argumentations in the chain contributes to the defense of the standpoint and only the series as a whole can constitute a conclusive defense. In contrast to "horizontally linked" coordinatively compound argumentation, "vertically linked" subordinatively compound argumentation does not consist of single argumentations that all refer directly to the same standpoint.

In subordinatively compound argumentation, the standpoint has only been conclusively defended if the listener regards the last subargumentation in the chain as an acceptable defense of the substandpoint to which it refers. Naturally, all the subargumentations coming between the primary argumentation and the last subargumentation must also be acceptable to the listener. In subordinative argumentation, the defense of the primary standpoint is always by way of one or more intermediate steps.[5]

The simplest form of subordinative argumentation arises when the argumentation for a standpoint consists of one argument and this argument—which now serves as a substandpoint—is defended by one subargumentation which is also single. Repeated subordination leads to subsubargumentation, subsubsubargumentation, and so on. The structure of subordinatively compound argumentation can be schematically represented as follows:

[5]It is important to realize that a standpoint can only be sufficiently defended by subordinative argumentation if the unexpressed premises are also acceptable and that this applies equally to steps that contain only one explicit argument. (1) Tweetie can fly, for (1.1) Tweetie is a bird, because (1.1.1) Tweetie is a penguin, could otherwise be taken to be acceptable because (1.1.1) seems to justify (1.1) and (1.1) seems to justify (1), whereas adding the unexpressed premise (1.1′), All birds can fly, makes clear what is wrong here: penguins are birds, but they cannot fly (so, without any rebuttal, 1.1′ is unacceptable). In our opinion, cases like this clearly demonstrate why there is much reason in analyzing every "one premise" argument as a part of a single argumentation in which a premise has been left unexpressed. We are grateful to Frank Veltman for reminding us of the problem.

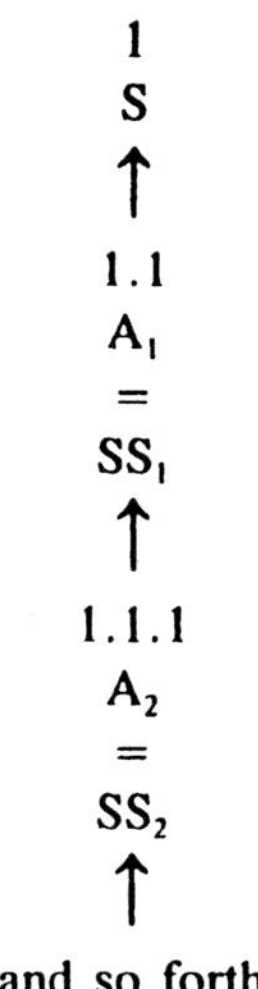


In this diagram, $A_1$ is the primary argumentation for the primary standpoint S, $A_2$ is the secondary argumentation (or subargumentation), $A_3$ the tertiary argumentation (or subsubargumentation), and so forth. $A_1$ serves as the first substandpoint $SS_1$, $A_2$ as the second substandpoint (or subsubstandpoint) $SS_2$, and so forth. 1.1 stands for the primary argumentation and the first substandpoint ($A_1/SS_1$), 1.1.1 for the subargumentation and the subsubstandpoint ($A_2/SS_2$), and so on.

It is a characteristic feature of subordinative argumentation that it consists of a conditional series of single argumentations. It is only on condition that one single argumentation offers sufficient support to the other that the primary standpoint will ultimately be conclusively defended. If the speaker assumes that his argumentation requires no further argumentation because it is acceptable to the listener, he can bring the subordination to a close.

If a particular substandpoint in a subordinative argumentation is inconclusively defended, all the standpoints lying "above" it will also be inconclusively defended, so that ultimately the primary standpoint itself is inconclusively defended. Subordinative argumentation consists of a step by step defense of the primary standpoint which can be seen as a chain of reasoning in which the weakest link determines the strength of the whole, regardless how strong the other links may be.

Subargumentation supporting a single argumentation which serves as the primary argumentation may consist of one single argumentation, but it may also be multiple or coordinatively compound. The same can, by the way, be the case if the primary defense consists of coordinatively compound or multiple argumentation. One of the arguments which is a constituent part of a coordinatively compound argumentation may, for example, be supported by three multiple subargumentations, and one of the constituent parts of a multiple argumentation by two coordinatively compound subargumentations. These subargumentations could themselves be backed by further subsubargumentations and so forth. In argumentative practice, all kinds of combinations of argumentation structures do occur:

> President Corazon Aquino yesterday gave evidence in a civil action she says she initiated in defense of the truth. Mrs Aquino told a libel hearing in Manila she had reason to be angry after reading Mr Beltran's column about a recent coup attempt. According to her, the column was a blatant lie. "I did not hide under the bed," she said. "Besides it is physically impossible for me to hide there because the bed I use is a platform bed and there is no space between the bed and the carpet." (*The Guardian*, February 12, 1991)

Another illustration of a combination of multiple, subordinative and coordinative argumentation is:

> She won't worry about the exam. She's bound to pass. She's never failed before, she's prepared well, she's not nervous, and she also has a feeling for the subject. Besides, she doesn't care whether she'll pass or not.

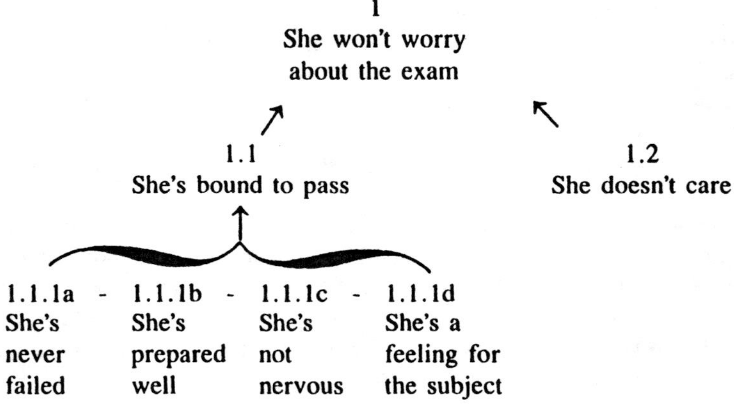


If subordinative argumentation occurs in support of one of the arguments in a multiple argumentation, the consequences of rejecting one of the arguments that constitute the subordinative argumentation are different from those of rejecting it if it were part of an argumentation that consists only and solely of one line of pure and simple subordinative argumentation. In the example, the argumentation for the standpoint consists of a two-part multiple primary argumentation 1.1 and 1.2, and a coordinatively compound subargumentation 1.1.1a-d for the first primary argumentation. If the subargumentation 1.1.1a-d were to be rejected, the first primary argumentation would also have to go, but this would not affect the second. As a consequence, the primary standpoint 1 might still be conclusively defended.

Subordinative argumentation is often not verbally marked as such. The general indicators of argumentation can also be used for subordinative argumentation: "for," "because," "since," "hence," "thus," "therefore," "that is why," "as," "in view of," "consequently," and so forth. In the case of progressive presentation, the direction of the subordination is the precise opposite of that in retrogressive presentation. Strictly speaking, it would perhaps be more accurate to speak of subordination in the one case and superordination in the other.

One exclusive indicator of subordinative argumentation is the reduplicated "because because" or "since because," although not everyone will regard this as an elegant construction. Here is an example:

> The Ego (the "Self") is, because it is independent of space and time, not "mortal" in the usual sense of the word. Since it is independent of time, it cannot "die." On the other hand we cannot say exactly what happens to it when the body has died.
>
> Moreover the Ego is free, *since because* it is independent of space and time it is detached from causal links and there are no material causes of action.

Some words may be used for all argumentation structures. A very common example is "and." At first sight, subordinative argumentation with "and" often appears to be coordinative. However, in Boultbee's criterion, for instance, where "and ought" means "and *therefore* it ought," "and" is used for subordinative argumentation:

> If the converse of a statement is absurd, the original statement is an insult to the intelligence and ought never to have been made.

Luckily, there are also indicators of argumentation structure which make it clear that we are *not* dealing with subordinative argumentation: "incidentally," "furthermore," "moreover," and "especially as."

## COMPLEX ARGUMENTATION AND UNEXPRESSED PREMISES

As we explained in chapter 6, in every single argumentation, as a rule, one of the premises will have been left unexpressed. The antagonist's doubts may then relate to the explicit premise as well as to the unexpressed premise. In the following argumentation, there is subargumentation that concerns an unexpressed premise:

> Jack is spoilt because he is an only child. In such cases, parents always feel guilty for not having provided the child with a playmate and try to eliminate their guilt feelings by sanctioning whatever the lonely boy or girl wants.

The coordinative subargumentation in the second sentence does not relate to the explicit premise "Jack is an only child," but to the unexpressed premise "Only children are spoilt." In cases like this, the unexpressed premise should be made explicit in order to get an adequate analysis of the argumentation structure. The argumentation structure of the example can be represented schematically as follows:

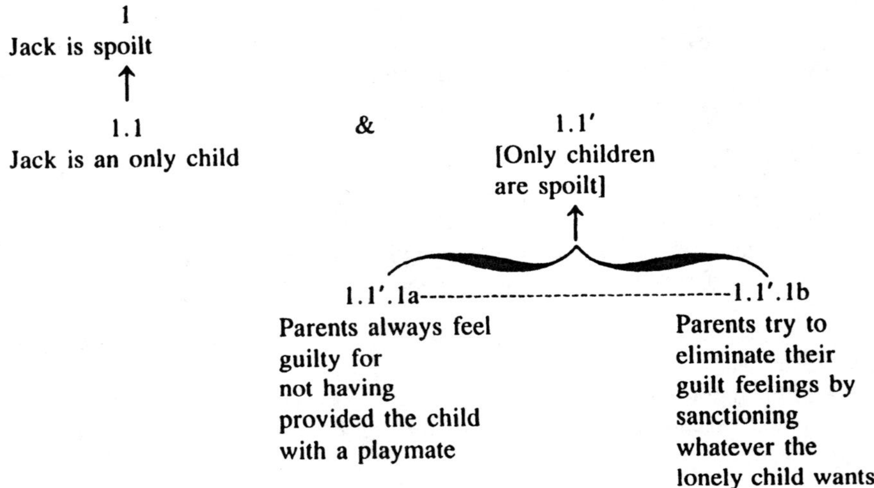


In the diagram, the unexpressed premise (1.1′) is indicated by a prime, put in brackets and linked to the explicit premise by means of an ampersand.

Here is a logically more complicated example of subargumentation that is related to an unexpressed premise:

> If it were really true that God existed, there would not be so much misery in the world. Half the world's population is starving. That is why God does not exist.

The argumentation structure of this example can be reconstructed as follows:

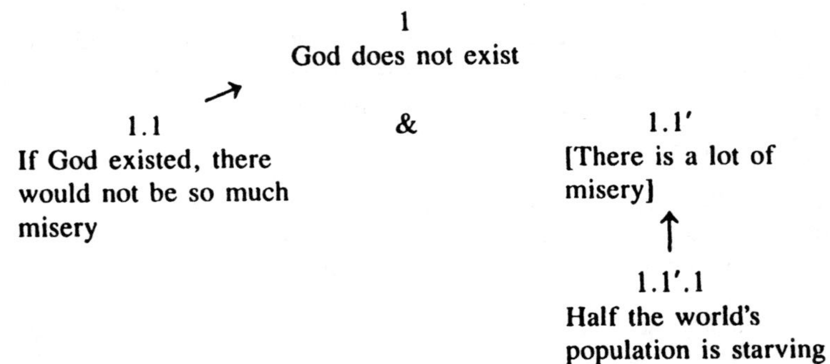

If he makes unexpressed premises explicit in accordance with the procedure recommended in chapter 6, in his endeavor to determine the pragmatic optimum, the analyst might sometimes be inclined to formulate the unexpressed premise in such a way that a more complex underlying argumentation structure is presupposed. In "Maggie is a liberal, therefore, she is progressive," in the absence of a well-defined context, the most likely candidate for the pragmatic optimum is "Liberals are progressive." Alternative reconstructions of the unexpressed premise could have been "People with an interest in politics are progressive" and "All women are progressive." If the analyst does indeed opt for "Liberals are progressive," the argumentation structure is not affected: The argumentation remains singular. The structure can then be represented as follows:

If the analyst opts for one of the two alternatives, the argumentation structure *does* change. By adding either of these premises the argumentation structure becomes subordinatively compound:

*Alternative 1*

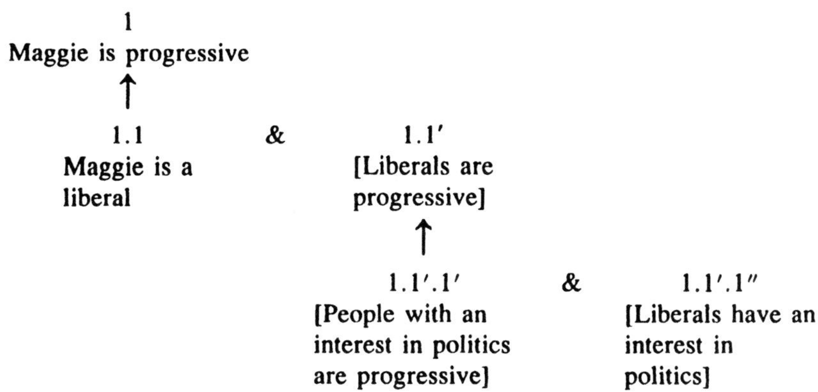

*Alternative 2*

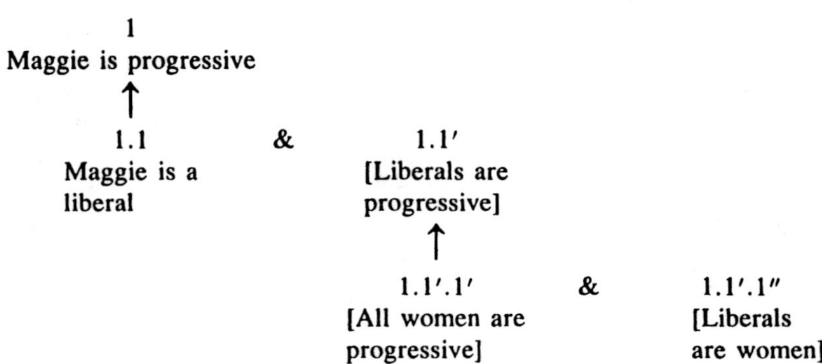


"Liberals are progressive" recurs in both alternative 1 and alternative 2. In fact, it would be more correct not to label "People with an interest in politics are progressive" and "All women are progressive" as *alternatives* to the pragmatic optimum "Liberals are progressive" (1.1′), but as possible *supplements* to 1.1′, which may be appropriate additions in a certain well-defined context.

What this example shows, is that reconstructing an unexpressed premise in an undefined context always requires formulating the pragmatic "minimum" that is part of the single argumentation that links the explicit premise to the standpoint. Any reconstruction that goes further than this minimum presupposes a subordinatively compound argumentation structure and, hence, one or more other unexpressed premises. Unless a well-defined context clearly indicates otherwise, the best policy in reconstructing unexpressed premises is therefore to start from the assumption that the argumentation is singular and to stick for the time being to the premise that fits in best with this structure. In other words, until further notice the pragmatic minimum is then also taken to be the pragmatic optimum. Only if the context becomes more clearly defined, this minimal pragmatic optimum can be supplemented with other premises so that the pragmatic optimum is substantiated in a more complex argumentation structure.

The reconstruction of standpoints that are left unexpressed can sometimes also be legitimated by the (verbal or nonverbal) context of the argumentation. In the following advertisement, for example, the general background knowledge that advertisements are designed to persuade people to buy something, makes it possible to identify both the standpoint which is being defended and crucial parts of the subordinatively and coordinatively compound argumentation that offers implicit support for it:

> Facts, news, and the background to the news. All in The Telegraph. The Telegraph. The common-sense newspaper. The Telegraph.

The message of this advertisement can be paraphrased like this:

> The Telegraph contains news, facts and background information. The Telegraph is a common-sense newspaper. So: The Telegraph is a good newspaper. Therefore, you should buy The Telegraph.

The argumentation structure incorporated in the discourse can be reconstructed as follows:

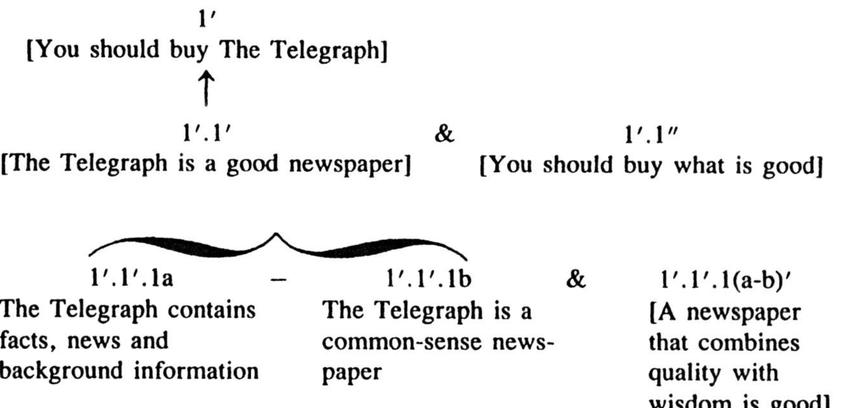
1′
[You should buy The Telegraph]
1′.1′
&
1′.1″
[The Telegraph is a good newspaper]
[You should buy what is good]
1′.1′.1a
–
1′.1′.1b
&
1′.1′.1(a-b)′
The Telegraph contains facts, news and background information
The Telegraph is a common-sense newspaper
[A newspaper that combines quality with wisdom is good]

# PART II

# COMMUNICATION AND FALLACIES

CHAPTER 8

# Analyzing and Evaluating Argumentative Discourse

## COMPONENTS OF AN ANALYTIC OVERVIEW

In order to get an overview of those aspects of the argumentative discourse that are crucial for resolving a difference of opinion, the following analytic operations must be carried out:

1. determining the points at issue,
2. recognizing the positions that the parties adopt,
3. identifying the explicit and implicit arguments, and
4. analyzing the argumentation structure.

An *analytic overview* shows the differences of opinion, the distribution of dialectical roles, the expressed and unexpressed premises which make up the arguments, and the argumentation structure. What the construction of an analytic overview entails can be illustrated with the help of a letter to the editor, which was published by a Dutch newsletter:

> *Pornography is not an infringement of human integrity*
> How can pornography be an infringement of human integrity? Women who claim this must be mad. I'd like to see them substantiate their claim. If the normal rules of logic mean anything to them, I can explain that pornography has nothing to do with an infringement of human integrity. Pornography does not prohibit anyone anything, nor is there a question of condescension, because nothing is thrust on anyone. It seems quite clear to me. Which is why I believe I am right.

According to the letter, some women adopt a positive standpoint toward the proposition that pornography is an infringement of human integrity. At the beginning, the author makes clear that she does not accept this standpoint. As is illustrated in the heading, she adopts a negative viewpoint toward the proposition. So, there are two protagonists: the women who support the standpoint that pornography is an infringement of human integrity, and the author, who disputes this. Here, the dispute is single and mixed.

The women's standpoint that pornography is an infringement of human integrity, together with the author not accepting this standpoint are part of the confrontation stage. The same goes for the author's opposite standpoint that pornography is not an infringement of human integrity, which may taken to be not accepted by the other women. As no account is given of any further developments in the other women's position, any contributions they may have made to resolving the dispute are not recorded in the analytic overview.

The opening stage starts when the author challenges the women to defend their standpoint and anticipates being challenged herself. She refers to the discussion rules by suggesting that the normal rules of logic should apply.

The argumentation stage is represented by the author's coordinatively compound argumentation that in accepting pornography no one is prohibited anything, and that neither is there a question of condescension. The last part of the argumentation put forward by the author is supported by the subordinative argument that nothing is thrust upon anyone.

In the concluding stage, the author maintains her standpoint. Consequently, she claims that the dispute has been resolved in her favor.

The structure of the author's argumentation can be schematically represented as follows:

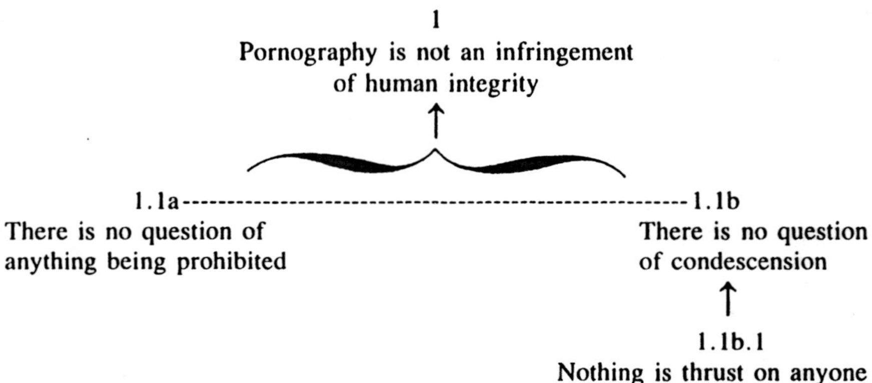


## ARGUMENTATION SCHEMES AS DIALECTICAL TOOLS

The analytic overview contains the points that are relevant to the evaluation of the argumentative discourse. After all, if it is unclear which standpoint is being defended, there is no way of telling whether the argumentation is conclusive.

In case more than one standpoint is being defended, it must furthermore be clear which language user is acting as the protagonist of which standpoint. For one thing, it would otherwise be impossible to tell whether the various arguments for a standpoint constitute a coherent whole. And where crucial unexpressed premises are overlooked or the argumentation structure is misrepresented, an adequate evaluation of the argumentative discourse is impossible.

Starting from the analytic overview, the evaluation of the quality of the argumentative discourse can best be made to move from coarse to fine. First, attention must be paid to the explicit or implicit discussion of which the argumentative discourse is a part, second, to the specific arguments that are put forward in the argumentative discourse.

As for the discussion as a whole, the evaluation process entails establishing whether the discussion has actually progressed along a route that may lead to the resolution of the difference of opinion. All discussion moves that are an obstacle to this goal must be recognized as such and unmasked as fallacious. The remaining chapters of this book are devoted to the fallacies. In the next section we explain our approach, the present section deals with the assessment of individual arguments.

In evaluating the various arguments that are put forward in the discourse, it must first be determined whether the argumentative discourse contains any inconsistencies. If something can be both one way and another at the same time, what are we supposed to believe? Logical contradictions, pragmatic and other kinds of inconsistencies weaken the strength of the argumentative discourse more or less seriously.

The general importance of avoiding contradictions has been stressed with considerable emphasis, and great force, by the analytic philosopher Frits Staal:[1]

> If someone wants to maintain that the statements "*I am in Montparnasse*" and "*I am not in Montparnasse*" can be true at the same time, he is not being rational. It is easy to say you reject the straitjacket of logic, that life is freer, warmer and more vital without logic, but in fact you're talking nonsense. Since Aristotle and the Indian logicians people have always taken the view that statements like that should be avoided. No rational human being would claim that "*The telephone is over there*" and "*The telephone is not over there*" can both be true at the same time. No rational human being: Only some philosophers insist that it is so.
> (*Vrij Nederland*, April 28, 1984)

[1]In everyday discourse, contradictions are sometimes difficult to spot. Often, it is also hard to decide whether there really is a contradiction or any other kind of inconsistency ("Governments have no right to control women's bodies"/"Abortion is murder"). As Perelman and Olbrechts-Tyteca (1958) have pointed out, contradictions need not be rhetorically unacceptable: in "quasi-logical" arguments apparent contradictions can be effective means of persuasion. Nor need they automatically be unacceptable in a pragma-dialectical perspective: It may, for instance, be clear from the context in which it occurs that the same expression is used in two different meanings ("(Physically) I am in New York"/"(In the spirit) I am in Montparnasse").

In order to assess the quality of the individual arguments, it must be determined whether the underlying reasoning is logically valid and starts from premises that are acceptable. There is no need, however, to immediately assume that somebody who puts forward an argument is indeed involved in demonstrating how the conclusion is logically derived from the premises.[2] Still, in some way or other, the step from the arguments to the standpoint must be such that the acceptability of the premises is transferred to the conclusion.[3]

In his endeavor to transfer the acceptability of the premises to the conclusion and to achieve the interactional effect that the listener accept his standpoint, the speaker tries to put forward his argument in such a fashion that it convinces the listener. He communicates, as it were, that he knows the way that leads from what is already accepted to the standpoint.

When contemplating his argumentation for the standpoint that Daniel will be concerned about the costs, he may, for example, have started from a thought like *It is typical of Americans that they are materialistic* and back up his standpoint by saying: "As Daniel is an American (and Americans are inclined to care a lot about money), he is sure to be concerned about the costs." Starting from a thought like *We are now faced with the same problem as last year*, he might argue "The method I propose worked last year (and this problem is similar to the one we had last year), so it will work again." And starting from a thought like *Heavy drinking is bound to cause a hangover*, he might argue "Because Tom has been drinking an excessive amount of whiskey (and drinking too much whiskey leads to a terrible headache), Tom must have a terrible headache."[4]

In arguing in one of these ways, he relies on a ready-made *argumentation scheme*: a more or less conventionalized way of representing the relation between what is stated in the argument and what is stated in the standpoint.[5] In our opinion, each argumentation can be characterized by the argumentation scheme that is being employed. We make a distinction between three main categories of argumentation schemes, which characterize three different types of argumentation.

In the first type of argumentation, someone tries to convince his interlocutor

---

[2]Just like Harman (1986), who identified principles of reasoning with principles for revising one's beliefs and intentions, we do not simply equate principles of reasoning with principles of logic.

[3]On this point, logic has not much to offer. In spite of important differences in the way logicians define the object, scope, and method of their work, they seem unanimous in thinking that their concern with validity is about formal rather than substantive relations between premises and conclusions, syntactico-semantic rather than pragmatic aspects, reasoning in isolation rather than in context, implications rather than inferences and—most important to us at this juncture—transmission of truth rather than acceptance.

[4]We can only speculate about what the speaker "really had in mind" when connecting the explicit argument with the standpoint. For all we know, Peirce may be right in saying that a "habit of thought" is active "in such a way that, upon contemplating the believed premiss, by a sort of perception the conclusion is judged to be true" (1955, p. 131).

[5]The concept of argumentation scheme is also used by authors such as Hastings (1962), Windes and Hastings (1969), and Perelman and Olbrechts-Tyteca (1958).

by pointing out that something is *symptomatic* of something else. This type of argumentation is based on an argumentation scheme in which the acceptability of the premises is transferred to the conclusion by making it understood that there is a relation of *concomitance* between that which is stated in the argument and that which is stated in the standpoint. The argumentation is presented as if it is an expression, a phenomenon, a sign or some other kind of symptom of what is stated in the standpoint, as in "As Daniel is an American (and Americans are inclined to care a lot about money), he is sure to be concerned about the costs."

In the second type of argumentation, someone tries to convince by pointing out that something is *similar* to something else. This type of argumentation is based on an argumentation scheme in which the acceptability of the premises is transferred to the conclusion by making it understood that there is a relation of *analogy* between what is stated in the argument and what is stated in the standpoint. The argumentation is presented as if there were a resemblance, an agreement, a likeness, a parallel, a correspondence or some other kind of similarity between that which is stated in the argument and that which is stated in the standpoint, as in "The method I propose worked last year (and this problem is similar to the one we had last year), so it will work again."

In the third type of argumentation, someone tries to convince by pointing out that something is *instrumental* to something else. This type of argumentation is based on an argumentation scheme in which the acceptability of the premises is transferred to the conclusion by making it understood that there is a relation of *causality* between the argument and the standpoint. The argumentation is presented as if what is stated in the argumentation is a means to, a way to, an instrument for or some other kind of causative factor for the standpoint, or *vice versa*, as in "Because Tom has been drinking an excessive amount of whiskey (and drinking too much whiskey leads to a terrible headache), Tom must have a terrible headache."

Of course, there are many subcategories of argumentation schemes. Among the (sub)types of argumentation based on a relation of concomitance, for instance, are those presenting something as an inherent quality or as a characteristic part of something more general. Argumentation (sub)types based on a relation of analogy are, for example, making a comparison, giving an example and referring to a model. Argumentation (sub)types based on a relation of causality include those pointing to the consequences of a course of action, presenting something as a means to a certain end, and emphasizing the nobility of a goal in order to justify the means.

Just as logical argument forms such as *modus ponens*, argumentation schemes are abstract frameworks that can have an infinite number of substitution instances. As all substitution instances of an argumentation scheme can, following the established tradition of considering the hypothetical conditional as the logical minimum, be logically analyzed as involving a *modus ponens*-like inference from premises to a conclusion, their logical argument form by itself provides no distinctive feature between the various argumentation schemes. More importantly, merely reconstructing the logical argument form is by no means enough for an adequate evaluation of argumentation.

In our typology, argumentation schemes are categorized according to the way in which the various types of argumentation should be evaluated. Each type of argumentation corresponds to certain assessment criteria that pertain to the relation represented in the argumentation scheme.

Therefore, in order to evaluate an argumentation adequately, one must first determine which argumentation scheme is employed. An argumentation scheme is a pointer to a certain dialectical route. A person who puts forward an argumentation anticipates criticism, and by choosing a particular type of argumentation, using the one argumentation scheme rather than the other, he implies that he thinks he knows which route will lead to the justification of his standpoint. At any rate, whether he really thinks this or not, if he is to be taken seriously by the other party, he may held to be committed to deal with the critical questions which pertain to a justification via the argumentation scheme that is inherent in his argumentation.

In relying on a certain argumentation scheme, the arguer invokes a particular testing method in a dialectical procedure, in which certain critical reactions are relevant, and others not. Each argumentation scheme calls, as it were, for its own set of critical reactions. In conjunction with each other, these reactions constitute a well-rounded test for checking the soundness of an argumentation of the type concerned.

If the speaker does make it clear to the listener which argumentation scheme he is using, he may assume that the listener will know what kind of testing method is being invoked in using this scheme. The speaker may also assume that the listener knows that this is what he assumes, so that the listener knows that the speaker is prepared for his critical reactions. If these assumptions are indeed justified, the communicative prerequisites for critical discussion are, at least, effectuated.

The speaker may, for instance, indicate which argumentation scheme he is using by adding a proverb, or any other kind of *topos*, in which the quintessence of the argumentation scheme is being expressed.[6] He may also make use of certain more or less standardized expressions for indicating a particular argumentation scheme, such as "X is characteristic of Y," "X is typical of Y," and "X's are essentially Y" for pointing out a relation of concomitance:

I think that Mary is pig-headed, because she is a teen-ager and

- it is characteristic of teen-agers that they are pig-headed
- teen-agers *are* pig-headed

[6]Cf. Goodwin and Wenzel (1979), who regard proverbs or *topoi* as "warrants" (or "backings" for "warrants").

- being pig-headed is a mark of being a teen-ager
- teen-agers are pig-headed by nature
- teen-agers are by nature pig-headed
- pig-headedness is typical of teen-agers
- pig-headedness is a typical characteristic of teen-agers
- being pig-headed is part of being a teen-ager
- teen-agers are all potentially pig-headed
- in fact teen-agers are pig-headed

Among the expressions used for pointing out a relation of analogy are "X is comparable to Y," "X corresponds to Y," and "X is just like Y":

The Dutch educational reform of the 70s had to flop, because the British educational reform also flopped and the Dutch educational reform

- is comparable to the British educational reform
- congrues with the British educational reform
- reminds one of the British educational reform
- is the same as the British educational reform
- is analogous to the British educational reform
- is related to the British educational reform
- corresponds in a crucial way to the British educational reform
- is defined along major lines (criteria etc.) as the British educational reform
- is just like the British educational reform, an enterprise doomed to fail

A relation of causality may, for instance, be pointed out by expressions such as "X leads to Y," "X is a means of getting Y," and "Y results from X":

The victim must have had sexual contact, because she appeared to be pregnant and

- pregnancy is caused by sexual contact
- pregnancy results from sexual contact
- pregnancy is the result of sexual contact
- sexual contact leads to pregnancy
- from sexual contact you get pregnant
- sexual contact ends with pregnancy
- sexual contact ends up with pregnancy
- sexual contact is the cause of pregnancy
- sexual contact is the means of getting pregnant
- sexual contact contributes to pregnancy

If the argumentation scheme is not, in some way or other, indicated by the speaker, the listener must find it out by himself. He has to detect the implicit justification that is involved in putting forward a certain argument in support of a certain standpoint, thus defining the *topos* or *locus* that designates the argumentation scheme that is employed. For this purpose, he has to identify the premise which has been left unexpressed in the argumentation.

It should be stressed again that identifying an unexpressed premise does not necessarily boil down to trying to retrieve the bridging premise the arguer really had in mind when carrying out his argumentation. For all we know, it might well be the case that he has just been arguing associatively, having no bridging in mind at all, let alone the premise which is to be reconstructed as the unexpressed premise. Perhaps, he intuitively thinks the association that happened to occur to him to be convincing to the audience. Methodologically, it would also be very hard to find out what exactly he had in mind.

Fortunately, for a dialectical evaluation one need not really know this, because it is the speaker's commitments that count: The analyst should try to establish what exactly the speaker can be held responsible for. As is explained in chapter 5, in ordinary discourse, normally a speaker does not say everything he could have said, because there is neither the time nor the need for it. As all experienced language users know, much is taken to be understood. Speakers know that they have, in many respects, undertaken more than the words they have used literally mean. As long as they want to be considered to be reasonable, they are liable for commitments well beyond what they have actually said.[7]

Suppose Joe and Charlie are talking about Francisca, whose bike has been stolen:

Charlie: "She will be stoic about it."

Joe: "Uh?"

Charlie: "Well, she is an Amsterdammer, isn't she?'

Charlie's argumentation about Francisca's stolen bike could be reconstructed as "Francisca will be stoic about the stealing of her bike, because she is an Amsterdammer."

Of course, we do not know what Charlie truly thought. It might have been something like "Amsterdammers tend to be careless about their belongings." Other possibilities are "Amsterdammers such as Francisca do not take an interest in the material aspects of life," "Amsterdammers are used to having their bikes stolen," "Amsterdammers do not care at all about bikes," and "Amsterdammers are always stoic." We cannot really be sure. Therefore, we cannot tell which unexpressed premise, if any, he had in mind. In fact, we do not have to know, as

[7]Logical and pragmatic presuppositions and implications are simple illustrations of such commitments. The speaker, for instance, who has asked the question "How long have you been married?" can afterwards not reasonably deny that he assumed the listener to be married.

long as we can "follow" him. As he is communicating with Joe, Charlie knows that we, or at least Joe, should somehow, and minimally, be able to follow him. And if it is not clear to Joe that the type of argumentation is used all right, Charlie can not reasonably expect his argumentation to make his standpoint acceptable to him.

In order to be able to determine the soundness of Charlie's argumentation, an analysis is needed of its argumentation scheme, so that Joe can respond with the critical reactions that are appropriate to the employment of that particular scheme. In certain situations, Joe could, in order to get hold of the argumentation scheme, simply ask Charlie which unexpressed premise he had in mind, but even then there is no guarantee that Charlie would report what he actually thought. He might rather come up with the unexpressed premise that seems, in retrospect, the most favorable to him. Even so, however, he would not be free to say just anything that suited him, for by speaking in the way he has spoken he has undertaken certain commitments which cannot be denied afterwards. Basically, Charlie does not so much have to report a premise, but he has to reconstruct it, just like Joe and any other analyst, from what has been said in the context of the conversation.

When reconstructing Charlie's argumentation, the analyst—whoever he or she may be—has to establish which factors in the communicative context are relevant for determining to which unexpressed premise Charlie may pragmatically be held committed. If there is no evidence to the contrary, he should start from the assumption that Charlie genuinely intends to overcome Joe's doubt concerning his standpoint. Then, "Amsterdammers are used to having their bikes stolen" is preferable as an unexpressed premise to its alternatives, because it fits in best with what can be known in this conversational context about Amsterdammers, their bikes, and their attitudes. According to this unexpressed premise it goes with being an Amsterdammer not to be disturbed by having one's bike stolen, so the argumentation that is being used here is of the symptomatic type, where an attempt is made to make the standpoint acceptable by pointing out that there is a relation of concomitance between what is stated in the argument and what is stated in the standpoint.[8]

After the symptomatic character of Charlie's argumentation has been established, his argumentation is amenable to the particular dialectical testing method that is appropriate for this type of argumentation. The set of critical reactions that are relevant to argumentation with an argumentation scheme based on a relation of concomitance includes the following evaluative questions. Is Francisca really an Amsterdammer? Is it typical of Amsterdammers to be stoic? Or is stoicism also typical of citizens of other big cities? Do Amsterdammers by any chance have other predominant characteristics as well?

[8]In other cases, where the argumentation scheme is clearly indicated by the arguer, this scheme is already part of the context that can be used to identify the unexpressed premise. For practical purposes, the analyst should always start from what is clear and go from there to what is unclear.

If the argumentation had been of the type where it is pointed out that there is a striking similarity between the present case and a more familiar one, with an argumentation scheme based on a relation of analogy, the following questions would have been relevant critical reactions. Is the situation to which the present case is compared indeed correctly described? Does it really resemble the present case? Or are there crucial differences between them? Are there perhaps other situations that better resemble the present case?

In case of instrumental argumentation, with an argumentation scheme based on a relation of causality, the relevant reactions would have included the following evaluative questions. Is the announced effect of the proposed measure really so desirable? Will this effect indeed follow? Or could it be achieved more easily by way of another measure? Does the proposed measure not have any serious negative side-effects?

## FALLACIES AS VIOLATIONS OF DISCUSSION RULES

For practical reasons we first discussed the assessment of the individual arguments, but in evaluating the quality of argumentative discourse the evaluation of the discussion as a whole comes methodically first. In our pragma-dialectical perspective, this evaluation concentrates on the fallacious moves that hinder the resolution of the difference of opinion.

According to its standard definition, a fallacy is an argument that "seems to be valid but is not so" (Hamblin 1970). Many instances of generally recognized fallacies, however, clearly fall outside the scope of this definition. In some cases there is not the slightest question of there being arguments (e.g., the fallacy of *many questions* and the *argumentum ad baculum*). In other cases, logically speaking, the argument concerned is not invalid at all (as in *circular reasoning*). In still other cases (as in *argumentum ad verecundiam* and *argumentum ad populum*) it would be highly overdoing things if one looked for the error in the invalidity of the argument.

Thanks to Hamblin's book *Fallacies* (1970), one may take it to be common knowledge that the so-called Standard Treatment of fallacies suffers from serious theoretical and practical defects. Although Hamblin's devastating criticism has not seemed to worry some writers of textbooks, it elicited strong and divergent reactions from others. At the one end of the spectrum there are people who want to banish fallacies until further notice as a subject from logic textbooks.[9]

[9]This radical exclusion of the topic of fallacies from the textbooks, as in Lambert and Ulrich (1980), seems an over-reaction to the flaws of the Standard Treatment. It carries the danger that, in the end, the study of fallacies will totally disappear from systematic intellectual scrutiny.

At the other end there are authors who favor a more positive appreciation of the fallacies.[10]

The work of John Woods and Douglas Walton provides a more constructive reaction to Hamblin's criticism of the Standard Treatment.[11] Their point of departure is their belief that the Standard Treatment fails to work because it only uses classical syllogistic logic, propositional logic and predicate logic. In their opinion, the remedy could be to call on other, nonclassical, logics. Woods and Walton set about showing that in many cases it *is* possible to give a satisfactory analysis of the fallacies.

The systematic exploration of advanced logical systems in order to analyze fallacies is characteristic of Woods and Walton's approach. They use, for example, inductive logic for the analysis of the fallacies of *secundum quid* and *post hoc ergo propter hoc*. For the analysis of *argumentum ad verecundiam*, they use the logic of plausible reasoning, for the analysis of *many questions* and *petitio principii*, dialectical game theory, and for the analysis of *ignoratio elenchi*, relatedness logic. Apart from these logics, they discuss the usefulness of epistemic, doxastic, and modal logics for clarifying a number of other fallacies.

This approach amounts to applying an appropriate logical system in analyzing a particular fallacy. Every fallacy needs, so to speak, its own logic. For practical purposes this approach is not very realistic.[12] In order to be able to carry out the analyses, a considerable amount of logical knowledge is required. There are also some theoretical disadvantages inherent in this approach. By relying on so many different logical systems, one only gets fragmentary descriptions of the various fallacies, and no overall picture of the domain of the fallacies as a whole. Ideally, one unified theory that is capable of dealing with all the different phenomena, is to be preferred. No doubt, the fallacies constitute a heterogeneous category, but this need not automatically mean that they can only be analyzed by means of varying theoretical instruments.

In our opinion, in dealing with the fallacies it is important not to exaggerate the role of logic, even if the absolute certainty that a purely logical approach appears to offer is thereby sacrificed. The practical significance of "logical" errors in comparison with other fallacious moves can only be properly assessed if it

---

[10]They claim, for example, that *tu quoque* (Gerber, 1974), *slippery slope* (Govier, 1982), or *composition and division* (Broyles, 1975) need not always be condemned as malpractices, but can be perfectly legitimate arguments. In our opinion, referring to mitigating circumstances which make a fallacy no fallacy after all only creates new and serious problems. As each case then has to be examined on its own merits, the identification and detection of fallacies becomes very much ad hoc and it becomes extremely difficult, if not impossible, to develop a general and workable method for distinguishing between fallacious and nonfallacious arguments.

[11]See Woods and Walton (1989) and Woods (1988). Other interesting alternatives are provided by Finocchiaro (1981, 1987a) and Hintikka (1987).

[12]Ultimately, unlike quantum theory, the theory of fallacies should have practical applications that are, after appropriate instruction, accessible to ordinary language users.

is first clear what place the argumentation or other speech act in which they occur, occupies in the wider context of a critical discussion. Argumentation, just like any other speech act, is a functional element in the verbal exchanges between ordinary language users. Only if the communicative and interactional context is taken into account it becomes clear that argumentation has a "repairing role": It aims to remove one language user's doubt concerning the standpoint of the other. Without making allowances for such pragmatic knowledge, the analysis of these discussion moves can not be justified.

Which requirements should an adequate theory of fallacies, in our view, fulfill? First, it should provide norms for distinguishing between reasonable and unreasonable moves in argumentative discourse. Second, it should provide criteria for deciding when such a norm is violated. Third, it must provide interpretation procedures for determining whether an utterance satisfies these criteria.

As we see it, the analysis of fallacies always proceeds in three steps: The utterance must be interpreted as a specific speech act, this speech act must be recognized as a violation of a general norm, and it must be established whether the situation in which the utterance occurs is indeed within the scope of this norm. Agreement on the general norms for reasonable behavior in a critical discussion does not automatically coincide with agreement on the criteria for deciding what counts as a violation of these norms, nor with agreement on the interpretation procedure that determines whether an utterance satisfies the criteria.

In the literature about fallacies, norms and criteria are often confused and interpretation problems are usually ignored or trivialized. The confusion of norms and criteria creates unrealistic expectations about what a certain theory of fallacies can do. The neglect of interpretation problems results in a theory of fallacies that is inadequate for achieving its practical goals.

What are the outlines of our alternative? We present an ideal model in which the rules for reasonable argumentative discourse are specified as rules for the performance of speech acts in a critical discussion aimed at resolving a dispute. For each stage of the discussion, the rules indicate when participants intending to resolve a dispute are entitled, or indeed obliged, to carry out a particular move. They must observe all the rules that are instrumental to resolving the dispute.[13] Any infringement of a discussion rule, whichever party commits it and at whatever stage in the discussion, is a possible threat to the resolution of a dispute and must therefore be regarded as an incorrect discussion move. Fallacies are analyzed as such incorrect discussion moves in which a discussion rule has been violated.

In our approach, the term *fallacy* is thus systematically connected with the

---

[13]Only in conjunction with the fulfillment of the appropriate "higher order conditions," observance of the rules can also constitute a sufficient (first order) condition for resolving a dispute. For second order conditions pertaining to the attitudes and dispositions of the discussants and third order conditions pertaining to the circumstances in which the discussion takes place, see van Eemeren and Grootendorst (1988).

rules for critical discussion. We think that all traditional categories have their proper place in our system, but even if one or more of the traditionally listed fallacies could not be analyzed pragma-dialectically, this would not automatically mean that there is something wrong with the theoretical apparatus. It would be a mistake to treat the traditional list as a sacrosanct gift from heaven.[14]

In our approach, committing a fallacy is not automatically considered to be tantamount to unethical conduct: It is wrong in the sense that it frustrates efforts to arrive at the resolution of a dispute. The very fact that they all represent indispensable components of a code of conduct for resolving differences of opinion is the rationale for the 10 discussion rules we present in chapters 9-18.[15] It is precisely because of this problem-solving capacity that they should be acceptable to discussants who want to sort out their differences.

Our approach to fallacies is broader and at the same time more specific than the traditional logico-centric approach. It is broader because, right from the start, all violations of the discussion rules, not just the "logical" errors concerning validity, are brought into the analysis. It is more specific because the fallacies are systematically connected to the resolution of a difference of opinion. The most crucial consequence is that this approach provides an insight into why it is that something is called a fallacy.

For a realistic appreciation of the scope of our theory of fallacies, it is important to note that it is not always justified to use the norms provided by the rules for critical discussion. They apply only where the discourse is actually aimed at resolving a dispute. Although it is in many cases of argumentative discourse pretty obvious (or at least reasonable to assume) that the main purpose of the discourse *is* to resolve a difference of opinion, in many other cases it is equally obvious that resolving the difference of opinion is *not* the main object. There are also a lot of cases in which it is not so clear what the object of the discourse really is. The identification of fallacies is therefore always conditional: Only given a certain interpretation of the discourse, is it justified to maintain the allegation that a fallacy has occurred.

In practice, a discourse will hardly ever be either completely resolution-oriented or not resolution-oriented. In unclear cases, if the discourse could or could not be aimed at resolving a dispute, it is a good policy to employ the strategy of *maximally dialectical analysis* and interpret the (part of the) discourse concerned as if it were (part of) a critical discussion.

In principle, the rules for critical discussion provide all the various norms which

[14]In principle, we can explain of all the traditional fallacies what their place is in our system (cf. chapters 9–18), but we have to allow for the possibility that some of the traditional fallacies are not quite rightly listed as such. Otherwise we would slip back into the same ad hoc approach as the severely criticized Standard Treatment.

[15]These rules are, in fact, a simplified version of the more elaborated and theoretically motivated rules we discussed in van Eemeren and Grootendorst (1984).

play a role in resolving a dispute.[16] Whereas the traditional, logico-centric approaches have just one norm—formal validity, in one sense or another—the 10 pragma-dialectical rules amount to 10 different norms. They do not only cover formal validity, or rather invalidity, but also many other things that can go wrong in argumentative discourse.

A norm can be violated in many different ways and this may lead to different kinds of fallacies. In order to comply with the norms, various kinds of criteria need to be satisfied. So far, the pragma-dialectical theory does not yet provide all the criteria that are necessary for deciding whether or not a certain speech act satisfies the norms. In its present state, it is basically a theory of norms, not a theory of criteria.[17]

In principle, the pragma-dialectical theory does provide the necessary interpretation procedures for determining whether or not an utterance satisfies a certain criterion. But that is not to say that these procedures are put in such a form that they lead automatically to the only right interpretation. In any case, all characteristic features of ordinary discourse, notably implicitness and indirectness, are systematically taken into account. In the logico-centric approaches, these phenomena are either completely ignored or treated as "infirmities" of natural language which have to be disposed of as soon as possible. At best, they get some superficial attention, leading only to ad hoc observations.

---

[16]For the rationale for the proposed norms, see also van Eemeren and Grootendorst (1988). It should be remembered that in order to be able to make well-grounded and systematic practical recommendations for resolving a dispute, not only these first order conditions but also second and third order conditions concerning attitudes and circumstances must be taken into account. Here, our position is similar to that of Siegel (1988) and some other representatives of the Critical Thinking Movement. Although we agree with Paul (1982) that an "atomistic" conception of critical thinking as the mastery of a battery of technical skills does not suffice, we value Ennis's list of a critical thinker's fundamental proficiencies (1987), which correspond to avoiding the fallacies of the standard list. Because in our approach these proficiencies are systematically put in a general and comprehensive perspective, the problem of atomization does not arise.

[17]To develop precise and unequivocal criteria for distinguishing between different kinds of violation of the same norm and similar kinds of violation of different norms further pragma-dialectical research is required; this research can benefit from the type of work done by Woods and Walton (cf. Woods & Walton, 1989).

CHAPTER 9

# Fallacies in the Confrontation

## ADVANCING STANDPOINTS AND DOUBT

A dispute arises when someone advances a standpoint and someone else casts doubt upon it. Though it may sound paradoxical, in order to further the resolution of disputes the expression of differences of opinion must also be furthered.[1] It is only when a dispute has fully come to light that it becomes possible to make systematic attempts at resolving it. Ideally, the dispute should become clear at the confrontation stage, which precedes the actual resolution process in a critical discussion.

Furthering the externalization of disputes means aiming for the creation of a climate in which people are enabled to advance any standpoint they wish and to cast doubt on any standpoint they wish. To begin with, it must be acknowledged that everyone has, in principle, the right to advance a standpoint on any subject and to call any standpoint into question, whatever it may refer to. Because arguments in support of a standpoint may themselves be regarded as substandpoints which can be called into question, this starting point also applies to advancing arguments and casting doubt on arguments.

The requirement of freedom of speech means that no restriction whatever is placed on the standpoints or arguments that may be put forward or criticized, nor on the persons permitted to do so. The speech acts by which these standpoints are expressed need not necessarily consist of factual statements, they may also be value judgements or aesthetic evaluations. Their propositional content may vary from something very simple to something very complicated.

[1]This does not always apply to differences of opinion in diplomatic and other negotiations, but then the principal aim of the discourse is not resolving the conflict by way of critical discussion.

That standpoints can relate to anything at all is expressed in the rules for a critical discussion by emphasizing the *non*-imposition of any condition regarding the kind of proposition the standpoint may refer to. The absence of any restriction on the persons permitted to advance or question a standpoint means that the speech acts that have to be performed in order to do so cannot be subject to special preparatory conditions with respect to the status or position of the speaker. In a critical discussion, everyone is entitled to assert something or to cast doubt on it.[2]

To be able to make the best use of this fundamental right to externalize their differences of opinion, the discussants must not be hindered from advancing their standpoints and from calling into question the standpoints of their opponents. This prohibition against limiting one's opponent opportunities to resolve a dispute by restricting his right of free speech is formulated in Rule 1 for a critical discussion: *Parties must not prevent each other from advancing standpoints or casting doubt on standpoints.*

Rule 1 can be broken in various ways. A discussant can impose certain restrictions on the standpoints that may be advanced or called into question, he can also deny a certain opponent the right to advance the standpoint he likes to advance or to criticize the standpoint he likes to criticize. In the first case restrictions as to content of the standpoints are imposed, in the second the other party's personal liberty is infringed.

Restrictions as to content mean that certain standpoints are in fact excluded from the discussion. This may also happen by declaring particular standpoints sacrosanct, so that the opponent is prohibited from casting doubt on them and they are rendered immune to criticism: "Then out comes my copy of the latest *Watchtower*, and I study it picking out the main points of each article. I mean you can't dispute what's in the Bible" (Viv Nicholson interviewed by *The Sunday Times*, November 25, 1990). Excluding a standpoint from the discussion, whether this is done by immunizing it or otherwise, is putting obstacles to the development of a critical discussion.

Infringing the opponents's personal liberty by denying him the right to advance a standpoint or to criticize it is an attempt to eliminate him as a serious partner in the discussion. This may be done by putting pressure on him to refrain from advancing a particular standpoint or casting doubt on it. It may also be done by discrediting his expertise, impartiality, integrity or credibility. Such maneuvers are generally executed not directly but by sophisticated and devious detours. Rather than being addressed directly to the opponent, they are often intended for consumption by a third-party audience.

---

[2]In the confrontation stage there are no exceptions to this rule, but this does not automatically lead to an obligation to defend a standpoint against any unreasonable antagonist who in the opening stage of the discussion proves to be not willing to accept anything at all or is in some other way uncooperative.

## PUTTING PRESSURE ON THE OPPONENT

Putting pressure on one's opponent in order to prevent him from advancing a standpoint or casting doubt on a standpoint is just as much putting an obstacle to the development of a critical discussion. It may have the result that the discussion gets no further than, or not even as far as, the confrontation stage. In that case, there will be no question of bringing the dispute to a resolution.

Every attempt to nip a discussion in the bud like this is a violation of Rule 1 and must, therefore, be regarded as a fallacy. In principle, either party can be guilty of this fallacy. If an attempt is made to prevent a standpoint from being advanced, the discussant who would have played the part of the antagonist is responsible for the fallacy; if an attempt is made to prevent doubt from being expressed, the protagonist is the guilty party.

The most extreme way of preventing one's opponent from advancing a standpoint or casting doubt on a standpoint is to make it literally impossible for him to speak. The most effective way of doing that is, of course, to eliminate him physically. Yet the threat of violence alone may well be sufficient, and threats of other sanctions can also be very effective. It is the element of threat that provides this type of violation of Rule 1 with its generic and established title: *argumentum ad baculum*.[3]

The Latin term *baculum*, which means stick, refers then, by extension, to a threat of any kind of violence ("fallacy of the stick"). If things do not stop at threats, the name gives a literal description. But if a stick is brought into play there is, of course, really no question any more of a discussion, let alone a critical discussion.

When an opponent is eliminated by methods such as shaking one's fist or drawing a knife, the very failure to use verbal means already damages the fundamental character of a critical discussion. Directives like "Shut up" and "I forbid you to raise this matter for discussion" also aim to bring about effects that conflict with that character. But in the case of verbal threats there is just as well a violation of Rule 1, because the speech act that is performed in uttering a threat is designed to achieve the interactional effect that the opponent links a particular consequence to the fact that he realizes that he is being threatened ("I'd better shut up"), whereas the only interactional effect that is sought in a critical discussion is that the opponent party be convinced of the wrongness of his standpoint or his doubt.

Threatening one's opponent amounts to putting pressure on him to refrain from taking up a position. Usually, the threat will not be issued in so many words: There will merely be some suggestion of possible tiresome consequences for the opponent if he prevents the speaker from getting his way. This is perhaps be-

[3]Woods and Walton (1989) gave a logical analysis of *ad baculum*, but they rightly suggested that the proper place for dealing with this fallacy is not logic (cf. Jason, 1987; Walton, 1987b; and Kielkopf, 1980).

cause it might otherwise be too obvious that the speaker is obstructing the development of the resolution process and infringes the rules of critical discussion. Appearances of reasonableness must be kept up at all times.

Due to the indirect way in which threats are generally issued, an *argumentum ad baculum* is in practice often difficult to pin down. Sometimes it is a useful pointer if the speaker takes refuge in wordings that emphatically assure the listener that *no* pressure is being put upon him: "Of course, I leave it entirely to you to take your stand," "Naturally it is for you to know what you will or won't accept," and so on. Such reassuring statements are often followed by a disclaiming *but*: "but you must realize that we are your biggest advertiser" (and if you publish that article about our role in South Africa you can forget about our advertising account).

A sophisticated, although not uncommon, way of using threats to put pressure on the opponent is to work on his emotions. The opponent is then, for instance, made to understand that he will be held responsible for hurting or disappointing the person who advanced the standpoint if he starts questioning it. The threat contained in this moral blackmail makes him feel that he is no longer free to cast doubt on the standpoint.

Because the technique of restricting the other party's freedom to advance or criticize a standpoint plays on his feelings of compassion, this particular type of violation of Rule 1 involved is called *argumentum ad misericordiam*.[4] Such attempts to speculate on pity to silence the opponent and have things one's own way are most commonly undertaken in the case where one party wishes the other party to do something for him. The sanctions that are used to back up the threat can then vary from pointing out the tiresome consequences that will arise if the complainant does not get his way ("If you fail me, my grant will be cut") to fits of weeping and worse.

## ATTACKING THE OPPONENT PERSONALLY

A personal attack on one's opponent is another attempt to eliminate him as a serious partner in the discussion by undermining his right to advance a standpoint or to cast doubt on a standpoint. By portraying him as stupid, unreliable, inconsistent, or biased, one effectively silences him, because if the attack is successful he loses his credibility. Strictly speaking, he is not prevented from advancing a standpoint or criticism, but, for practical purposes, he might as well be. Every attempt to bring about this effect is a violation of Rule 1 and must be regarded as a fallacy. Both the protagonist and the antagonist can be guilty of such a

[4]Walton, again, believes that *ad misericordiam* is not a fallacy of logic: it rather involves pragmatic and psychological matters (1987b). According to Hamblin (1970) and Kielkopf (1980) not all cases of *ad misericordiam* are fallacious.

violation. Because personal attacks are aimed at convincing an audience rather than one another, this is a typically rhetorical technique.

Currently widespread for all personal attacks is the Latin term *argumentum ad hominem.*[5] Neither of these attacks is aimed at the intrinsic merits of the opponent's standpoint or doubt. Instead,they are aimed at his person. There are three variants of the *argumentum ad hominem.*

The first variant consists of cutting down one's opponent by casting doubt on his expertise, intelligence, character, or good faith. This is a *direct personal attack*, often known as the "abusive" variant of the *argumentum ad hominem.*

In the second variant, the motives of one's opponent for his standpoint or doubt are made to appear suspect: He has an interest in the matter and is thus biased. This is the "circumstantial" variant of the *argumentum ad hominem*, which amounts to an *indirect personal attack.*

In the third variant of the *argumentum ad hominem*, an attempt is made to find a contradiction in one's opponent's words or between his words and his deeds and to undermine his credibility in doing so. Usually, such a discrepancy between a person's statements or between his ideas and his actions in present and past is referred to by its Latin name *tu quoque. Tu quoque*, in its basic form, occurs when someone casts doubt on a standpoint of which he himself is an adherent.[6]

In a direct personal attack, it is assumed that someone who is stupid or bad can never hold a correct opinion or have justified doubts. The man is played, not the ball. This generally happens in direct confrontations when tempers begin to rise, but it also occurs in written polemic, as illustrated by the postscript to a letter in a professional journal for advertising:

> I know Gianotten as a failed advertising man who as a sly economist of exceptional egocentricity could communicate better with money than with people in his working environment and markets in general. Apart from the fact that he reads me wrongly (but then he has never been able to listen) his scraggy little thesis amounts to saying

---

[5]Historically, the term *argumentum ad hominem* had a very different meaning (cf. Finocchiaro, 1974). The first person to have employed the term *argumentum ad hominem* as a technical term was Locke. In *An essay concerning human understanding* of 1690, he also introduced three other types of *ad*-arguments (*argumentum ad verecundiam, argumentum ad ignorantiam* and *argumentum ad judicium*) (1961). Locke is thus sometimes called the "inventor" of the *ad*-fallacies category. He himself, however, does not say in so many words that he considers the four *ad*-arguments to be fallacies and this is also not apparent in his explanations.

[6]Hamblin (1970) adhered to the view, commonly held in the Standard Treatment, that a circumstantial *ad hominem*, in contrast to an abusive *ad hominem*, need not always be fallacious. Gerber (1974) contended that in many cases *ad hominem* constitutes a valid argument. Govier (1981) pointed out that the *tu quoque* variant is a common and often legitimate way of arguing. According to Walton (1987a), *ad hominem* has a critical function in shifting the burden of proof by pointing out a pragmatic inconsistency in the arguer's position. See also Hoaglund (1982), Johnstone, Jr. (1952, 1970), Parker (1984), Walton (1985b), Woods and Walton (1989). For a dialectical analysis of *ad hominem*, compare Barth and Martens (1977).

> that advertising is only a part of the total marketing mix, but I was not unaware of that. The final line of his reaction is characteristic of the man, who handled people carelessly and advertising clumsily. A communicative cripple in both directions. And as far as lying awake is concerned: No, Evert, you've never bloody well lain awake from anything or anyone apart from yourself.

In the case of an indirect personal attack, a person's opinion is traced back to his stake in the matter and his arguments are "unmasked" as rationalizations. The chairman of Holland's Mother Tongue Education Commission, Mr. Bolle, having suggested that essay-writing should be abolished from schools, was treated to the following indirect personal attack in a newspaper:

> Writing essays? That's a load of rubbish, thought Bolle. The point is, he is himself incapable of writing essays, as may easily be determined merely by looking at a report written by him. What Bolle cannot, another shall not. Bolle shudders at the thought that the son or daughter of a dustman might one day turn out to be better at putting his thoughts down on paper than Bolle himself will ever manage to be. So, "Away with essays," minister Bolle recommends.

In the *tu quoque* variant of the *argumentum ad hominem*, the assumption is that a person who is not consistent cannot be right. The name *tu quoque* ("you too") reflects the fact that, originally, it referred first and foremost to someone who casts doubt on a standpoint of which he himself has always been an avowed adherent (or who stands up for a standpoint which he has always rejected). Today, the term refers to any form of inconsistency: quietly changing one's mind, chomping through a prime steak while pleading fervently for vegetarianism, and so on.

Whoever fails to practice what he preaches, applies double standards or continually reneges on himself is, of course, inconsistent. But this does not necessarily mean that his most recent standpoint is incorrect. To be able to establish that, it is first necessary for any arguments in favor of that standpoint to be tested in a critical discussion. Establishing that in similar questions one's opponent has adopted two diametrically opposed standpoints may bring to light a discrepancy in his attitude, but it cannot substitute for testing his present standpoint.

The complexity of this problem is nicely illustrated by a passage from an interview with the chairman of Holland's Christian Democratic Party, Piet Steenkamp. To Steenkamp's observation that catholics' consciences are underdeveloped because of their upbringing, the interviewer reacts as follows:

> Yet there's an inconsistency here somewhere. You are asking for a sort of clemency for behaviour like that displayed by some catholic politicians, really because they are not quite *au fait* with the difference between right and wrong, in fact because they aren't quite *au fait* with what life is all about. But on the other hand when it comes to abortion, for example, catholic politicians suddenly think they *do* have a monopoly on wisdom: Suddenly people can't think about things for themselves.

Here, the interviewer is drawing attention to a contradiction in Steenkamp's attitude. He does not explicitly link to this the conclusion that he regards as wrong Steenkamp's attempt to justify certain dubious financial transactions of catholic politicians, but this is the implication of his comparison with the attitude of catholic politicians towards abortion. Going by what he actually says, the interviewer cannot be accused of a *tu quoque* fallacy, but the suggestion contained in his words may well thought to be strong enough to think otherwise.

## COMPLICATIONS REGARDING THE CONFRONTATION

Rule 1 formulates the fundamental right to advance or criticize any desired standpoint without being hindered in any way by someone else. In practice, however, in certain situations one or more restrictions may be imposed on the exercise of this right. This happens most commonly in formal and institutionalized contexts in which the required procedures are laid down in rules, regulations, or statutes.

The clearest instance of this is provided, of course, by the law of the land. For example, in an appeal against sentence, the facts of the case are not open to discussion because they have already been established. Another example is the inadmissibility of testimony from spouses and other family members of the first degree. But there are plenty of instances outside the law too. At official meetings, for example, the discussion will be confined not only to the subjects on the agenda but also to those who have a right to speak.

These and similar restrictions are designed to further the orderly process of law or of the meeting. Because they are imposed with the direct or indirect agreement of those involved, they are not an infringement of Rule 1. This can also be the case with limiting agreements in less formal discussions. But as soon as the restrictions, without having a clear function in furthering the resolution process, are imposed unilaterally and against the wishes of those concerned ("You're only here to watch, so shut up"), there is a violation of Rule 1. Whether the restrictions are really accepted by all those involved is, of course, not always so clear. In principle, the burden of proof is always on the party wishing to impose the restriction.

A personal attack on one's opponent by depicting him as stupid or unreliable or by making his motives appear suspect is a violation of Rule 1 because it is an attempt to eliminate him as a serious partner in the discussion. In practice, however, situations can occur in which a direct or indirect personal attack may well be justifiable. Suppose, the standpoint at issue has a direct bearing on the person of one's opponent. For example, if he has made himself out to be an expert archaeologist or a manager of upright character and these qualifications are called into question, then it is obviously going to be relevant to point out any gaps in his archaeological knowledge or to cite any examples of corruption in his past.

Recognizing the relevance of such accusations of lack of expertise or incorruptibility is no exception to the basic rule that one's opponent cannot be eliminated by attacking him personally. In such a case, a reference to his person is after all part of the propositional content of the standpoint under discussion, and remarks about the person are, in principle, relevant arguments in the discussion. If they were ruled out of order, a resolution of the dispute would be made impossible right from the start. How can you show that someone is dishonest if you are not allowed to give examples of his dishonesty?

Another situation in which a personal attack can be justified is when witnesses give evidence in legal proceedings. The reason for calling the evidence of witnesses is that there is no other way of discovering the true sequence of events. The reliability of the testimony is thus of crucial importance. Ultimately, this reliability depends directly on the reliability of the person giving the evidence. What happened, and how it happened, is accepted on his authority. If there are grounds for doubting his powers of observation or his good faith, it is relevant to point this out by adducing the fact that he is near-sighted or has a vested interest. To do so does not then make one guilty of committing either the fallacy of the direct or the fallacy of the indirect personal attack.

The *tu quoque* variant of the *argumentum ad hominem* can also cause complications. This form of fallacy is, for example, committed if one rejects one's opponent's standpoint on the grounds that he held a different opinion at some time in the past. Yet no fallacy is committed by pointing out contradictions in the standpoints and arguments that the opponent has advanced *in the course of the discussion*. On the contrary, such criticism is a highly relevant contribution to the resolution process. Admitting inconsistent statements within one and the same discussion makes it impossible to resolve the dispute. It is therefore necessary to differentiate between discrepancies inside and outside the discussion. Only in the second case can there be a *tu quoque*. Unfortunately, where exactly one discussion ends and the next begins is in real life sometimes hard to determine.

Another complication is that it is not always immediately apparent whether or not one is dealing with a contradiction. Is wearing leather shoes incompatible with a vegetarian way of life? Is refusing to join the army on pacifist grounds irreconcilable with knocking out a burglar or a mugger? In contemplating the answering of such questions, there is always a risk that the more fundamental point will fade into the background: Even if there *is* a contradiction, this has nothing to do with the rightness or wrongness of the standpoint that is under discussion.

There are still more complex variants of the *tu quoque* fallacy, in which the discrepancy does not relate to the opponent's own behavior but to his assessment of the behavior of others. Suppose someone is accused of moonlighting and he retaliates by pointing out that his opponent's wife moonlights as a cleaning lady. This defense could mean that the party that is first attacked believes that he has the same rights as his opponent's wife, and wants to make this point, but usually such a reaction means more than that. The speaker rather wants to imply that the opponent is inconsistent: He deplores in the one instance what he evidently condones in the other. Therefore, he has no right to judge the aggrieved party on this point. Even if it is less obvious here that the argument is a fallacy of the *tu quoque* type, it nevertheless is. That is why it is important to be on one's guard when the other side in a discussion is implicitly or explicitly accused of applying double standards.

CHAPTER 10

# Fallacies in the Distribution of Discussion Roles

## BEING OBLIGED TO DEFEND A STANDPOINT

To be able to resolve a dispute about a standpoint, the person who has called the standpoint into question must be prepared to assume the role of antagonist in a discussion about the standpoint and the person who has advanced the standpoint must be prepared to assume the role of protagonist and defend his standpoint. This allocation of discussion roles takes place at the opening stage, in which those involved determine whether there is enough common ground (mutually agreed rules, presumptions and other starting points) to make it worthwhile to undertake a serious attempt at resolving the dispute. If this is not the case, there is no point in embarking on the argumentation stage. Then, there is in effect no true discussion at all and a resolution of the dispute remains out of reach. Whether the conditions for a critical discussion have been fulfilled is something that is in practice usually determined tacitly.

Such problems as may arise in allocating discussion roles will generally have no bearing on the antagonist. One of the parties has after all of his own accord challenged the other party by casting doubt on his standpoint and he can therefore hardly object to taking on the role of antagonist. So, problems concerning the discussion roles will almost always relate to the role of protagonist. Where a dispute has arisen it is the person who has advanced a standpoint who is faced with opposition. It is up to him to decide whether the point of departure of the discussion and his commitment to his own standpoint are indeed such that he is prepared to act as protagonist and defend the standpoint against the antagonist rather than retract it.

To the right, established in Rule 1, to advance any standpoint one wishes or cast doubt on it, the equally fundamental right must be added to challenge someone who has advanced a standpoint to defend it.[1] This would be an empty right if it were open to everyone to decide arbitrarily whether or not to take up the challenge. That is why Rule 2 for a critical discussion explicitly states an obligation to defend: *A party who advances a standpoint is obliged to defend it if the other party asks him to do so.*

The question is, however, whether a party who has advanced a standpoint can in reasonableness be expected always to take up the challenge. In our opinion, there are two important cases to which the rule does not apply.

The first case occurs when the same standpoint has to be defended against an attacker against whom it has already been conclusively defended while nothing has changed in the point of departure (the same rules, presumptions and other starting points). The obligation to defend a standpoint has then lost its pragmatic point. Otherwise, the discussants could be required to repeat the same discussion *ad infinitum*. Against a different challenger or with different discussion rules, presumptions or other starting points the situation is, of course, different because it is conceivable that the defense of the standpoint might lead to a different result.

The second case in which Rule 2 does not apply occurs when the challenger refuses to tie himself down to any discussion rules, presumptions or other starting points. If it becomes clear at the opening stage that there is no pragmatic base at all for common understanding, it is also apparent that the chance of resolving the dispute is zero anyway. In that case there is no point in prolonging the discussion.

## EVADING THE BURDEN OF PROOF

The obligation under Rule 2 to defend a standpoint that has been called into question has traditionally been known as the *burden* (or *onus*) *of proof*: The party whose standpoint has been questioned must prove that it is acceptable.[2] In fact, the allocation of the burden of proof is already determined by the distribution of roles that follows from Rule 2, because the party who is challenged must, in principle, assume the role of protagonist of the standpoint that has been called into question.

An obvious way of evading one's own burden of proof is to present the standpoint in such a way that there is no need to defend it in the first place. This can

[1]Of course, the antagonist should not offend against the Principle of Communication and the communication rules explained in Part I (chapter 5). This would happen if he challenged the protagonist to defend a standpoint already accepted by the antagonist.

[2]The concept of "burden of proof" originates from the context of law. In a criminal case, he who asserts must prove beyond reasonable doubt. In everyday argumentation, the requirement of proof is often less strict: some convincing evidence will suffice (cf. Hamblin, 1970; Walton, 1988a).

be done by giving the impression that the antagonist is quite wrong to cast doubt on the standpoint or that there is no point in calling it into question. In either case, the protagonist is guilty of the fallacy of *evading the burden of proof.*

The first way of evading the burden of proof amounts to presenting the standpoint as self-evident. In practice, attempts to do this can often be recognized by wording emphasizing the indisputability of the standpoint:

- "It's as clear as daylight that . . ."
- "Of course, there is no need for me to tell you that . . ."
- "It will be clear to everyone that . . ."
- "Nobody in his right mind would deny that . . ."
- "It goes without saying that . . ."
- "It cannot be denied that . . ."

The suggestion made by such phrasing is that someone who fails to see immediately the self-evidence of the standpoint must be incredibly stupid, whereas, in fact, the words may only be a smokescreen designed to conceal the weakness of the standpoint. Whoever allows himself to be overwhelmed by it may well drop his doubts. That, at any rate, is what the protagonist in such a situation is hoping for.

Such formulations should, instead, be taken as warning signs that the protagonist may be trying an easy way of getting out of his obligation to defend his standpoint. Something similar applies to phrasing by which the protagonist attempts to indicate that he, as it were, guarantees the rightness of the standpoint:

- "I can assure you that . . ."
- "You can take it from me that . . ."
- "I cannot imagine any other interpretation than that . . ."
- "There's no doubt in my mind that . . ."
- "I am absolutely convinced that . . ."

By giving his personal guarantee of the rightness of his standpoint the protagonist makes it very difficult for the antagonist to persist in his doubt. That would be, after all, to cast doubt directly on the protagonist's expertise, or even on his integrity. Therefore, phrasing of this kind can be used to force one's opponent to make a choice: Either he must accept the standpoint and put up with it, or he must abandon his faith in the protagonist. The latter would mean causing loss of face for the protagonist, and, if at all possible, the antagonist will normally want to spare him that embarrassment. If the protagonist is not gambling on this social mechanism, there is every reason for him to assume that the antagonist will simply ignore such phraseology. The antagonist may think that a protagonist who is really so sure of his case ought not to find it too difficult to produce a successful defense of his standpoint.

Another way of evading the burden of proof is to formulate the standpoint in such a way that it is protected from any adequate assessment. Here are some examples of such "hermetic" wordings:

- "The Frenchman is essentially intolerant."
- "The real young person of today is lazy."
- "The church is conservative by nature."
- "The squatter is open to anarchist tendencies."

When are standpoints like these undermined by criticisms? If they did not refer to "the" Frenchman, "the" real young person and so forth, it would be easier to imagine what an appropriate attack and an adequate defense would look like. If, instead of the definite article, there had been quantifiers such as "all," "some," "most," or "the average," it would at least have been clear that the protagonist, in order to defend his standpoint satisfactorily, should have been asked to come up with some examples.[3]

Precisely because there are no such quantifiers and intangible essentialistic qualifications such as "essentially," "real," and "by nature" are added, it is unclear in what case the standpoint in question would be conclusively defended or, for that matter, refuted. How many examples to the contrary are needed? If words like "all" or "some" were used this would be basically clear. Essentialistic statements with these quasi-definite articles (or with indefinite articles) evade all empirical testing and cannot be refuted. Therefore, they do not lend themselves for being used in a critical discussion.

Formulating a standpoint in a nonfalsifiable way can be seen as an attempt to render it immune to criticism. This "immunization strategy" is a sophisticated way of evading the burden of proof.[4] The immunizing effect is often reinforced by choosing even more general formulations in which no article is used:

- "Women are, by nature, possessive."
- "Frenchmen are essentially intolerant."
- "Squatters are open to anarchist tendencies."

If an attempt is made to refute the standpoint that women are by nature possessive by citing one or more examples of women of whom there is nothing possessive, the opponent often finds these examples irrelevant. It turns out that such statements are supposed to be treated as statements relating to the "essence" of women, Frenchmen, and so on and not as quantified statements in which the quantifier happens to have been omitted. The statements concerned are true because

---

[3]For logoforic uses of the definite article in generic sentences, see Barth (1974).

[4]Albert introduced the term *immunization strategy* when discussing ways out of the "Münchhausen trilemma" (1975).

women, Frenchmen and so on "just are that way." The women cited as examples to the contrary suddenly turn out not to be "real" women or they make themselves out to be what they are not. All attempts at an attack thus simply rebound from an armor of immunity.

## SHIFTING THE BURDEN OF PROOF

Apart from evading the burden of proof, the protagonist can also rid himself of the defensive obligation resting on him under Rule 2 by shifting the burden of proof to the challenger. This violation of Rule 2 is called the fallacy of *shifting the burden of proof*. What it amounts to is that an attempt is made to get the challenger to start proving why the standpoint that he has called into question is wrong.

In a nonmixed dispute, only one party has advanced a standpoint, and only that party can be the protagonist. As a consequence, this party is then also the only party who can have an obligation to defend a standpoint. If he tries to shift the burden of proof onto the party who is deemed to fulfill the role of antagonist, this is a fallacy. The failed protagonist is the only party who can be held liable for this fallacy.

In a case like this, shifting the burden of proof means that the prospective antagonist must prove that the standpoint that he has called into question is untenable. This amounts to his being saddled with the role of protagonist of the contrary standpoint. Because the antagonist himself has advanced no standpoint, he is in fact under no obligation to defend one, not even the one that is the opposite of the standpoint that he has called into question.

Here is an example of a denial of the burden of proof for a standpoint and the (implicit) shifting of the burden of proof onto those who do not meekly accept the standpoint. It is provided by W.J. Geertsema, the Queen's Commissioner in the Dutch province of Gelderland:

> In an interview with a weekly, Geertsema expresses his belief that money from bank raids has been used in squatting campaigns and campaigns against nuclear energy. As an example he cites the recent squatting campaigns in Nijmegen. Geertsema: "Thousands took the train to Nijmegen and stayed there for several days. That money must have come from somewhere. . . . I can't prove it," he says, "and it is not my job to do so."

In mixed disputes, the situation is somewhat more complicated. In such disputes, there are two opposed standpoints. One party, for example, may have advanced the standpoint that pornography is damaging to the health of the nation; the other may have advanced the view that this is absolutely not true. Thus, each party implicitly casts doubt on the acceptability of the other's standpoint. The question is then, on which party does the burden of proof rest?

Because both parties have advanced a standpoint, according to Rule 2 both discussants bear the burden of proof for a standpoint. There is, in other words, a *double* burden of proof. The problem here is not how to apportion the burden of proof, but the order in which the two parties must acquit themselves of their burden of proof.

In practice, this problem of the order of acquitting burdens of proof is usually presented as a problem of choice. Often, each party makes an attempt to force a decision and lay the burden of proof at the door of one of the parties. In such cases, a way out is sometimes found by assuming that the burden of proof rests on the party who is attacking a received wisdom, a prevailing tradition or an existing state of affairs. The burden of proof then rests on the party who wishes to change the *status quo*. He must prove that the alternative he is propounding is better. This means that the *status quo* has the status of a *presumption*.[5]

The Dutch author Piet Grijs gives an example of the application of the principle of presumption. He attacks the "NATO professor" van Staden, who has put forward the view that American cruise missiles should be deployed in the Netherlands:

> Van Staden has given his argument the form of answers to a series of objections, raised by himself, to the deployment. That is strange, for the burden of proof rests with the deployers.

According to Grijs, van Staden ought to have given pro-arguments for deployment, because in the *status quo* there are no cruise missiles. Instead of that, van Staden is content to discuss the objections to deployment—objections that, moreover, he has thought of himself.

The principle of presumption cannot be used in all cases. There is not always really a clear *status quo*. Take a dispute between someone who thinks that he and his partner should start saving and his partner, who thinks that saving is a waste of time. Which of them has presumption on his side?

Furthermore, there is a suggestion in the principle of presumption that the apportioning of the burden of proof that the principle leads to is also the most just. This need not be the case. It is certainly the most conservative, and the principle thus soon acquires an ideological connotation, even though it is intended to be purely practical.[6]

If the parties are basically agreed as to the application of the principle of presumption, there will be no objection to this. So, faced with the dilemma of

[5]In criminal law, presumption refers to the principle that a fact or state of affairs is taken to be true until proven otherwise: The accused is presumed to be innocent until his guilt has been established. The implication is that the accuser has the burden of proof (cf. Hamblin, 1970; Walton, 1988a).

[6]Goodnight (1980) made a distinction between conservative and liberal presumptions, where the liberal presumption is to embrace change unless there are good reasons for avoiding it (cf. Willard, 1983).

which party must lead with his defense, the principle will sometimes present a solution. But the application of the principle must not be allowed to result in the burden of proof being placed unilaterally on one party.

There is another principle that can provide a way out of the impasse of determining the order in which standpoints are to be defended in a mixed dispute. This is the principle of appealing to the criterion of *fairness*.[7] This principle holds that the standpoint that can most easily be defended should be defended first, so that the lightest burden of proof prevails. Albrecht Lier, according to his own testimony an illegitimate son of Prince Hendrik of the Netherlands, appeals to the criterion of fairness in an interview with a newspaper when it is suggested to him that he will have to come up with some sort of proof for his assertion that the only thing that ever gets published about his father is "mudslinging" and "drivel":

> Proof? It's impossible to prove the opposite of something negative! How can I prove to you that I don't go into the woods at night to look for young boys? Try proving that. No, it's the man who says I do it who must come up with the proof.

## COMPLICATIONS REGARDING DISCUSSION ROLES

It is often not only very difficult to establish which standpoint should be accorded the status of a presumption, but also to apply the criterion of fairness. It is not always possible to predict what standpoint is going to be easier to defend and hence has the lightest burden of proof. The practical usefulness of the principle of presumption and the criterion of fairness is thus somewhat limited.

In fact, both can only be used if the parties are agreed as to who has presumption on his side and what is the easier standpoint to defend. This is in any case something that cannot be decided unilaterally by one party against the wishes of his opponent. In some institutionalized discussion situations, such as a court of law, there is a third party, for instance a judge, who is in a position to break the deadlock. In everyday discussions, the parties must themselves try to get past the impasse. If they fail, there is no alternative but for one of the two simply to go ahead and begin his defense. Otherwise, the discussion reaches a stalemate at the opening stage.

If there *is* a clear status quo, which is also recognized as such by both parties, then there is, of course, no difficulty in applying the principle of presumption, but then, indeed, the problem will generally not arise at all. This is simply because if there is a recognized status quo there will probably not be two rival standpoints but only one, because the status quo is unlikely to be formulated in a standpoint unless there is some particular reason to do so. To advance what everyone

---

[7]In law, in certain cases, when the one thing is easier to prove or to refute than the other, the principle of fairness assigns the burden of proof to the party with the lightest task.

already knows and accepts is, in principle, to perform an unnecessary speech act and, hence, to violate the communication rule of efficiency.

Advancing a standpoint that goes against the status quo is, naturally, not an unnecessary speech act, and is thus more likely to occur in practice. In most cases, therefore, where there is a clear status quo, only one standpoint will be advanced, and that means that at that moment there exists a defensive obligation for only one standpoint. The person advancing that standpoint is obliged to defend it, not because it goes against the status quo but because according to Rule 2 the obligation to defend a standpoint goes with advancing it. As this obligation to defend the standpoint is conditional on the other party's challenge to do so, the protagonist's obligation is only activated if there is indeed expressed dissent.

The fallacy of shifting the burden of proof in a nonmixed dispute is traditionally referred to by the term coined for it by the English philosopher John Locke: *argumentum ad ignorantiam*. Locke too saw it as an attempt by the protagonist to get the antagonist to try to demonstrate that the standpoint that he has merely called into question is wrong. The fallacy lies in the fact that the protagonist represents matters in such a way as to make it appear that by expressing his doubt about it the antagonist has taken upon himself the obligation to prove the standpoint wrong.

In more recent publications, the term *argumentum ad ignorantiam* has been used to designate the "ignorance" or "stupidity" fallacy, which amounts to concluding from the fact that something has *not been proved* to be the case that it *is not* the case. Or concluding from the fact that something has not been proved *not* to be the case that it *is* the case. Although misunderstandings about the burden of proof play an important part in this fallacy, it is, nevertheless, quite a different kettle of fish. To avoid misunderstandings, in this book, the term *argumentum ad ignorantiam* is reserved for the modern interpretation.

One of the most important differences between the fallacy of shifting the burden of proof and the *argumentum ad ignorantiam* is that the first is a violation of a discussion rule at the opening stage and the second is a violation of a discussion rule at the concluding stage, which is discussed in chapter 17.

CHAPTER 11

# Fallacies in Representing a Standpoint

## ATTACKING STANDPOINTS

A dispute about a standpoint is resolved if the person who has cast doubt on it sees that his doubt is unjustified and ultimately accepts the standpoint. It is also resolved if the person who had advanced the standpoint sees that it is untenable and retracts it.

An effective way of making someone abandon his standpoint is to create a mixed dispute and prove the opposite standpoint. Someone who can be convinced that smoking is bad for you is likely to cease maintaining that it is good for you (although it is by no means necessary for him to do so). As a successful attack on the original standpoint consists then of a successful defense of the opposite standpoint, here at least we could justly say that defense is the best form of attack.

In this defense, the antagonist of the original standpoint is the protagonist of the opposite standpoint, and the original protagonist is now the antagonist. So, in such an attack on a standpoint, both parties have to play the part of protagonist and antagonist. If the opposing standpoints relate to one and the same proposition, the dispute is a mixed single dispute.

In a mixed single dispute, there is always a danger that the original antagonist will start attacking a standpoint that is slightly different from the one advanced by the original protagonist. There is then a shift in the proposition with respect to which one party adopts a positive and the other a negative standpoint (so that in effect the dispute becomes multiple). This may happen at the very beginning of the discussion, but it may also happen later on. For example, one discussant may start off by asserting that smoking is nothing like as harmful as people say, whereas the other discussant may behave as if his opponent had asserted that smoking is harmless, and may then try to prove that this is far from being the case.

If the parties talk at cross purposes like this, it will be impossible for them to resolve the original dispute. It is, therefore, essential that the propositions with respect to which standpoints are adopted should be the same for both parties and that they do not change unnoticed during the course of the discussion. The argumentation advanced in defense of a standpoint must refer to the same proposition as the doubt or contradiction that led to the argumentation being advanced. And if at the end of the discussion the opposing party adopts the same standpoint, this standpoint must relate to the same proposition as the original standpoint—otherwise the dispute will still not have been resolved.

If a shift takes place in the proposition with respect to which standpoints are advanced, doubt is expressed and attacks and defenses are carried out, the discussion can, at best, lead to a spurious resolution. What one party has unsuccessfully attacked and what the other party has successfully defended is different from the standpoint that was originally at issue. Or, even worse, what the one has successfully attacked and the other has unsuccessfully defended is different from the original standpoint. Then, the attack violates Rule 3 for a critical discussion: *A party's attack on a standpoint must relate to the standpoint that has indeed been advanced by the other party.*[1]

The danger that Rule 3 will be violated is always there throughout the discussion. The doubt expressed by the antagonist at the confrontation stage can straight away relate to a slightly different proposition from the proposition that is at issue in the protagonist's standpoint. At the opening stage, both the protagonist and the antagonist may be starting from a proposition that is at variance with the one that led to the original difference of opinion. The arguments and the criticisms that are put forward at the argumentation stage may not always refer to the same proposition. And at the concluding stage, when establishing the final result the protagonist as well as the antagonist may easily refer to a proposition somewhat different from that in the original dispute. It may, for example, be that in their conclusion they redefine the dispute more narrowly or, for that matter, less narrowly.

Rule 3 can, in principle, be broken by both the protagonist and the antagonist. It is most likely to be broken in a mixed discussion, when it is easier for both antagonists to attack a different standpoint from the one actually advanced by the protagonist. With the discussion situation being so complex and the protagonist so occupied in devising his defense, there is a good chance that the offense will go unnoticed.

---

[1]It is, of course, quite another matter that the antagonist should—in line with the Principle of Communication—respond to what the protagonist may be taken to have said rather than to what he has literally said. Routinely, teachers and psychotherapists carry this sometimes a bit further (and for our purposes a bit too far) by responding to what they think the speaker should have said if he would have been sincere about it or conscious of his "real" feelings.

## IMPUTING A FICTITIOUS STANDPOINT TO THE OPPONENT

There are two important techniques for attacking standpoints not genuinely advanced by the opponent. A fictitious standpoint can be imputed to him, or his actual standpoint can be distorted. In either case, the maneuver is more likely to succeed with an audience not entirely sure exactly what the other party has asserted than with the opponent himself. In the case of a polemic in a newspaper, for example, the readers will rarely be able to lay hands on the article that they need in order to be able to check whether a standpoint has been accurately represented.

In extreme cases, the opponent may have a standpoint attributed to him that in no way resembles what he said or even might have said, but the whole thing can also be less blunt than that. However it is done, imputing a fictitious standpoint to one's opponent is a case of the fallacy of the *straw man*.[2] In the fallacy of the straw man the opponent and his standpoint are caricatured in such a way that they can more easily be attacked.

If there is really no resemblance between the standpoint being attacked and the original standpoint, the discussion takes on something of the eerie quality of a phatasmagoria. Even so, the attacker and the attack are genuine enough: Only the standpoint is not.

One clever way of suggesting that one's opponent has adopted a particular standpoint, when in fact he has not, is to put forward the opposite standpoint with great emphasis. In a discussion situation, if one person is emphatic in his support for something, he soon creates the impression that others are against it, and from there it is only a short step for the audience to assume that the speaker's opponent belongs to that group. For example, if a woman says firmly: "I personally regard the defense of our democracy as being of the highest priority," she thereby suggests that there are those who think otherwise. If her opponent does not hasten to declare that he too is a great champion of democracy, he immediately heaps upon himself the suspicion that he could not give a damn about democracy.

This mechanism seems to work to even greater effect when the standpoint presented contains a negation: "I don't think church schools should be allowed to practice discrimination." Who thinks they *should*? The opposing party?

It is only relevant to present an opinion with emphasis if it is not shared by others. This is why putting a standpoint forward can in itself have the effect of the contrary view being ascribed to the opposing party. Because it is one of the communication rules that nothing that is superfluous may be adduced, the audience will tend to assume that a standpoint that has been advanced must be relevant, and that its relevance must be due to the fact that it is not subscribed to by others. If the opposite side in the discussion does not rush to deny this, he

[2]Cf. Naess (1966) and Walton (1984, 1987b).

will soon find himself accused of subscribing to the opposite standpoint.

Another way of imputing a fictitious standpoint to the opponent is to refer to the party or grouping to which the opponent belongs and to link them with the fictitious standpoint:

> As a communist he's bound to think Mrs Thatcher is an untrustworthy politician.

Here it is taken for granted what the group will think of the matter and that what applies to the group applies to every individual member of it. The suggestive power of this manner of presentation is so strong that the victim may have considerable difficulty in shaking off the standpoint attributed to him:

> He may say he thinks Thatcher is a good prime minister, but as a communist, of course, he still really thinks she is a lackey of capitalism.

The creation of a fiction goes even further if it is not clear precisely who it is that actually adheres to the standpoint being attacked. The opponent is then a fantasy who, because he does not actually exist, cannot say anything in retaliation. Because it is often difficult to say whether the victim of the attack and his standpoint actually exist or whether they are the product of the attacker's imagination, this technique is particularly likely to bring success where the audience is completely ignorant about the subject concerned.

The Dutch writer Karel van het Reve uses this technique of making up the opposition in a clever way by presenting its standpoints as *idées reçues:*

> Everyone thinks Philips are perfectly capable of making lamp bulbs that don't burn out.

> In all schools the teacher will tell you that you must avoid using the same word twice.

By casting the propositions of his fictional opponents in a generalized and absolutized mold, van het Reve makes it easier for himself to show how stupid they are. References to surveys or other evidence that there are people who really adhere to the standpoint are, of course, absent. A single example of the contrary would be enough to refute the idea of the cliché. "Name one" is therefore the first critical reaction that should be given to such standpoints beginning with phrases like "every," "most," and "virtually all."

## DISTORTING THE OPPONENT'S STANDPOINT

The second technique of surreptitiously attacking a standpoint not genuinely advanced by the opponent consists in first distorting the standpoint and then attacking it. In practice, the differences between the attacked standpoint and the original standpoint will often be quite subtle. By design, the opponent's words are so twisted that it becomes at the same time easy for the distorter to tackle and difficult for an outsider to tell whether justice is being done to the original standpoint.

A knowledge of the maneuvers that may be carried out in distorting a standpoint can be helpful to recognizing a straw man. Among the devices that are employed here are simplification, exaggeration, absolutization, generalization, and the omission of nuances or qualifications. Often, they are used in combination, as in the following complaint by a psychologist about criticism leveled against a doctoral thesis written under his supervision:

> The result is very discouraging for the way he goes about things: quoting some sentences completely out of context, himself suggesting meanings that aren't there, and finally, with a few well-aimed exaggerations – which aren't there either – making the prey ripe for his omniscient and omnivorous voracity. I find this rather an easy way of discussing academic work.

The rest of the complaint consists of pointing out twisted meanings, omitted specifications, and exaggerations.

Probably the most commonly heard complaint of anyone who has ever seen his own standpoint discussed in print is that things are being taken out of context. Even in cases in which there is a pretense of quoting the author literally, as in interviews and newspaper reports, such and similar distortions do occur. The leader of the Dutch Labor Party, Wim Kok, gives a clear example of the omission of nuances when illustrating his claim that certain journalists "treated him in bad faith":

> Kok, invited to speak at the official opening of the academic year, reflected on the fact that in our society there are essential jobs for which it is becoming increasingly difficult to find the people. Why not, by analogy with national service in the forces, have a sort of national service in social well-fare, he suggested. "It was just an idea," says Kok, "but the next day *The Telegraph* came out with a 7-column headline on page 3: Kok wants forced labour! I felt I'd really been taken for a ride."

Exaggerating a standpoint by generalizing it, may be done by leaving out such quantifiers as "some," "a few," and "a couple" so that the standpoint is made to appear to refer to "all." The resulting standpoint is much easier to attack. For example, if you are defending the standpoint that some men are oversensitive, your job is over as soon as you have given a couple of examples of oversensitive men. Ways of defending the thesis that *all* men are oversensitive are naturally much thinner on the ground. Moreover, your opponent only has to indicate one tough guy to show that the standpoint is untenable.

In this case, the standpoint has become easier to attack because the possibility of falsification has been increased. There is no need for any specialized knowledge to be able to see that. In order to come up with the appropriate critical reactions it is useful to have an insight into the logical means available for attacking and defending standpoints containing the quantifiers "all" and "some"—the two standard types to which most of these cases can be reduced.[3] For the unmasking of other types of generalization as straw man fallacies specialist knowledge is often indispensable.

In many cases of potential distortions, the most one can do is to make a close comparison of the original standpoint and the version in which it is now presented. If no original is available, all one can do is harbor one's suspicions regarding the accuracy of the representation. An example of such a suspect representation of a standpoint occurs in an M.P.'s reaction to a Junior Health Secretary's argumentation for his plan to stimulate sport as a leisure activity:

> The first argument, the unsoundness of which is plain to the naked eye and which presumably serves to divert attention from the true motives, relates to the cost of the health services. The Secretary is afraid that little-used limbs soon go brittle or fall off, after which the help of the medical establishment has to be called in at a cost of an average monthly salary every day. Because in the world market sports trainers are cheaper to come by than surgeons, prevention is also better than cure with an eye for the public spending borrowing requirement.

By presenting the Secretary's argument in such a way that it appears ludicrous from the outset, the writer has made attacking it a simple matter. Because the Secretary is not quoted literally, we are forced to take the M.P. at his word. In this case, because of its absurdity, it is safe to assume that the Secretary's position is being ridiculed.

If the original were available it would be possible to use it to check the accuracy of the way the standpoint is represented, as in the following example taken from an article by a journalist called Poll:

> Renate Rubinstein once wrote that she almost choked with anger at the very thought of the grey trousers and tweed jackets that were my daily apparel.

According to Rubinstein herself she never wrote this, and she was so angry at having a "quotation or quasi-quotation" thrown at her like this that she offered Poll a prize of a thousand guilders if he could name the location of the quotation. A week later, Poll responded by quoting an old article by Rubinstein:

> Actually, with all his cultural snobbery he is a very boring, rancorous little man.

With this quotation, Poll believes he has found the conclusive evidence for his assertion, and goes on: "Next week she'll doubtless publish a rectification or think

[3]For dialogical definitions of the quantifiers specifying the formal possibilities for attacking and defending quantified sentences, see Kamlah and Lorenzen (1984). Cf. Hintikka (1976, 1981) and Krabbe (1982).

up some excuse to wriggle out of it." However, now that both the original and the quoted version are available in their literal form, it is perfectly clear that the quotation differs considerably from the original.

## COMPLICATIONS REGARDING THE REPRESENTATION OF STANDPOINTS

Through replacing quantifiers like "some," "a few," and "a couple of" with "all," a standpoint can be exaggerated by generalizing it. One complication is that these quantifiers are often not in so many words present in the original wording. The protagonist may, for example, have said that men are oversensitive. His opponent can then attack this standpoint as if he had said that *all* men were oversensitive. Is this a case of a straw man?

In practice, quantifiers are often omitted without this leading to any difficulties, because in most cases the context will make it clear whether the "all" or the "some" interpretation is the right one. If the opposite party's attack assumes the "all" interpretation whereas the context clearly points to the "some" interpretation, then there is clearly a case of a straw man. However, the context is not always as clear as that.

It is not unheard of for a protagonist to intend the "all" interpretation but then suddenly fall back on the "some" interpretation as soon as the standpoint is being attacked. Because of the absence of explicit quantifiers, he can, for instance, always claim not to have said that *all* men were oversensitive. The omission of quantifiers can thus be one of the protagonist's devices to cover himself against criticism. It is then, in effect, a variant of the immunization strategy.

Many instances of the straw man fallacy relate to the propositional content of the assertion by means of which a standpoint is advanced. In case of an exaggeration, the propositional content is attributed a greater scope than it actually has. Yet it also happens that a standpoint is accorded greater communicative force than the protagonist intended.

This occurs if the protagonist presents his standpoint as a conclusion which is plausible on the grounds of certain information and the antagonist—whether deliberately or not—treats it as a necessary conclusion and proceeds to demonstrate (in his role as protagonist) that the conclusion need not necessarily follow from the available information. The protagonist intended to point out an inductive probability or plausibility argument, whereas, in his attack, the antagonist (as protagonist) assumes that it is supposed to be a deductively valid argument. Because the precise reach of the communicative force, like the scope of the propositional content of the standpoint, often remains implicit, it is difficult to put one's finger on such a misrepresentation.

If the original version of the standpoint being attacked is still available for comparison, it may be possible to determine how accurately it is represented.

In some other cases, the standpoint as represented by its attacker may be so unlikely as to arouse suspicion on that count alone. Certain signals in the representation may also be helpful. In dubious cases, there are quite likely to be spurious confidence-inspiring introductions such as "The author clearly believes that . . ." or "The author is fascinated by the notion that. . . ." Although such wording suggests otherwise, many times the author in question will not have formulated the standpoint that is ascribed to him. If excessive stress is placed on the obviousness of a standpoint or on the correctness of the way it is represented, some suspicion is generally not misplaced.

Besides distorting the opponent's actual standpoint and imputating a fictitious standpoint to the opponent, attacking the opponent's weak arguments while ignoring his strong arguments and attacking insignificant opponents while disregarding more powerful opponents are also regarded as straw man fallacies in the literature.[4] Concentrating on the opponent's weak arguments and concentrating on a weak opponent amount, in fact, to the same thing: In both cases, the attacker chooses the path of least resistance by avoiding more serious opposition. All these attacking strategies go straight to the heart of the straw man, which lies essentially in representing the other party as weaker than he actually is.

[4]Cf. Damer (1980) and Govier (1985).

CHAPTER 12

# Fallacies in Choosing the Means of Defense

## CHOOSING THE MEANS TO DEFEND A STANDPOINT

At the argumentation stage of a critical discussion, the argumentation is put forward that is calculated to remove all doubts concerning the acceptability of the disputed standpoint. This argumentation is advanced by the protagonist of the standpoint. Rule 4 formulates the requirement that the argumentation in a critical discussion must genuinely pertain to the disputed standpoint: *A party may defend his standpoint only by advancing argumentation relating to that standpoint.*

Rule 4 can be violated in two ways. First, a standpoint may be defended by means other than argumentation. Second, a standpoint may be defended by argumentation not relating to the standpoint advanced at the confrontation stage. In the first case, we are dealing with *nonargumentative means of persuasion*; in the second, with *irrelevant argumentation*.

The fallacy committed by using nonargumentative means of persuasion is that a real resolution of the dispute is prevented by the disputed standpoint not being defended by means of rational arguments. The various means employed instead are all such that they fail to fulfill the identity and correctness conditions for the complex speech act of argumentation.

It is, in particular, the essential condition for the speech act of argumentation that is in these cases violated: There is no serious attempt to rationally justify or refute the disputed proposition. In other words, there is no genuine attempt to convince. Generally, someone who takes this line will himself not really believe that the chosen means bring about an acceptable justification or refutation of the proposition. In that case, the responsibility condition is not fulfilled either. Indeed, even the preparatory condition may not have been met, because the listeners can not be expected to accept the nonargumentative defense as an acceptable justification or refutation.

In the context of a critical discussion, means of persuasion that fail to meet the conditions of the complex speech act of argumentation must be regarded as spurious or, at best, as surrogate arguments. The danger of using such surrogate arguments lies in the fact that they are presented as genuine arguments. It is a danger exacerbated by the effect of the Communication Principle, which makes that all contributions to the discussion are, in principle, treated as relevant. As a result of the strategy of the maximally argumentative interpretation, all the contributions made by the protagonist that are capable of being interpreted as argumentative are so interpreted.

The use of nonargumentative means of persuasion can hardly be intended as a rational attempt to convince the opponent. These means are not employed to determine in a rational way which of the two parties who are in disagreement is actually right, but to win the audience over. Nonargumentative persuasion is usually aimed at a third party. The rhetorical techniques used in the endeavor primarily consist of ruses for gaining the victory in the eyes of an audience of outsiders. These rhetorical ruses can be divided into two groups: The protagonist can play on the emotions and prejudices of the audience, or he can sell his standpont by parading his own qualities, thus deliberately bringing himself into the discussion.[1]

The fallacy that is committed by irrelevant argumentation is that the disputed standpoint is defended by argumentation that has no bearing on it so that no real resolution of the dispute can be achieved. In effect, the argumentation supports a standpoint that is quite different from the one about which the opinions differ. Just as with a straw man, compared with the proposition originally at issue, there is a shift in the proposition with respect to which a standpoint is being adopted.

The main difference between the fallacy of irrelevant argumentation and that of the straw man is that in the case of a straw man the shift results in the standpoint being easier to attack, whereas in the case of irrelevant argumentation it becomes easier to defend. By changing "some" to "all," a standpoint can be made easier to attack; by changing "all" to "some," it can be made easier to defend. The fallacy of advancing argumentation that is only relevant to a standpoint that is not actually at issue is traditionally called *ignoratio elenchi*.[2]

---

[1]For rhetorical persuasion techniques, see Kennedy (1963), Simons (1976), and Sproule (1980). Van Dijk (1984) discussed the role of prejudice.

[2]Cf. Hamblin (1970).

## PLAYING ON THE AUDIENCE'S EMOTIONS

Violations of Rule 4 in which nonargumentative means of persuasion are used by exploiting the emotions of the audience are known by the generic term of *argumentum ad populum*.[3] Such violations play directly at the audience's feelings. In this respect, they differ from the *argumentum ad hominem* and the *straw man*. In the case of *argumentum ad hominem*, the intention is to damage the opponent's credibility, thus eliminating him as a serious opponent in the eyes of the audience. The straw man fallacy only works if the opponent (who will often be absent) has first been subjected to fraudulent modification.

The purpose of exploiting the audience's emotions is to play on prejudices of the audience that are not directly relevant to the standpoint being defended rather than defend this standpoint starting from the premises mutually agreed upon by the discussants: *Pathos* then takes the place of *logos*.[4] For this reason, such violations of Rule 4 are sometimes called "pathetic fallacies."

The *argumentum ad populum* is a fallacy that can frequently be observed at public demonstrations, political meetings, and religious gatherings. Its effect depends on sociopsychological factors that play a part in meetings of large groups of people. Whoever succeeds best at manipulating the emotions of those present is the most likely to get his way. The true demagogue knows how to play on both positive and negative emotions and how to touch both the group as a whole and the individuals composing it.

The positive emotions that may be exploited include, for example, feelings of safety and loyalty; the negative ones, fear, greed, and shame. Negative group emotions often have to do with social and ethnic prejudice. To the extent that group-related emotions are involved, identification with the group interest plays an important role. The more powerful the presence of these emotions in an audience, the more effectively they can be exploited in an *argumentum ad populum*. A speaker, for example, who wishes to restrict the numbers of foreigners in a fashionable residential area may only have to appeal to the audience's group interest by invoking their prejudice that letting in more foreigners will endanger their own identity, to sway them to his way of thinking. If he can at the same time appeal to their individual interests by invoking their materialistic prejudices with a suggestion about the falling of house values, a critical discussion about the subject may become quite unnecessary.

For an *argumentum ad populum* to be effective, there is usually no need to bring *topoi* such as common cultural identity or the value of personal property

[3]According to Hamblin (1970), the arguments *ad passiones* were in the early 18th century added to Locke's list by Isaac Watts. *Ad populum* is a controversial fallacy: some authors think that it is not always fallacious. (cf. Kielkopf 1980; Walton, 1987b).

[4]For the distinction between *logos*, *pathos*, and *ethos*, see Braet (1991). Wisse (1989) discussed *ethos* and *pathos* from Aristotle to Cicero, Gill (1984) post-Ciceronian approaches.

as an explicit argument into the discussion. It is enough to emphasize to give them emotional "presence": The audience will itself make the desired connection with the standpoint at issue. The audience is thus, as it were, softened up, so that it will more easily accept its manipulator's standpoint. If prejudices *are* advanced explicitly as arguments they need to be evaluated as any other (bad) argument. For rhetorical purposes, it is probably much more effective to make use of prejudices only to create the right atmosphere. Such maneuvers may also have a diversionary effect by preventing the audience from realizing, until it is too late, exactly how shaky the standpoint's foundations really are.

Generally speaking, the *argumentum ad populum* thrives best in discussions on a broad scale, in which many people consider themselves involved. Not surprisingly, then, it is a fallacy committed not infrequently by politicians and other public figures. Rhetorical ruses of this kind do not resolve differences of opinion but they can, of course, have other functions to the speaker and his audience. They may, for instance, be important in an epideictic sense by emphasizing the group's unitedness.

## PARADING ONE'S OWN QUALITIES

The second way of using nonargumentative means of persuasion to win the audience over is parading one's own qualities or qualities one attributes to oneself. When the protagonist does so, he deliberately brings his own person into the discussion. He employs *ethos*, the third category of the rhetorical means of persuasion. According to Aristotle, *ethos* is generally even more effective than *logos* and *pathos*.

In conformity with Aristotelian terminology, violations of Rule 4 in which the protagonist's personal characteristics, expertise or other qualities are emphasized in order to persuade the audience to accept a standpoint, are usually called *ethical fallacies*. Where an ethical fallacy is committed, the protagonist attempts to get a standpoint accepted by the audience just because of the authority he derives in the eyes of the audience from his expert knowledge, credibility, or integrity. Therefore, this fallacy can be regarded as an *argumentum ad verecundiam*.[5]

An *argumentum ad verecundiam* can be effective due to the psychological mechanism that the audience is more likely to accept what someone says the more confidence they have in him. In extreme cases, a particularly strong *ethos* can even render argumentation for a standpoint superfluous. There is no need for it because the audience takes the speaker at his word, going along with whatever he says or proposes.

---

[5]In the literature on fallacies, little attention is paid to *ad verecundiam* as an ethical fallacy.

*Ethos* can also play a part in a less extreme way. According to the Dutch prime minister, Mr Ruud Lubbers, without *ethos*, even the good arguments lack force. Answering a question from an interviewer as to whether convincing is merely a matter of argumentation, he says:

> Arguments are important, but not enough by themselves. Who uses them is also important. That is a question of authority and respect. Integrity is part of it too, in the sense that people feel they are not being tricked.

If a powerful *ethos* can make argumentation, from a rhetorical perspective, unnecessary for certain audiences, conversely a weak *ethos* may make powerful argumentation a necessity. This is well illustrated by the following quotation from the journalist Renate Rubinstein, who wonders, referring to a polemic about a doctoral thesis, why the opposing party thought it unnecessary to advance arguments for his standpoint, whereas she herself felt she did have to argue her case:

> I think it is because I am not a professor. If I had been a professor, preferably a China specialist, it would have been enough for me to write what I did, and the statement would have been an argument in its own right. Since I am an outsider, I have to prove it. It is not true just because I say it is true. So proof is something you provide because you have to. If you had a degree or a sign on your door you would not have to, unless you felt you had to. Professors, collectives and believers in an ideal (however bloodthirsty they may be, but that is true of many ideals) have no need to earn their rightness because the professor relies on his mental capital and the others rely on mental unemployment benefit or, more graphically, on poor relief.

In relying too heavily on *ethos*, blind faith may take the place of rational considerations. People then accept the standpoint not because they have been convinced by sound arguments, but simply because they have faith in the authority of the protagonist. If *ethos* takes in this way over from argumentation, we are dealing with the fallacy of the *argumentum ad verecundiam*:

> *Professor Mary Elderly:*
> Women have quite a different logic from men; as a professor I can say that with some emphasis.

There is nothing inherently objectionable to *ethos*. We all regularly have to accept certain things on the authority of experts; it could not be otherwise. Some subjects require so much specialized knowledge that it is simply impossible for the layman to evaluate all the standpoints on their merits. So far so good, but we do have to realize that a real resolution of the dispute is then precluded: We let the experts "settle" it.

If a protagonist plays on the ignorance of his audience, he runs the risk of creating an obstacle to a critical discussion. This is only a proper course of action if the subject is recondite, the audience wholly ignorant of it and the protagonist indeed a real specialist in it. If these conditions are not fullfilled, the protagonist is guilty of an *argumentum ad verecundiam*. And if he does, in fact, not even possess the specialized knowledge that he pretends to have, he is even guilty of deceit.

Somebody who wishes to take part as an antagonist in a critical discussion, or who wishes to evaluate a discussion critically, is well-advised to bear in mind that the process of resolving the dispute can easily be frustrated if the protagonist unnecessarily tries to settle it on the basis of his expertise. The protagonist may claim a degree of expertise that he does not possess. Even if he is as expert as he claims, his expertise may be completely irrelevant to the question at issue in the discussion. This might be the case, for example, if a person labels herself a professor and as such makes pronouncements about female logic, and then turns out to be a professor of Egyptology.

In theory, the effect of the deception can be undone as soon as we become aware that a protagonist is falsely pretending to have expert knowledge. What then probably happens is that a direct personal attack is set against the misplaced claim to authority. This implies a departure from the plane of a critical discussion, albeit perhaps only a temporary one: The critical discussion is, as it were, interrupted, but can be taken up again at a later stage. During this intermezzo, the protagonist's *ethos* may be brought back into its proper perspective, but this does not, of course, refute his standpoint.

## COMPLICATIONS REGARDING THE MEANS OF DEFENSE

The dividing line between nonargumentative means of persuasion and irrelevant argumentation is sometimes difficult to draw. It is not always so clear whether the conditions for the performance of the complex speech act of argumentation have indeed been fulfilled. In borderline cases, the strategy of maximally argumentative interpretation may provide a solution, but this solution is not always truly satisfactory.

Another complication is that the term *argumentation* itself is sometimes used in a rather different sense in colloquial speech. Indeed, the difference can be so considerable that it is hard to see any correspondence of meaning at all with the technical sense in which it is used in the theory of argumentation. Here is an extreme example, taken from a letter to the editor referring to rioting connected with the eviction of squatters from a building in Amsterdam:

> It is my conviction that the rule of law is not in danger when a particular group disputes the policies or measures of the proper authorities, even if unorthodox means are employed, as was the case in the squatter campaigns in the Vondelstraat

> and on the Keizersgracht. The rule of law is put at risk when the authorities fail to take the core of protests seriously, when the protest itself is not seen as a radical form of argumentation but merely as a threat directed against everything and everyone.

If the meaning of the word *argumentation* departs so grossly from that of the technical term as it does here, this will generally not lead to any misunderstandings. It is different when the differences are smaller:

> Nobody is going to fool me into believing that Phillips arrived at the standpoint that the public display or sale of pornography should be prohibited, along the path of argumentation described by him. He undoubtedly already held that standpoint—and he also has an interest in that standpoint, with his institute being round the corner from the streets where pornography is on display—and fabricated the argumentation to go with it.

By suggesting that Phillips' standpoint is inspired by self-interest and that the argumentation was "fabricated" to go with it, the sincerity of Phillips' argumentation is questioned. But this is not the main problem. The manner in which Phillips' argumentation was arrived at is also questioned. The author appears to assume that there are certain requirements for the "context of discovery" of argumentation, but no such requirements are laid down in the "happiness" conditions for the performance of the complex speech act of argumentation. The question is now what precisely the consequences are that the author attaches to this predicament. Is Phillips' argumentation unsound? Is it irrelevant? Or is it, after all, no argumentation at all?

The rhetorical ruses of the protagonist playing on the audience's emotions and parading of his own qualities can cause some extra confusion because the second is, in fact, a form of the first. The difference is that when the protagonist parades his own qualities he is not so much mobilizing emotions or prejudices that already exist in the audience as putting himself on the line. He can only do so successfully, however, if the audience has sufficient confidence in his expertise and integrity, that is, if he is in sufficient credit with the audience. So, here too the audience plays a central role, albeit a different one.

The *argumentum ad verecundiam*, incidentally, need not always imply an emphasis of the protagonist's own excellence. The opposite strategy may also be extremely effective. The protagonist then very modestly presents himself as a layman. By electing for the position of an underdog he attempts to sow the seeds for a climate of sympathy and benevolence on the part of the audience, so that it will be more inclined to believe what he says. Because here too improper use of the protagonist's *ethos* plays a central role, violations of Rule 4 caused by using this technique are likewise ethical fallacies. If the protagonist starts exploiting his modesty by exaggerating it, an ethical fallacy imperceptibly becomes an *argumentum ad misericordiam.*[6]

An *argumentum ad misericordiam* can be used either to put pressure on the audience or to sway the audience in the protagonist's favor. If he does the former, at the confrontation stage, there is a violation of Rule 1; if he does the latter, at the argumentation stage, there is a violation of Rule 4. When identifying fallacies it is important to keep these two variants of the *argumentum ad misericordiam* well apart, because they have different implications for the resolution of the dispute.

The protagonist's parading of his own qualities in an *argumentum ad verecundiam* can also occur as a violation of two different rules. Besides being a violation of Rule 4, at the argumentation stage, it can also produce a violation of Rule 2, at the opening stage. It is then an attempt at evading the burden of proof for a standpoint. The protagonist gives, as it were, a personal guarantee of the rightness of his standpoint, so that it is more difficult for the antagonist to cast doubt upon it and the protagonist slides out of his obligation to defend the standpoint. This violation of Rule 2 can be regarded as a variant of the *argumentum ad verecundiam.* Here again, the two variants should be carefully distinguished.

Just as with the *argumentum ad hominem*, with an *argumentum ad verecundiam* situations can arise in which it appears not to be a violation of any of the discussion rules. Just as with the *argumentum ad hominem*, this is most likely to occur with an eyewitness report or a statement given in evidence. If the protagonist was the only person in a position to make a particular observation and his report is called into question, he can do very little else but insist that he really did see what he says he saw.

Something of the kind happens in cases in which the protagonist is the only person in a position to judge the accuracy of an utterance. This might be so, for example, in the case of pronouncements concerning his own state of mind or physical well-being. How otherwise can he convince others that he is sad or has a headache, than by *saying* he is sad or has a headache?[7] The listener will either have to take him at his word or abandon confidence in his sincerity. If the listener does the latter, he leaves the protagonist with no means whatever of convincing him.

A third group of cases in which something is so because the protagonist says it is so arises when a declarative is performed. A chairman opening a meeting, a clergyman christening a child, and a referee awarding a point all possess the authority, by virtue of their office, to do so. Anybody who doubts whether the meeting has really been opened, whether the child has really been christened, or whether the point was really scored, can only be convinced by pointing out

---

[6]Walton (1987b) argued that *ad misericordiam* is a fallacy because it involves irrelevance rather than because it is an appeal to mass enthusiasm.

[7]Cf. Austin (1970).

that the chairman *said* "I hereby open the meeting," and so on.

Just as has happened with the *argumentum ad hominem*, here again we must emphasize that these are not exceptions to the general rule that a protagonist cannot evade his burden of proof by setting himself up as a guarantor of the rightness of a standpoint or by overwhelming the audience with his expertise, without giving any arguments for his standpoint. In all these cases, special circumstances simply leave no alternative to trying to remove the other party's doubt by personally guaranteeing the rightness of the observation, the statement or the declaration concerned. The observation, the statement or the declaration can only be accepted so on the authority of the protagonist. A real resolution can in these cases thus not be achieved. Of course, that is not to say that it would always be unwise, let alone irrational, if the other party, for lack of any alternative, would go by the protagonist's compass.

CHAPTER 13

# Fallacies in Dealing With Unexpressed Premises

## MAKING EXPLICIT WHAT HAS BEEN LEFT UNEXPRESSED

The argumentation that a protagonist, at the argumentation stage, advances in defense of his standpoint is crucial to the resolution of the dispute. As explained in chapter 6, besides explicit premises, the argumentation will generally also contain unexpressed premises. They throw, as it were, an invisible bridge between the explicit premises and the standpoint that is being defended. In a critical evaluation of the discourse, both the explicit and the implicit components of the argumentation must be considered.

In itself, the fact that unexpressed premises are being used does not necessarily imply that something is being held back or covered up. Usually, such premises have not been left unexpressed in order to manipulate or deceive, but simply because they, literally, go without saying. Advancing them in full would, in other words, be superfluous and hence inefficient. It might indeed arouse irritation, or even suspicion, if in the argumentation all sorts of things were advanced explicitly that the listener was already well aware of or could work out for himself.

All the same, sometimes certain elements *are* with less noble intentions omitted from the argumentative discourse. In this way, the protagonist may try to conceal some weak or dubious link in his argumentation from the antagonist's attention. And something that has been presented as self-evident need, of course, not always be so. Therefore, in order to be able to carry out a critical evaluation of the discourse, the crucial unexpressed premises must first be made explicit.

We may assume that the protagonist is violating one of the rules for communication only if there are good grounds for such an assumption. From the observation that his argumentation is "incomplete," it cannot simply be deduced that the reasoning underlying that argumentation is invalid. If at all possible, the apparently invalid reasoning must be augmented by the addition of an extra premise to turn it into valid reasoning. A valid argument is produced by formulating the "logical minimum" in the form of an "if . . . then . . ." premise. This reconstruction is not yet really satisfactory because the logical minimum merely repeats that the standpoint follows from the explicit premise. If in any way possible, besides making the argument valid, the additional premise must also be more informative than the logical minimum. In fact, it must be the most informative of the commitments that, in the particular context at hand, can be attributed to the protagonist. Only if these conditions are met in the best possible way, the "pragmatic optimum" has been reached.

Sometimes, the reconstructed unexpressed premise can be put before the protagonist, so that it can be adjusted in mutual consultation. In many cases, especially if written texts are concerned, there is no opportunity for this. One problem that often arises is that the text may well contain insufficient clues for ensuring that the reconstruction of the unexpressed premise will not only satisfy the validity requirement but also the requirements concerning commitment and informativeness. Only if justice has indeed been done to each of these requirements, an appeal can be made to Rule 5 for a critical discussion: *A party may not falsely present something as a premise that has been left unexpressed by the other party or deny a premise that he himself has left implicit.*

## MAGNIFYING AN UNEXPRESSED PREMISE

Rule 5 essentially means that the protagonist can be held to nothing he is not really committed to and to everything he really is committed to. If the antagonist attacks the protagonist by producing a reconstruction of the unexpressed premise that goes further than to what the protagonist can actually be held, the antagonist violates Rule 5, thus committing a fallacy. The fallacy consists of going beyond the pragmatic optimum that is justified by the verbal and nonverbal context in which the argumentation occurs. It is a form of exaggeration that amounts to *magnifying what has been left unexpressed.*

By thus "maximizing" the unexpressed premise, the antagonist may try to facilitate his attack. Take the following example:

> William is at home, because his car's in the drive.

Starting from the logical minimum "If his car is in the drive, then William is at home," and taking into account the specific background knowledge that William is a disabled person, the pragmatic optimum can be determined as "William never goes out without his car." A broader reconstruction such as "People never go out without taking their cars," which in other contexts might be the obvious choice, would in this case mean blowing up the unexpressed premise illicitly. It should be little trouble to find an example of someone who sometimes leaves the house on foot or by bicycle.

Magnifying an unexpressed premise is, in fact, a special variant of the *straw man* fallacy. In the "ordinary" case of the straw man, a standpoint is falsely attributed to the protagonist whereas here it is a premise that is falsely attributed to him. Just like an attack on a fictitious or distorted standpoint in ordinary straw man fallacies, an attack based on a blown-up unexpressed premise may be undeservedly successful—a situation that is naturally more likely to arise with an inattentive audience or unwary reader than with the opponent himself.

It is difficult to give a hard and fast rule for exactly when a unexpressed premise has been magnified to unacceptable proportions. In the example of William, it is quite clear what is wrong, but usually the distinction between right and wrong is more subtle and less easy to make. As long as the context fails to clarify what has been left unexpressed, in order to avoid the risk of magnifying the unexpressed premise, the strategy of "minimal complementization" should be adopted. This can be illustrated with the help of an example:

> "In the old days, on the production line, things were much better. Why? Because you all sat closer to each other and your attention wasn't all taken up by what you were doing, so you could talk to each other while you were working."

If the argumentation in this example is simplified, for the sake of convenience, to "In the old days things were better because you could talk while working" and the rest is ignored, the logical minimum here is "If you can talk while working, things are better" and the pragmatic optimum something as "Talking while working is good." A more general unexpressed premise such as "Talking is always good" cannot be attributed to the old worker who is quoted because he cannot be held committed to this premise as the context provides no reason why "talking while working" could be generalized into "talking in general."

The author who quotes this argumentation, Simon Carmiggelt, furnishes himself a nice example of magnifying an unexpressed premise:

> An old production line worker said: "Things will be better for my children than for me, because I've given them an education." When you hear something like that it makes you go cold. That dear old belief that knowledge and happiness go together makes you suspect the man has never met an intellectual.

The old man's standpoint is that things will be better for his children than they were for him. His argumentation for this standpoint is that his children, unlike him, have had an education. What has been left unexpressed is the premise which links having had an education with things being better for them. The logical minimum of what remains implicit is: "If my children have had an education, things will be better for them than for me." Because it can hardly be assumed that the old man thinks that the beneficial effects of education apply only to his own children, there is nothing against an expansion beyond this logical minimum into "Things are better for those who are educated than for those who are not." The context provides no reason for going further than this, so that it must be regarded as the pragmatic optimum.

Carmiggelt, however, in his own ironic way, does go further than the premise just chosen as the pragmatic optimum in making out the unexpressed premise. In his reaction to the old worker's words, he assumes that those who are educated are happier than those who are not. This is possible because "things being better" can be given the wider, immaterial interpretation that people are being happier now instead of the materialistic interpretation that more money is being earned. Completely out of the blue endorsing the immaterial interpretation, Carmiggelt imputes to the old worker the adage that knowledge brings happiness (and sets the opposite against it). In doing this, he makes himself guilty of the fallacy of magnifying up what has been left unexpressed.

## DENYING AN UNEXPRESSED PREMISE

The protagonist too can violate Rule 5 and thus commit a fallacy. That happens if he evades the responsibility assumed in his argumentation by denying that he is committed to an unexpressed premise that is correctly reconstructed as such. The fallacy is then *denying an unexpressed premise*.

What this fallacy amounts to is that a protagonist whose standpoint has been questioned, despite the fact that this commitment has been correctly uncovered, refuses to accept his commitment to the unexpressed premise. He, as it were, seeks to play down his responsibility. His standard reaction could be something like "I never said *that*." Strictly speaking, of course, this is true: It is characteristic of premises that are left implicit that they *are* unsaid. But, viewed pragmatically, this reaction is just as unwarranted as denying something that *has* been explicitly stated.

Again, the example of the old man who thinks things were better on the shop floor in the old days may serve as an illustration. If the unexpressed premise has been made explicit correctly as "Talking while working is good," the old man cannot deny that this is what he believes. Otherwise, his behavior would be equally strange as if he denied to believe that in the old days people used to be able to talk to each other while working. True, he has not actually *said* that he thinks talking while working is good, but anyone taking what he says seriously is entitled to infer it from what he *has* actually said.

Especially if it was the protagonist's intention to conceal a debatable or controversial view from the antagonist's attention, making unexpressed premises explicit is rather like an unmasking. In such cases, the protagonist naturally perceives the unexpressed premise as embarrassing and uncovering it is undesirable to him. To escape from it, he may seek refuge in bluntly denying any responsibility for the view contained in the premise, thus trying to undo the damage caused by the unexpressed premise that "betrayed" him.

In argumentation where moral considerations or principles play a part, it can sometimes be revealing to make the unexpressed premises explicit. Suppose someone is defending the standpoint that imprisonment is wrong because it does nothing to actually help the offender. A critic might advance against this the argument that imprisonment is not primarily intended to help offenders. The protagonist who then reacts by saying that he never said it was, evidently feels he has been caught adhering to an untenable principle. If he tries to get out of it by denying that he can be held to that principle, he denies an unexpressed premise that can very well be attributed to him on the basis of what he actually said.

The inclination to deny an unexpressed premise will be even stronger if it concerns a judgment which the protagonist regards as socially unacceptable. That is to say: If he assumes that not just the antagonist but also many others, not only do not subscribe to the opinion concerned but actively detest it. A clear example of this can be found in the following passage from a radio broadcast by an extreme right-wing political party:

> "But surely not all foreigners are criminals?" "No, and we've never said they are! Some of them are perfectly prepared to adapt to our way of life."

The makers of the program were probably well aware that the view that all foreigners are criminals is one that is not shared, and even detested, by most of their listeners. In their anxiety to stress that the party does not think all foreigners are criminals either, they give themselves away, because the unexpressed premise in the argumentation that some foreigners are perfectly prepared to adapt to our way of life is, of course, that whoever adapts to our way of life is not a criminal. From there, for some people, it is only a short step to conclude that those who do *not* adapt to our way of life *are* criminals. Though the party pretends that it has nothing to do with it, by this reasoning, foreigners are clearly confronted with a simple choice: Either they adapt to our way of life, or they are regarded as criminals. The following text contains a similar example:

> I've got nothing against homosexuals. I just think the age of consent for homosexual relations with children ought not to be lowered, because otherwise there is a danger that they will turn into homosexuals.

In his first utterance, the speaker makes it appear as if he wishes to make no distinction between homosexuals and heterosexuals. But this "tolerant" attitude is belied by the use of the word "danger" in his argumentation for the standpoint that the age of consent for homosexual relations should not be lowered. The unexpressed premise in this argumentation is that homosexuality is something that should be avoided if possible. The speaker would be unlikely to support the standpoint that heterosexual relations with children are undesirable by claiming that there was a danger that they would become heterosexuals.

These two examples illustrate how making unexpressed premises explicit can reveal views that the protagonist would probably prefer not to proclaim in public. Yet, in his argumentation, they are all the same used as a covert means of persuasion.[1] Precisely because they are implicitly there it is wrong—and in the examples given pretty hypocritical—to deny responsibility for them. Making unexpressed premises explicit is in such cases not only beneficial to the clarity of the discourse but also to its mental hygiene.

## COMPLICATIONS REGARDING UNEXPRESSED PREMISES

To be able to establish that the antagonist or the protagonist is committing a violation of Rule 5, it must first be determined what the correct reconstruction is of an unexpressed premise in the protagonist's argumentation. Otherwise, it is impossible to ascertain that the antagonist is magnifying this unexpressed premise to unjustifiable proportions or that the protagonist is wrongly denying his commitment to this premise. Although it is not always possible to determine exactly what a correct reconstruction entails, in most cases the worst blunders can be avoided by following the method of starting from the logical minimum and then, taking into account the verbal and nonverbal context, defining the pragmatic optimum.

Generally, determining what the definition of the pragmatic optimum should be amounts to broadening the scope of the proposition that represents the logical minimum, but it may also occasionally mean that the scope of this proposition will be narrowed down. This can be illustrated by the example "Agnes is at home, because her car's in the drive." If Agnes said yesterday that today she was going for a drive and would otherwise stay at home, it is clear that "Agnes never goes out without taking the car" would go too far. To ignore this context, is to commit a violation of Rule 5. In this particular case, a more limited formulation of the unexpressed premise such as "Today Agnes would only go out for a drive" seems more like it.

Unfortunately, the context does not always provide sufficient clues for saying with certainty whether the scope needs to be broadened or narrowed down. A further complication in determining the correct reconstruction of an unexpressed premise is that, as a rule, the argumentative discourse will also contain elements which, although implicit, are not unexpressed *premises*, but (for example) *pre-*

[1]See for the role of prejudice in argumentative discourse aimed at persuasion Billig (1988), van Dijk (1983, 1988), and Sykes (1985).

*suppositions*.[2] In practice, it can be extremely difficult to distinguish between the various sorts of implicit elements.

The difference between unexpressed premises and presuppositions can be illustrated through the help of the example "Things will be better for my children than for me, because I've given them an education." The pragmatic optimum "Things will be better for those with an education than for those without," which may be regarded as the premise that has been left unexpressed, is only relevant if the speaker himself has not had an education. There is thus a further implicit element in the discourse, namely "I never had an education." This element, however, is a presupposition, and does not serve as an unexpressed premise in the argumentation.

The confusion of presuppositions and unexpressed premises is here made more likely by the fact that both elements are necessary for a meaningful interpretation of the discourse. The functions they fulfill, however, are different. "Things will be better for those with an education than for those without" serves to bridge the ratiocinative gap between the explicit premise "I gave my children an education" and the standpoint "Things will be better for my children than for me." "I never had an education" serves to explain the underlying rationale of the comparison between the speaker and his children: If the speaker had had an education himself, in that respect there would be no difference between him and his children, so that it would be meaningless to compare the two.

Not only premises may be left unexpressed in argumentative discourse, but standpoints too can remain implicit. The problems of making them explicit are basically the same as those encountered in making unexpressed premises explicit: The antagonist may go too far in reconstructing an unexpressed standpoint, the protagonist may refuse to acknowledge a correct reconstruction. The "Those aren't my words" effect can be illustrated by looking at the following passages from a "brief grammar of politics" by the journalist John Jansen van Galen:

> The bluntest conclusions to be drawn from your exposition can best be left to your interrogator. Two instances from real life, both from the Prime Minister. What does he think of the national union leader? "I believe he is trying with perfect sincerity to do what he can in his members' interests." I say, concludes the interviewer, praise indeed. The Prime Minister: "Yes, well, praise . . . that's what *you* may call it."
>
> And what does the Prime Minister think of the opposition's remark about the postponement of the decision to deploy the missiles, which under the influence of the peace movement will be stretched as long as it can be?
>
> "I believe that remark fails to reflect the situation perfectly. So far there has been no question of any postponement." So, the interviewer concludes, the opposition do not know what they are talking about. The Prime Minister: "That is *your* way of putting it."

[2]Cf. for presuppositions Rescher (1961), Kempson (1975), and Stalnaker (1977), and for the difference between unexpressed premises and presuppositions Ennis (1982) and Burke (1985).

> Improvise a tirade about the way the socialists never fulfill their promises, always break agreements and are constantly contradicting themselves. Your wife, who is playing the interviewer, says: "You think the socialists are undependable." To this you reply, straight-faced but with a twinkle in your eye that betrays your pleasure at this interpretation: "That is not what I said."

In the example, the three cases are treated as if they were equal: In all three, the speaker evades his responsibility by making the interviewer responsible for the standpoint concerned. Yet, in fact, there are important differences. In the first case, the Prime Minister can justifiably dissociate himself from the interviewer's conclusion because the observation that the union leader sincerely does what he can in his members' interests does not imply that the Prime Minister has to approve of the objectives that this leader is aiming for or the way in which he goes about it.

Even more obvious is the difference between the Prime Minister's words and the conclusion arrived at by the second interviewer. A single remark by the opposition which according to the Prime Minister fails accurately to reflect the situation does not mean that they do not know what they are talking about. There may also be other reasons for an inaccurate presentation besides a complete lack of knowledge or understanding. In other words, here again, the Prime Minister is perfectly entitled to dissociate himself from the conclusion hung on his words by the interviewer.

In the third case, the situation is different. What else does undependability mean than not keeping promises, breaking agreements and contradicting oneself? If all this is regarded as applying to the socialists, one cannot dissociate oneself from the conclusion that the socialists are undependable. True, this conclusion has not been stated in so many words, but it is impossible to interpret the speaker's words in a way that does not lead to this conclusion. To pretend otherwise is to be guilty of denying a correctly reconstructed standpoint.

CHAPTER 14

# Fallacies in Utilizing Starting Points

## DEALING WITH STARTING POINTS

To be able to resolve a dispute, the protagonist and antagonist must be able to call on at least a minimum number of common starting points. Otherwise, there would be no point in the discussion at all, because it would be clear from the start that the protagonist had no chance of ever convincing the antagonist. For in that case, there is no realistic basis for achieving this interactional effect.

The joint point of departure for the argumentative discourse is made up by the starting points that the protagonist and the antagonist have in common at the opening stage of the discussion. These starting points may include facts ("Yerevan is the capital of Armenia"), suppositions ("Pjotr's doubtless taken early retirement by now") and truths ("Influenza is caused by a virus") as well as values ("Incest is sinful"), norms ("Lawyers must not be allowed to advertise"), and value hierachies ("Creativity is more important than knowledge").

To be able to make proper use of the common starting points in the defense of his standpoint, the protagonist must naturally be able to see clearly which propositions are among them. In the most extreme case, the protagonist and antagonist will have come to an explicit agreement about their common starting points, such an agreement being reached at the opening stage of the discussion and remaining valid throughout the argumentation stage.

Of course, prior agreements about the point of departure are the exception rather than the rule. Almost always, however, the discussants will have certain ideas of their own of exactly what the common starting points are. The better they are acquainted with one another, the better they will know what starting points they really have in common. Eventually, it then makes little practical difference whether there is an explicit agreement or not.

Even so, it is only through explicit agreement that the discussants can be a hundred per cent certain about what may be regarded as belonging to the common starting points. Even if they know each other quite well, they may be sorely mistaken about one another's views. This naturally applies the more strongly the less well they know each other, the extreme case being a written text meant to be read by an indefinable and probably heterogeneous group of potential antagonists who are unknown to the protagonist.

A proposition that has the status of an accepted starting point may not be called into question during the discussion. This does not mean, of course, that the proposition concerned can never be called into question again, but if this does happen, it at once loses its status as a common starting point.[1] To exclude the possibility of questioning the proposition altogether would, of course, be a direct violation of the principle that *everything* can be called into question (Rule 1). Nevertheless, a party who feels that such a proposition needs to be questioned, can best leave it until later. A meaningful discussion aimed at resolving the dispute becomes impossible if everything is called into question at the same time.

Having common starting points does not mean that the protagonist and the antagonist both really have to believe that the propositions that together constitute the joint point of departure are actually all equally acceptable. No sincerity requirement is attached to giving a proposition the status of a starting point. Whether they really believe in the proposition or not, the point of accepting it as a starting point is that the protagonist and the antagonist may treat it as if they really believed in it. Under the circumstances, there is no need to replace this externalized responsibility condition by a purely psychological sincerity requirement.

Imposing a sincerity requirement would also be undesirable: That would make it impossible to conduct a discussion in which certain starting points are adopted provisionally, as commonly happens when scientific hypotheses are being tested, or as assumed premises in conditional proof or as tentative suggestions. It would then be impossible to use the method of *reductio ad absurdum*, so highly valued in logic and mathematics, where the proposition being discussed is temporarily assumed to be true so that it can be used in order to discover whether it gives rise to a contradiction that would indicate that it was actually false.

Demanding genuine sincerity, rules out the possibility of certain types of exploratory discussion for the very purpose of determining whether there is a basis for meaningful discussion. It is better not to have such a requirement and to leave the discussants entirely free to choose what propositions they feel ought to serve as their common starting points. Should they so desire, they can even include patent falsities among them. The only restriction is that the whole of the starting

[1]Then, the starting point becomes the standpoint at issue in a new discussion.

points must be consistent: It may not contain any apparent logical contradictions or pragmatic inconsistencies.[2]

How can the protagonist wishing to defend his standpoint make use of common starting points? First and foremost, by pointing out, at the argumentation stage, that the antagonist has questioned a proposition in his argumentation that is actually part of their joint point of departure. If the protagonist rightly does so and is not making things up, he then shows that the antagonist casts doubt on a proposition that ought not have been called into question because of its status as a common starting point. If the antagonist, nevertheless, persists in his doubt, he violates, just as the protagonist who departs from agreement that is nonexistent, Rule 6 for a critical discussion: *A party may not falsely present a premise as an accepted starting point nor deny a premise representing an accepted starting point.*

## FALSELY PRESENTING A PREMISE AS A COMMON STARTING POINT

If the protagonist acts as if a proposition expressed in his argumentation were one of the common starting points when in fact it is not, he is violating Rule 6. Because, in practice, it is very rare for there to be any explicit statement of what propositions have the status of common starting point, it will not always be immediately clear whether the protagonist is breaking this rule or not. Generally, in determing what the point of departure is, the protagonist will have to rely on any knowledge he happens to have of the views the antagonist has expressed in the past, and of what can be inferred from those views.

In falsely promoting a proposition to the status of a common starting point, the protagonist tries to evade the burden of proof: He prevents the proposition from being questioned and thus requiring a defense. The techniques that he may employ in this violation of Rule 6 are basically the same as those used in evading the burden of proof for a standpoint. One way to evade the burden of proof is to pretend that the proposition has no need of defense, so that it is understandable that it is not among the original starting points that were explicitly agreed at the opening stage. In an article in *The Sunday Times* (December 9, 1990), Neil Lyndon accused "modern feminism" of wrongly suggesting, in pseudo-Marxist propositions, such an inviolable and common starting point, "despite its shaky basis in reason and fact":

> It became axiomatic that women, as a class, were oppressed by men, as a class, and that a state of war existed between them.

---

[2]Some epistemologists insist that it is never really possible to establish whether this is the case, because inevitably we hold beliefs that are, due to various complicated theoretical presuppositions and implications, implicitly inconsistent in subtle ways we have not yet discovered.

The impression that a proposition need not be defended can be given by introducing it in a wording that suggests that this proposition belongs to the starting points shared by all right-thinking people, including, of course, the antagonist: "It goes without saying that . . . ," "Of course, there is no need for me to tell you that . . . ," "It will be clear to everyone that . . . ," "Obviously, . . . ," "Clearly, . . . ," "It is apparent that . . . ," and so forth. If something really does go without saying, then why say it? More often than not, this kind of wording is employed to suggest a degree of agreement that does not really exist. Then it signalizes an attempt on the part of the protagonist to smuggle things into the common starting points on a false passport.

Another way of preventing a proposition from being attacked is to put a debatable point in an obscure position in the formulation, so that it does not immediately strike the eye. This can be done by not actually stating it but "packaging" it in the form of a presupposition: something that the protagonist tacitly assumes. Karel van het Reve provides a nice example of this way of wrapping up the real message:

> Instead of saying bluntly "Pete's got scabies," for example, we say "It's amazing he does nothing about that scabies!" The real message is that Pete has scabies, but it is presented as if it is not *that* that is the real message, but our amazement.

Another example of packaging a proposition in a presupposition is to say "I find it very regrettable that I have to fire you" when the real message is "You're fired."

A presupposition can be exploited in the same way in a question. In this case it is precisely the proposition that is presupposed in the question that is at issue. There are in fact two questions, one is clearly presented as such, the other is not. In this way, the impression is given that the answer to the question not asked is one of the protagonist and antagonist's common starting points. This violation of Rule 6 constitutes the fallacy that is known as *many questions*.[3]

The fallacy of many questions is generally used when the protagonist does not expect the antagonist to be willing to agree to a particular proposition. This happens, for instance, frequently in police interrogation and also in political interviews. By a devious route the protagonist tries to make the antagonist agree with him. Because the many questions fallacy is designed to trick the interlocutor, it is also known as the *trick question*: "Where did you hide the murder weapon?"

Presuppositions can also be hidden in adjectives:

1. The *scandalous* policy of this conservative government towards the Tamils began 3 years ago.

---

[3]Cf. Belnap (1969), Fair (1973), Walton (1988b, 1989a, 1989b), Woods and Walton (1989).

2. The *objectionable* notion that intelligence is genetically determined is one of the central theses of sociobiology.
3. Exports of those *incredibly ugly* carnations have again increased.

If the point at issue in the discussion is whether the government's policy towards the Tamils is a disgrace, the presupposition in (1) is a violation of Rule 6, because this proposition is not among the common starting points.

Substantives, too, can be used to formulate debatable propositions in, as for presuppositions, veiled language:

1. The *delusion* that money brings happiness has a long history.
2. The Sellafield *trick* is used to fudge the public's memory.

A sophisticated way of making propositions appear to be common starting points is to let them play an implicit part as unexpressed premises in the argumentation. Unless the protagonist defends such unexpressed premises explicitly, it may be assumed that he counts them among the common starting points. If he hides something in an unexpressed premise which he knows very well not to be part of the joint point of departure, he is abusing Rule 6. Only if this point of departure has been clearly stated at the outset an outsider who analyses the argumentation can really know whether or not the unexpressed premise concerned is part of the common starting points.

A special case of wrongly assuming that a proposition is one of the common starting points is when the protagonist defends his standpoint by way of a premise that amounts to the same thing as the standpoint. Because he then knows that the propostion concerned is the very point at issue in the dispute, he also knows that it cannot be one of the common starting points. The protagonist who nevertheless adduces such a premise is trying, like Baron Münchhausen, to pull himself out of the morass by his own hair. The protagonist who thus turns round in circles is guilty of the fallacy of *circular reasoning*. This fallacy is known also as *petitio principii* or *begging the question*. A protagonist commits this fallacy if he acts as if his standpoint has been adequately defended when, in fact, the starting point on which he relies in his defense is identical to the disputed proposition.[4]

The simplest form of circular reasoning is "A, therefore A." To be persuasive, of course, the wordings of the two A's will generally have to be slightly different:

> I think Leo is a real hypochondriac, because he's a melancholy type of person who is easily depressed.

---

[4]Cf. Robinson (1971b), Sanford (1972), MacKenzie (1979), Walton (1985a), Walton and Batten (1984), Woods and Walton (1982b, 1989).

If this example were to explain what is meant by the word "hypochondriac," then it could be reconstructed as a perfectly acceptable language usage declarative. Assuming that it is already clear that a hypochondriac is a melancholy type of person who is easily depressed, and that the point at issue is whether Leo is a hypochondriac, then things are laid on a bit thick. In fact, the speaker could then easily be accused of circular reasoning.

Circular reasoning can occur in such cases where a concomitance relation of identity is conveyed, it can also occur in cases where the relation between the argumentation and the standpoint is more like causal interdependence:

> How do I know he is a man of taste? Because he smokes Willem II cigars. All men of taste smoke Willem II.

Here is another example:

> God exists, because it says so in the Bible and the Bible is the word of God.

The premise that the Bible is the word of God presupposes that God exists, because without God there could be no "word of God." The premise thus depends on the truth of the proposition "God exists," which is precisely the point at issue.

Logically speaking, the argument underlying circular reasoning is valid: In "A, therefore A," it is impossible for the conclusion to be false if the premise is true. So, even if the name suggests that circular reasoning is a logical error, it is not.

## DENYING A PREMISE REPRESENTING AN ACCEPTED STARTING POINT

The antagonist obstructs Rule 6 if he questions a proposition that is to be regarded as part of the joint point of departure. This may be a proposition that has already been agreed to be one of the common starting points. It can also be a proposition that the protagonist, provided that the antagonist has not indicated that this would be erroneous, is entitled to attribute to the antagonist on the grounds of available and verifiable background knowledge. Although it is for an outsider not always easy to tell exactly what the protagonist and the antagonist may expect the other party to accept, they themselves are often very well aware of it. That is a good thing too, for if speakers and listeners were unable to tacitly assume an extensive range of mutually presupposed knowledge and opinions, all communication and interaction would be impossible.

Of course, it is always possible for the protagonist to make a mistake or feign ignorance, and wrongly act on the assumption that a particular proposition is one of the antagonist's starting points. In that case, the antagonist is entitled to point this out to the protagonist: "As far as I know, I have never said that I thought that proportional representation is a fairer system." If the antagonist has indeed earlier admitted a proposition as an acceptable starting point, then the protagonist is entitled to exploit this fact and the antagonist may not suddenly start questioning the rightness of that proposition. Not, at any rate, in that particular discussion that is then going on. Otherwise, it could in principle become impossible ever to resolve the dispute because the antagonist could evermore come up with new starting points and the protagonist would never be able to provide an adequate defense for his standpoint.

The common starting points of protagonist and antagonist can be used for bringing about a conclusive defense of a standpoint, but a protagonist who succeeds in defending his standpoint conclusively cannot simply claim that the standpoint has now been proven true. All that has been proven is that the standpoint is tenable *given the common starting points*. It is only in virtue of the propositions that the antagonist is willing to concede that a successful and conclusive defense of the standpoint is achieved. Because of this, the defense is called *ex concessu*.[5]

An antagonist who falsely denies that a proposition is one of the common starting points denies the protagonist the opportunity of defending his standpoint *ex concessu*. If he can get away with this, having a discussion is pointless from the outset. Often, an antagonist will be moved to obstruct Rule 6 in this way by opportunistic motives. Gradually realizing that he is going to lose the discussion if he continues to uphold the original starting points, he may suddenly decide to deny one of them, thinking that rejecting this starting point is his last resort.

This maneuver is completely inept if the starting point is a proposition that has only been hypothesized in order to see how far one can get in basing one's defense on it. Both the protagonist and the antagonist know then that there is no question of any sincerity condition having been met and that this is of no further consequence. Indeed, they can even deliberately take a proposition that is patently false, in which case there is clearly no point in suddenly pointing out halfway through the discussion that one does not regard oneself as committed to it. An antagonist who nevertheless does that, sabotages any possibly meaningful discussion starting from a hypothesis or an unproven and as such exploration-worthy theory.

## COMPLICATIONS REGARDING STARTING POINTS

In the practice of argumentative discourse starting points do not constitute a static entity, but are basically subject to constant change. What may be an acceptable starting point today need not necessarily be one tomorrow and even a starting point that is accepted at the beginning of a discussion need no longer be acceptable later on so that it may be necessary to begin a new discussion with slightly

[5]Cf. Barth and Krabbe (1982).

other starting points. Even if it is perfectly clear at the opening stage which propositions are part of the joint point of departure, it is not always possible to answer absolutely and with certainty the question of whether Rule 6 is really being violated. This is particularly problematical if the wording of the proposition expressed in the protagonist's standpoint differs somewhat (or even by a wide margin) from that of the original starting point. Especially in the case of circular reasoning it is then difficult to see whether there actually is a circle. Is the standpoint really identical to the premise or are there relevant differences?

Another problem in identifying circular reasoning is that, as a rule, the circle is not directly and exclusively formed by the standpoint and the premise, but comes into being via one or more intermediate steps. The more intermediate steps, the larger the distance between the standpoint and the premise that ultimately amounts to the same thing. What we then have is subordinative argumentation in which the chain takes a detour to arrive back at the standpoint:

> Competition is good for the economy, because competition means that everyone wants to be the best, the fastest and the cheapest, because after all everyone wants to be competitive so as to be able to compete with others, because that is good for the economy.

The structure of this—still relatively simple—argumentation can be shown as follows:

1
Competition is good for the economy.

↑

1.1
Competition means everyone wants to be
the best, fastest, and cheapest.

↑

1.1.1
Everyone wants to be competitive.

↑

1.1.1.1
Everyone wants to be able to compete with others.

↑

1.1.1.1.1
Competition is good for the economy.

Subsubsubargument (1.1.1.1.1) is identical to the standpoint (1). The defense of the standpoint thus ultimately boils down to saying that the standpoint is true because the standpoint is true:

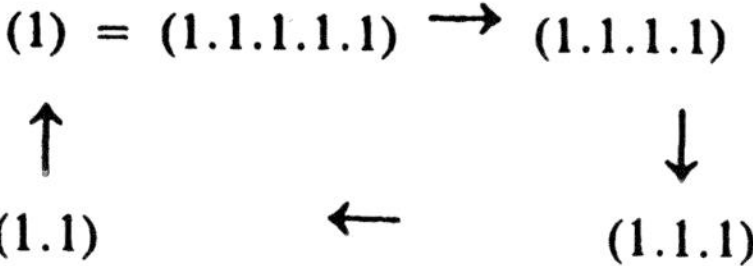

An extra complication in identifying circular reasoning is that it is sometimes cast in the mold of a statement so that it is not immediately obvious that a standpoint is being defended. The assertive concerned is of a tautological nature.

The following (grossly simplified) summary of Darwin's theory of evolution is an example of such a tautological statement:

"Evolution = survival of the fittest."

The tautological nature of this utterance comes to light when we try to establish what species of animals are "the fittest." We then discover that the way of doing this is to see what species have survived. In other words, what is actually asserted is that the survivors survive. Nobody would wish to deny that.

In this representation, the theory of evolution appears to be based on circular reasoning in which the standpoint is to be defended by a premise in which the truth of the standpoint is presupposed. The falsifiability of such a theory is, of course, nil: It is self-fulfilling. This may at first seem to be a strong point, but it is, in fact, a weakness because it means that a meaningful discussion on the subject is ruled out because any discussion of the theory is doomed to be pointless. A resolution of any dispute about a standpoint is by definition precluded if the standpoint is presented tautologically because in this way it is made immune to criticism.

CHAPTER 15

# Fallacies in Utilizing Argumentation Schemes

## DEALING WITH ARGUMENTATION SCHEMES

The method of evaluating the defense of standpoints by checking the relations between premises and starting points can be termed *identification procedure*: It is verified whether the propositions concerned can be identified as part of the joint point of departure. Yet it cannot be evaluated solely by means of the identification procedure whether the defense of the standpoint is indeed adequate for resolving the dispute. At a given moment, a proposition can just as well be questioned that is clearly not one of the common starting points and then there must also be a way of testing its acceptability.[1] Otherwise, the evaluative system would only allow for "closed" discussions, in which no new information is added to the agreed starting points and received wisdom that is available at the opening of the discussion. Moreover, even if a proposition can indeed be identified as a common starting point, the question remains whether it adequately supports the standpoint at issue.

In order to adequately support the standpoint, in every single argumentation that is put forward in defense of a standpoint the right kind of argumentation scheme must be used and this scheme must be used properly. Therefore, in addition to the identification procedure, there must also be a *testing procedure* relating to the argumentation scheme that is being used. The testing procedure is aimed at determining whether the argumentation put forward in defense of a standpoint

[1]With some propositions their acceptability is, in principle, still easy enough to check by looking something up in an encyclopedia ("The specific gravity of water is 1") or in a dictionary ("A leveret is a young hare"). In other cases, observations will be necessary ("The butcher's wife has lilac hair") or some research ("Not all AIDS patients have led a promiscuous life").

does indeed have an appropriate argumentation scheme that is correctly applied. What schemes are appropriate and what criteria they must meet is sometimes explicitly agreed at the opening stage of the discussion—just as the starting points which are the object of the identification procedure—but, in practice, these things will more often be tacitly assumed or presupposed.[2]

In case there are enough mutually acceptable starting points and argumentation schemes and it is perfectly clear what they are, it is, in principle, possible to answer the question whether an argumentation constitutes a conclusive defense for a standpoint. If both the identification procedure and the testing procedure produce a positive result, the standpoint has indeed been conclusively defended; if they both produce a negative result, it has been conclusively attacked.[3] Because of the crucial role of the testing procedure, in addition to the identification procedure, in determining whether or not a dispute has been resolved, Rule 7 for a critical discussion is stated as follows: *A party may not regard a standpoint as conclusively defended if the defense does not take place by means of an appropriate argumentation scheme that is correctly applied.*

In some cases, it has to do with the type and the scope of the proposition expressed in the standpoint which argumentation scheme is appropriate and how it is to be used. Three main types of proposition should be distinguished: *descriptive, evaluative*, and *inciting* propositions. Descriptive propositions describe facts or events ("The dollar rate is still falling"), evaluative propositions express an assessment of facts or events ("Saul Bellow's *The Dean's December* is an overrated book"), and inciting propositions call on to prevent a particular event or course of action ("The policy of apartheid must be combated with all possible means").[4] As the examples show, it is possible for all three types of proposition to be expressed in an assertive speech act. They can also be expressed by other types of speech act.

The scope of propositions can vary from a single individual member of a group or larger whole to all its members. There is also a wide range of possibilities in between. Propositions with the smallest possible scope are called *singular* ("Jack is talented"), propositions with the largest possible scope *universal* ("All chess-players are sensitive"), propositions whose scope lies between these extremes *particular* ("Some books are too expensive").

---

[2]Like the identification procedure, the testing procedure is, in principle, an intersubjective procedure. The discussants may allow a certain type of argumentation that others regard as questionable. Then it is doubtful if outsiders will take their conclusion to be a real resolution. In principle, in a critical discussion only those argumentation schemes are to be used whose problem validity for resolving a dispute is objectively secured, but in practice it is sometimes difficult to reach intersubjective agreement on whether this is the case.

[3]If only the identification procedure or only the testing procedure produces a positive result, no conclusive outcome has yet been achieved. Further deliberations are then required, either concerning the outcome of the testing procedure or concerning the acceptability of the unaccounted for premises.

[4]There is an old argument among philosophers as to whether all evaluative propositions are implicitly prescriptive (or inciting), as urging upon people that the valued item be chosen (or not, if disvalued). Compare, for example, Hare (1963, 1981).

Although there are no hard and fast rules for the appropriateness of argumentation schemes to propositions of a certain type and scope, some combinations seem to fit better than others.[5] Some argumentation schemes can be used with any kind of proposition, whatever its type and scope. Argumentation based on analogy, for example, can be used in all types of descriptive proposition for predicting an event ("The Flevo dam will be completed on time, because the Marken dam was too") as well as in all types of evaluative proposition for giving a judgment ("You can only have one person wearing the trousers at home; there's only one captain on a ship, too").

Combinations of speech acts in which facts or events are brought into a causal relation with one another form a special case of interrelated descriptive propositions: One fact or event is presented as the cause of the other ("Because the dollar rate is still falling, exports to the United States will fall"). In argumentation based on a causal relation it is in such a case possible to infer a particular effect as a prediction from a given cause, as in the dollar example. Given a particular state of affairs it is also possible to present the cause as an explanation for the state of affairs described in the effect proposition ("The standard of teaching is poor due to the poor training given to teachers in the 1970s"). It may also simply be clear that two facts must be causally linked because no other kind of linkage (analogy, concomitance) would make sense, whereas it is not yet so clear how exactly the causal relation should be interpreted, that is which of the propositions serves as the standpoint and which as the defending argument. (In "He smokes a lot, he coughs a lot," for instance, the standpoint that he smokes a lot could be defended with the argument that he coughs a lot, but it could also be that the standpoint is defended that it must be the case that he coughs a lot because it is an established fact that he smokes a lot.)

## RELYING ON AN INAPPROPRIATE ARGUMENTATION SCHEME

Some argumentation schemes are not universally acknowledged to be sound. This can be illustrated with the help of some examples of certain special cases from each of the main categories of argumentation schemes: the *argument from authority* (symptomatic argumentation), *argument from analogy* (similarity argumentation), and *argument from consequence* (instrumental argumentation). Arguments from authority and from analogy represent argumentation schemes which are indepen-

[5]Descriptive propositions, for example, often appear to call for argumentation of the causal type and evaluative and inciting propositions often invite the use of argumentation based on a relation of concomitance and analogy. And singular propositions can sometimes very well be defended by argumentation based on a relation of concomitance, whereas particular and universal propositions can often not be defended by this type of argumentation but require causal argumentation or argumentation from analogy instead.

dent of the type and scope of the proposition that is discussed: They can in principle be used for any kind of proposition. Arguments from consequence are dependent on the type and scope of the proposition: They can in principle only be used for a particular kind of proposition.

In arguments from authority, someone's expertise or special position is treated as a sign that the proposition ascribed to him is acceptable: The proposition is regarded as acceptable because an authoritative source says it is. To be able to use this argumentation scheme in the defense of a standpoint, it is necessary that the antagonist recognizes it as sound. If the protagonist chooses it even though he knows that this is not so, he is guilty of a violation of Rule 7 known as *argumentum ad verecundiam*.[6]

The authority appealed to need not always be a person. It may also be a book like the Bible or *Das Kapital*. However, because such a written source derives its status from its spiritual progenitor (God, Marx), here, too, authority is ultimately ascribed to a person. Tradition is a different body of authority: Something is good because it has always been that way.

Another body of authority is the number of people who believe something: Something is so, or good, because everybody thinks it is so, or good. If it is inappropriate to adduce the premise that the opinion of the mass of the people is decisive as an extra (so far unexpressed) premise to the argumentation, then the wrong argumentation scheme has been chosen. This particular violation of Rule 7 constitutes a variant of the *argumentum ad verecundiam* which is known as *argumentum ad populum*. Because of its appeal to the mass of the people, this form of the *argumentum ad populum* is also described as the *populistic fallacy*.[7]

An argument from analogy can, in principle, be used for any kind of proposition. The chairman of the Dutch football league division provides a nice example when discussing the question of whether the famous soccer player Johan Cruijff should be allowed to work as a trainer without having a trainer's certificate:

> Look, I have no opinion about Cruijff as a trainer (I expect he can do the job), but I recognize the system. You've got to have a driving license to drive a car, even if Bert Bloggs who's never taken his test is a much better driver than you are. The Cruijff question would not exist outside the game. Suppose the prime minister were to be caught without a driving license.

Whether this argumentation scheme is allowed to be used in a discussion, depends on whether the protagonist and the antagonist can agree on the conditions for its use. If they cannot and the protagonist nevertheless goes ahead using it, or if these conditions have not been fulfilled, he is guilty of one of the variants of the fallacy of *wrongful comparison* or *false analogy*.[8]

---

[6]Cf. MacKenzie (1981), Walton (1987b, 1989a, 1989c), Woods and Walton (1982a, 1989).

[7]Cf. Kielkopf (1980), Minot (1981), Woods and Walton (1989).

[8]Cf. Rescher (1964), Woods and Hudak (1991).

Opinions vary as to whether appealing to an authority and applying an analogy are in themselves admissible argumentation schemes. But if they are allowed, they may be applied to descriptive, evaluative, and inciting propositions, whether they are singular, particular, or universal. The type and scope of the proposition to be tested do not play a role.

In the case of arguments from consequence, where the difference between descriptive and inciting propositions is important, things are somewhat different. Here, the proposition to be tested is treated as the cause of a particular effect. This scheme may only be used if the proposition in which the cause is expressed and the proposition in which the effect is expressed are both suitable.

In the case of a suggested course of action, for instance, it is justifiable to examine the possible consequences. Positive consequences may lead to a decision to adopt the course of action; negative consequences may lead to a decision not to adopt it (in either case there may be other reasons for not accepting the recommendation). And when testing a hypothesis (descriptive proposition) it is justifiable to examine whether false assertions follow from it. Indeed, in science and scholarship this is a generally accepted method.

It is *not* permissible to test an assertion (descriptive proposition) by pointing out the undesirable effects of the assertion (evaluative proposition), because facts and values are then confused. In this case, examining the implications is an inappropriate argumentation scheme known as *argumentum ad consequentiam*:[9]

> Rationality and an analytical faculty cannot be called male attributes. If we do regard them as such, we give men an unwarranted advantage in job applications and promotion.

Whether the assertion that rationality and an analytical faculty are male attributes is true or false (descriptive proposition) cannot be decided by pointing out that giving men an advantage in job applications and promotion is undesirable (evaluative proposition).

## USING AN APPROPRIATE ARGUMENTATION SCHEME INCORRECTLY

If an argumentation scheme is rejected per se, any use of it will, by definition, be regarded as wrong. This does not mean, of course, that to approve of it in principle is to approve of every use of it indiscriminately. The argumentation scheme has been used correctly only if certain correctness conditions have been fulfilled. These conditions correspond to the critical questions that are associated with the argumentation scheme concerned.

---

[9]Cf. Rescher (1964).

In arguments from authority, for example, the fact that something is said by a particular person is taken as a sign of the acceptability of the proposition, but one of the critical questions that needs to be answered is whether his authority really guarantees its acceptability. For this to be so, at least, he must genuinely be an authority in the relevant field.[10] If he is not—his expertise lies in another field—then neither is he possibly a guarantee. The incorrect use of an argument from authority by falsely presenting someone as an authority, constitutes an *argumentum ad verecundiam.*

With arguments from analogy, one of the critical questions is whether the comparison is really justified or whether there are crucial differences. If the comparison is defective, the argument from analogy is used incorrectly and constitutes a fallacy of *false analogy.* The Cruijff example presented earlier could be considered as such a fallacy, but then it must be shown that training a football team without the required certificate is indeed not comparable with driving a car without a license. Neil Lyndon provides another example of clever but dubious reasoning by analogy when he criticizes the "new feminist" way of talking about men:

> *Bad mouthing*
> Julie Burchill writing in *Time Out*: "A good part—and definitely the most fun part—of being a feminist is about frightening men. American and Australian feminists have always known this, and absorbed it cheerfully into their act; one thinks of Shere Hite julienning men on phone-in shows, or Dale Spender telling us that a good feminist is rude to a man at least three times a day *on principle.* Of course, there's a lot more to feminism . . . but scaring the shit out of the scumbags is an amusing and necessary part because, sadly, a good many men still respect nothing but strength." [. . .]
>
> And yet . . . if you alter the specific vocabulary of those specimen lines you get the full strength of their intolerance. If you switch the terms you see that those declarations emerge from a general prejudice which—like all racist or nationalist prejudices—depends upon the presumption that everybody who shares a common origin shares a common classification of type and moral character. If, to take Julie Burchill's lines, you substitute the word "Nazi" for the word "feminist" and the word "Jew" for the word "man," you get (without much dickering) language that might have brought a stammer to the lips of Julius Streicher.
>
> "A good part—and definitely the most fun part—of being a Nazi is about frightening Jews. German and Austrian Nazis have always known this, and absorbed it cheerfully into their act; one thinks of Ernst Rohm julienning Jews in the ghettos, or Goebbels telling us that a good Nazi is rude to a Jew at least three times a day *on principle.* Of course, there's a lot more to Nazism . . . but scaring the shit out of the scumbags is an amusing and necessary part because, sadly, a good many Jews still respect nothing but strength."
>
> I am not saying that feminism is Nazism. I am saying that the language of vulgar intolerance is readily transportable.
> (*The Sunday Times*, December 9, 1990)

[10]As Wenzel (1989) rightly observed, the core problem is, of course, "how to decide when acquiescence to authority is reasonable and when it is not" (p. 304).

If disputes are to be resolved, false analogies must be avoided, but these examples illustrate that it is not always so clear when an analogy *is* false. For distinguishing false analogy from correct analogy, unequivocal criteria are badly needed.

One of the critical questions with arguments from consequence is whether what is presented as a consequence would actually occur. If a course of action is rejected on the grounds of the extremely negative result that it would have, when in fact that effect would not occur at all, then the scheme is being used incorrectly. A common abuse of this argumentation scheme, in which the speculation on unsubstantiated negative consequences is carried to an extreme, is known as *slippery slope*.[11] This fallacy entails erroneously suggesting that by taking the proposed course of action one will be going from bad to worse. A fallacy of this kind occurs—with others—in comments on a newspaper report on sex tourism in Asia:

> The implications of the suggestion that measures against sex tourism would be bad for the prostitutes are clear. Sex tours should not be discouraged but promoted, since they create jobs in the Third World. Might we not spend some of our overseas development aid on this good cause? Incidentally, there is no reason to restrict this argument to the Third World. Back here in Europe and in Holland we have an unemployment problem. Stimulating prostitution creates jobs. To go one twist further: crime prevention is bad for jobs in the police force; campaigns against child abuse cause unemployment among social workers.

The slippery slope is evident: Take a tolerant attitude to sex tourism in the Third World and you end up advocating death and destruction here at home.[12] Here is another example of how a slippery slope can go greatly over the top:

> If it was legitimate to say that all men are oppressors, then why should it be disreputable to say that they are all rapists? Or all child molesters? Idi Amin?

Two more argumentation schemes that are frequently used incorrectly are *cause-effect* arguments and *generalizations*. In the first, causally related descriptive propositions play a role, in the second, universal descriptive propositions.

The purpose of using causally related descriptive propositions is to establish that one event is the consequence of another, or that one event must be regarded as the cause of the other. To be able to say that there is a cause-effect relation between two events, it is necessary for one of them (the "cause") to precede the other (the "effect"). That in itself is naturally not enough: It is also possible for this chronological sequence to be purely coincidental, or there could be a third factor at work which causes first the one event and then the other. Most shops

---

[11]Cf. Govier (1982), Walton (1989a).

[12]Making use of Govier (1988), this example could also be analyzed as a consistency or precedent slippery slope.

are open on Saturdays and closed on Sundays, and this is always so, but the fact that the shops are shut on Sundays is not the result of their being open on Saturday. For a cause-effect relation it is necessary to establish that the second event could not have taken place if the first had not taken place before it.

To infer a cause-effect relation from the mere observation that two events take place one after the other amounts to committing the fallacy of *post hoc ergo propter hoc* ("after this, therefore because of this").[13] An alleged example of this fallacy is critically discussed in a consumer's reaction to the plan to institute a levy on video- and audiocassette recorders and unrecorded cassettes on the grounds that records are copied at home so that fewer records are sold:

> Just what do we object to in this arrangement? In the first place we do not think that the claim that home copying is responsible for the decline in record sales has been proved. It is a fact that record sales have slumped. It is also a fact that records are sometimes copied at home. But this does not necessarily mean that the first is a consequence of the second.
>
> For example, it has never been proved that someone who copies a record would have bought that record if he had had no means of copying it. You could equally well argue that copying music makes it better known and makes customers more inclined to buy more records.
>
> Be that as it may, this claim is just as unprovable as the claim made by the record industry. And we therefore find it incomprehensible that a new levy should be based on an unproved proposition.

General conclusions are sometimes arrived at by making observations that are regarded as particular instances of the general. Although the argumentation scheme underlying this method may at first sight appear to be that of instrumental argumentation, it is in fact rather a special case of symptomatic argumentation. The correct use of this argumentation scheme calls for observations that are representative and sufficient, otherwise the fallacy of *secundum quid* ("hasty generalization") is committed.[14] If you wish to argue that all white cats are deaf it goes without saying that it is not enough for you to refer your audience to your own cats.

## COMPLICATIONS REGARDING ARGUMENTATION SCHEMES

What reasons might be adduced by a protagonist and an antagonist for accepting or refusing an argumentation scheme? Suppose, they are presented with an argument from authority. Is it sound, or not? Opponents might simply point out that

---

[13]Cf. Walton (1989a), Woods and Walton (1989).

[14]Cf. Leddy (1986) on the more refined distinction between the fallacy of unrepresentativeness and the fallacy of small sample.

it cannot be deduced with certainty from the fact that an expert says something that it is in fact as he says. Proponents need not dispute this. They might counter it with the argument that it is simply impossible for everyone to know everything or find out about everything and that the opinion of an authority, while not providing certainty, does at least lend some plausibility to a point of view.

The problem with this controversy is that there are advantages and disadvantages and that they are hard to compare. It is unrealistic to aim for an objective decision as to whether arguments from authority are based on a sound argumentation scheme. The protagonist and the antagonist can only try to find a common criterion for weighing the advantages and disadvantages against each other and then decide about whether or not to allow this type of argument in their discussion. If they cannot reach an agreement, the protagonist should not use it.

Similar considerations apply to that subcategory of arguments from authority in which authority is ascribed to the number of people who believe something. The proponents of this argumentation scheme might argue that so many people can hardly be wrong, whereas its opponents might counter with the argument that history has plenty of striking examples to the contrary. Adherents of the first argument will admit this type of argument to the discussion, adherents of the second will reject it as an *argumentum ad populum*. At any rate, if no agreement can be reached, the protagonist should abstain from using it.

The decision is even more difficult if it does not concern descriptive propositions but inciting propositions. Must the number of people demonstrating against the deployment of nuclear weapons be treated as a legitimate argument? Many of the demonstrators may think so, but some politicians do judge otherwise:

> Politics is not made in the street. Numbers only count in elections and in parliamentary votes. You cannot make a direct connection between the numbers of demonstrators and the rightness of a particular opinion. Many or few people come along with things, urging, calling, singing, demonstrating. The only thing that counts is the idea that they support and the acceptability of that idea.

In elections and other voting matters, it is quite common for decisions to be taken on a straight majority. Should this *ad populum*-like approach always be regarded as completely unreasonable? Not, of course, if it is chosen out of necessity. In certain cases, decisions have to be taken, and they cannot be shelved indefinitely. Let the majority decide is then a civilized and nonarbitrary way of settling the matter. The fact that it is the number of votes that settles the dispute does by no means automatically mean that the quality of the argumentation no longer matters.

The fallacy of *hasty generalization* is generally regarded as an unacceptable way of arriving at general conclusions on the basis of specific observations. The trouble is that it is not always so clear that a generalization is based on observations that are insufficiently representative or not numerous enough. Usually, the generalization is presented as fully justified, as when prejudices are verbally "justified." One noisy foreigner for a neighbor leads then easily to the generalization that foreigners are disturbers of the peace whereas one noisy neighbor of one's own race will not so swiftly produce the conclusion that all the members of this race are noisy creatures.

Another illustrative example in which it is perhaps not immediately apparent that a hasty generalization has been made stems from a newspaper article in which a well-known professor of economics attacks a number of iniquitous situations that he believes become more and more prevalent in his university:

> No room for research is being asked for or offered. Not even asked for, because about 90% of all faculty teaching staff are incapable of any scholarly activity. They came to the universities on the waves of the tumult in the sixties, lured by the exceptional primary and secondary conditions of employment. To a man, they can now be unmasked as soured nonentities who frustrate not only their own lives but also those of others.

By referring to "about 90%," instead of "all teaching staff," the professor creates the impression that he has access to reliable statistics, but there is nothing to show that this is the case. We must therefore assume that he ascribes a general validity to his own experiences and that he is banking on his reputation as an economist with a statistical training to ensure that his readers will not doubt the reliability of his statements. In this context, the cautious "about" is well chosen: Here we have the academic with his devout respect for the facts.

For those who start from the traditional taxonomy of fallacies it may at first be somewhat confusing that the variants of certain fallacies that in the traditional taxonomy were lumped together in the same nominal category, are now differentiated into violations of different discussion rules. An *argumentum ad verecundiam*, for instance, can be a violation of Rule 2, Rule 4, or Rule 7. An *argumentum ad populum* can be a violation of Rule 4 as well as Rule 7. It is easy to see how functional these new divisions are.

If the *argumentum ad verecundiam* is a violation of Rule 2, at the opening stage of the discussion, the protagonist sets himself up as the guarantor of the rightness of his standpoint, thereby evading the burden of proof for his standpoint. If it is a violation of Rule 4, at the argumentation stage, he parades his own qualities to the antagonist or the audience instead of advancing arguments. If it is a violation of Rule 7, he does present argumentation, but the argumentation scheme is inappropriate or incorrectly used because the authority to whom the appeal is made is not an expert in the relevant field.

If the *argumentum ad populum* is a violation of Rule 4, the protagonist is playing on the emotions of the audience, instead of advancing arguments. If it is a violation of Rule 7, he is putting forward argumentation, but the argumentation scheme concerned is used incorrectly. The number of people believing something is taken as the basis for the conclusion that what they believe is actually true. Then, the *argumentum ad populum* is a variant of the *argumentum ad verecundiam*.

Although traditionally the variants of *argumentum ad verecundiam* and *argumentum ad populum* are in name variants of the same fallacy, the differences between them are so big that there is something to be said for regarding them as completely different fallacies which happen to have been given the same name. More important than the name is that the variants are violations of different rules for critical discussion.

CHAPTER 16

# Fallacies in Utilizing Logical Argument Forms

## DEALING WITH LOGICAL ARGUMENT FORMS

For a conclusive defense of a standpoint it is necessary for all the arguments used in the discourse to be logically valid. This validity requirement relates to the *form* of the arguments, which should be such that if the premises are true the conclusion of the argument cannot possibly be false. The *reasoning procedure* is the evaluative tool for establishing whether an argument is actually valid: It is aimed at checking whether its form does indeed guarantee that the conclusion follows from the premises.

To be able to determine whether an argument is logically valid, it is necessary to reconstruct the underlying reasoning of the protagonist's argumentation at the argumentation stage of the discussion. Reconstructing the underlying reasoning means establishing what exactly the premises and the conclusions are that constitute the arguments which are used in the argumentation. If there are any unexpressed premises, it will be necessary to make them explicit. The logical validity of the argument concerned is then more or less automatically guaranteed because making unexpressed premises explicit starts with formulating the "logical minimum" that links the explicit premise in a logically valid way with the conclusion.

Logical argument forms can only be evaluated if they are completely explicit. Leaving premises unexpressed is, in argumentative practice, rather the rule than the exception. Therefore, Rule 8 for a critical discussion is formulated as follows: *In his argumentation a party may only use arguments that are logically valid or capable of being validated by making explicit one or more unexpressed premises.*

In practice, the logical quality of their arguments will be thought to be quite important to the protagonist and the antagonist and they will do what they can to let their argumentation make a "logical" impression. Generally, when it comes to assessing the validity of each other's arguments, they will primarily, or even exclusively, rely on their own intuitions. A formal check will only be carried out if their intuitions lead to different results.

If he can see this coming, the protagonist will often try to avoid a critical examination of the validity of his reasoning by giving his words the appearance of logicality. By presenting something as "perfectly logical" he can try to prevent the antagonist from going into a closer examination of the logical merits of the argument underlying his argumentation:

> Now Geneva has failed, it is logical that Denmark will join the other countries and deploy cruise missiles.

The use of the term *logical* has less to do with the formal attributes of the argument and more with investing the standpoint with a veneer of logicality. In fact, the term is used here in the sense of *quasi*-logical.

But even without resorting to terms like *logical* and *logic*, the protagonist will often attempt to present his standpoint in such a way that it looks as if it is entirely logical to infer this standpoint from the premises. Often, he will suggest that he is only applying the principle of consistency that if you think one thing, you must, logically, also think the other thing:

> I have no objection to others not smoking, so they shouldn't object to the fact that I do smoke.

In evaluating the logical quality of the defense of a standpoint, before turning to the matter of whether the conclusion actually follows logically from the premises, first the question must be answered whether there are no inconsistencies in the set of premises. There is little point in checking an argument for its validity if the premises are inconsistent.

The most obvious type of inconsistency is when two premises are contradictory. This is the case if they contain propositions that can neither both be true nor both be false at the same time: "The fire is on" and "The fire is not on." The conjunction of the two propositions produces a compound proposition that because of its contradictory form is always false.

The chess player Viktor Kortsjnoi provides a somewhat more sophisticated example:

> Superstitious? Not me. That only brings bad luck!

A second type of inconsistency occurs where there are two contrary premises. Contrary premises cannot both be true at the same time, but they *can* both be false: "The coat is black" and "The coat is green," if, in fact, the coat is brown.

The crucial point about both contradictory and contrary premises is that the combination of the two propositions is always false, whatever their content.

If the inconsistency of premises were always as obvious as in these two examples, there would be little danger of the antagonist failing to detect it. Sometimes, it is not so immediately clear from the formulation that there is an inconsistency:

> Mrs. Janet Jones gave a remarkable answer to the question about her jealousy. "I haven't any," she replied. "I have a large dose of rationality. My mother always said: Jealousy rules the world, but it is not my greatest handicap. Though if my husband went to bed with someone else I'd take a shotgun to him."

Once it has been established which inconsistencies there are in a discourse, a decision must be taken as to whether it is still worthwhile (and feasible!) to start checking the logical validity of the arguments. One of the implications of Rule 8 is that the reasoning procedure must produce a positive result. Strictly speaking, checking the logical validity always calls for a reference to some system of rules of logic, but sometimes it will be evident straight away that an argument is invalid. In some other cases, it seems as if its invalidity can easily be demonstrated by means of an example, as in this article by the Dutch author Piet Grijs:

> The Christian faith is remarkable not for the improbability and incoherence of its pronouncements, but because it is so precisely the sort of faith we do not need. Briefly, it boils down to this: "God created the world. Mankind was very naughty. Then God sent his son, in the year nil. He committed suicide, and that is why mankind is redeemed from its naughtiness." Is each of those four sentences untrue? We cannot say with certainty. What worries me more is the complete lack of any coherent connection between them. The words "that is why" in the last sentence are an insult to the brain. These four sentences taken together seem to me to be just as true or false as any other arbitrary collection of four sentences that you might care to write down. For example: "The devil painted the world. But he cannot deduct the expenses for tax. Then his cousin appeared, in 1982. He is having an affair with the ex-leader of the conservatives, and that is why the trees are now growing green leaves."

Only in cases in which there is no need to make an unexpressed premise explicit, will it be necessary to check with the help of some system of rules of logic whether the argument itself is actually valid. The protagonist then violates Rule 8 if the reasoning procedure reveals that one or more of his arguments are invalid. The antagonist offends against Rule 8 if the reasoning procedure produces a positive result and he still rejects the argument as being invalid.

Traditionally, invalidity has been regarded as the distinctive criterion of fallacies.[1] Both the definition and the classification of fallacies were long determined

---

[1]Cf. Hamblin (1970).

by this criterion and many authors still maintain this position. To a certain extent, they are right: Some fallacies are indeed logical errors. But the invalidity of arguments is certainly not the most important cause of failure to reach a resolution of a dispute and a lot of fallacies need to be explained otherwise. Apart from the fact that arguments with unexpressed premises will already be made valid when they are completed, it is also often violations of rules other than Rule 8 that obstruct the resolution of the dispute.

## CONFUSING NECESSARY AND SUFFICIENT CONDITIONS

Violations of Rule 8 can take many different forms. Some of these logical invalidities occur with a certain regularity and are often not immediately recognized. Among them are fallacies that have to do with confusing a necessary condition with a sufficient condition (or the other way round) in arguments with an "If . . . , then . . ." premise.

The saying "There's no smoke without fire" can be cast in the "If . . . , then . . ." form: "If there is smoke, then there is fire." In a literal interpretation, this utterance means that the presence of smoke is a guarantee of the presence of fire and the absence of fire is a guarantee of the absence of smoke. Suppose that there is no fire and that someone does not see at once that there can then be no smoke, but instead thinks that there may be smoke. If it is assumed that there is smoke, then it must also, on the basis of the utterance "If there is smoke, then there is fire," be accepted that there is fire, whereas here the supposition is precisely that there is *no* fire. So, if someone wants to stick to this starting point, he cannot avoid conceding that there can be no smoke. The absence of fire is a guarantee of the absence of smoke.

The guarantee of the presence of fire that is provided by the presence of smoke means that, according to the utterance "If there is smoke, then there is fire," the presence of smoke is a *sufficient condition* for there being fire. Conversely, the guarantee of the absence of smoke provided by the absence of fire means that, according to this utterance, fire is a *necessary condition* for smoke.

Two valid arguments that can be constructed on the basis of the utterance "If there is smoke, then there is fire" are:

1. a. If there is smoke, then there is fire.
   b. There is smoke.
   c. *Therefore:* There is fire.
2. a. If there is smoke, then there is fire.
   b. There is no fire.
   c. *Therefore:* There is no smoke.

When sufficient and necessary conditions are confused with each other, the relation between smoke and fire is mixed up. Two such invalid arguments that can be constructed on the basis of the same utterance are these:

3. a. If there is smoke, then there is fire.
   b. There is fire.
   c. *Therefore:* There is smoke.
4. a. If there is smoke, then there is fire.
   b. There is no smoke.
   c. *Therefore:* There is no fire

In (3), it is deduced from the observation that a necessary condition of the presence of smoke has been fulfilled ("There is fire") that there is indeed smoke. The necessary condition is then erroneously treated as a sufficient condition, and no account is taken of the fact that on the basis of premise *a* (and in real life) it is possible for there to be fire without smoke. In (4) it is deduced from the observation that the sufficient condition of the presence of fire has not been fulfilled ("There is no smoke") that there is no fire. The sufficient condition is then erroneously treated as a necessary condition and, again, no account is taken of the fact that fire is possible without smoke.

The invalid arguments (3) and (4) entail an inversion of the valid argument forms of *modus ponens* and *modus tollens* respectively. In the inverted *modus ponens*, confirmation of the antecedent is inferred from the affirmation of the consequent (as in (3)), and in the inverted *modus tollens* disaffirmation of the consequent is inferred from disaffirmation of the antecedent (as in (4)). These two invalid argument forms are known as the fallacy of *affirming the consequent* and the fallacy of *denying the antecedent*.

Problems in recognizing these fallacies are often attributable to the acceptability of the conclusion drawn from the invalid argument. If somebody agrees with the conclusion, he tends to be less critical when it comes to checking the validity of the argument. This uncritical attitude is nicely criticized by Rob Sijmons in a newspaper:

> *Having sex may get you pregnant. If you get pregnant, you must have had sex.* The "inverted" assertion, while correct, does not necessarily follow from the first assertion, which in itself is also true. For homework, try inverting the equally true initial proposition: "Having sex may not get you pregnant."
>
> *Contaminated food can make you feel sick. If you feel sick you must have eaten contaminated food.* Nonsense, of course. Not only is the reasoning false, the inverted assertion is also false. Feeling sick can be caused by many other things. For example, by being pregnant. *So having sex can make you feel sick.* Homework: Is this last conclusion logically correct?

## CONFUSING THE PROPERTIES OF PARTS AND WHOLES

Another violation of Rule 8 is the erroneous attribution of a property of a whole to its constituent parts or vice versa. The properties of wholes and parts cannot always simply be transferred from one to another. Sometimes, the transfer produces an argumentation with a logically correct argument, but sometimes too the result may contain an incorrect argument. Here is an example where the argument is correct:

1. a. This chair is white.
   b. *Therefore:* The upholstery on this chair is white.

In this argument the whiteness of the chair is transferred to its upholstery. Because a chair's upholstery can be regarded as a constituent part of it and whiteness can be regarded as a property assigned to both chair and upholstery, this argument transfers a property ("whiteness") from a whole ("chair") to a part of the whole ("upholstery"). The general form of the argument in (1) can be represented as follows:

2. a. The whole X has property Z.
   b. *Therefore:* Part Y of X has property Z.

This argument form assumes that if a whole has a particular property, all the parts of the whole will also have that property. That this is not always the case becomes clear from the following argument, which has the same argument form as (1):

3. a. This chair is heavy.
   b. *Therefore:* The upholstery of this chair is heavy.

Argument (3) is clearly incorrect, and that means that the argument form of (3) cannot automatically be regarded as logically valid.[2]

Neither the attribution of properties of wholes to parts nor the attribution of properties of parts to wholes automatically produces a correct argument. The correctness of arguments of either one of these variants depends, among other things, on the *transferability* of the property concerned.[3] This transferability is determined by two factors: (a) the *nature of the property* to be transferred and (b) the *nature of the relation between the parts and the whole.*

[2]In pronouncing such a verdict it should, of course, be remembered that "logical validity" is a system-dependent notion. For the distinction between system-dependent validity and intuitive validity (or, as we have called it here, logical correctness), cf. Haack, 1978.

[3]Woods and Walton (1982a) spoke about compositionally and divisionally *hereditary* properties.

As for the nature of the property to be transferred, in the case of properties of persons, animals or things a distinction must be made between *absolute* and *relative* properties. Whether something or somebody possesses a particular absolute property can, in principle, always be assessed independently. With relative properties, by contrast, there is always some explicit or implicit comparison, whether directly with something or someone else, or with some yardstick, norm, or criterion.

Terms, words, and expressions that indicate absolute properties include the names of the colors of the material of which something is made and adjectives relating to shape or such fixed properties as flammability or toxicity:

4. This chair's feet are white.
5. This dress is made of cotton.
6. The village square is round.
7. This cleaning fluid is flammable.
8. The sap of the buttercup is poisonous.

Terms indicating relative properties or features may relate to weight, dimensions (length, breadth, depth, circumference, volume, etc.), strength, price, or qualifiers of character, appearance or other striking features:

9. That bag is heavy.
10. That elephant is small.
11. That bear is strong.
12. That boat is cheap.
13. My sister is nice.

The relativity of properties such as heaviness becomes clear from the comparative character (whether implicit or explicit) of the terms. A *heavy* bag, for example, is one that weighs more than an average bag. It is heavy when measured by the standards that apply to bags. We are not told by what yardstick exactly the weight of a bag is measured, but this is determined implicitly by the fact, known to every language user, that a bag is supposed to be capable of being carried. In the case of an aeroplane, for example, a different yardstick would apply.

Something similar occurs with terms like *large*. Their use depends on the yardsticks, norms, or criteria applying to the category to which the thing that is called "large," and so forth belongs. Within the appropriate category, a comparison is made with other members of that category. For example, the size of a mouse must be looked at within the context that belongs to the category of mice. A large mouse is not a large animal but a mouse that is larger than its conspecifics is large for a mouse.[4]

---

[4]Cf. Leisi (1952).

As for the nature or the relation between the parts and the whole, when assessing this relation it is important to draw a distinction between wholes that are *structured* and wholes that are *unstructured*.[5] An unstructured or "unordered" whole is no more than a collection of elements that together constitute the whole. The whole is, as it were, merely the sum of its parts. Examples are the peas in a tin, the drops in a puddle of water, and the grains in a heap of sand.

A structured or "ordered" whole is more than the sum of its parts. It is different in the sense that there is a qualitative difference between the collection of elements and the whole that they constitute. Examples of such structured wholes are a novel, consisting of a collection of sentences, a football team, composed by its players, and a machine, built up of various parts. Not every collection of sentences produces a novel: The sentences have to be ordered in a particular way to produce the required coherent whole. The same applies, *mutatis mutandis*, to the players forming the football team and the parts of the machine constructing the machine.

Some properties that can be ascribed to wholes are independent of the structure the whole has or does not have. Others are dependent on it. "Brownness," "being made of brass," "heaviness," and "largeness" are structure-independent properties. "Rectangularity," "edibility," "goodness," and "strength" are structure-dependent properties. A quantity of green peas taken together constitutes a whole that is also green, whether the peas are in a dish or still in the tin. But a collection of strong links does not automatically constitute a strong chain: They must first be connected to each other in the proper way.

As the example of the links shows, structure-dependent properties cannot simply be transferred from the parts to the whole. Nor is the converse possible. It does not follow from the observation that a jigsaw puzzle is rectangular that the pieces of the puzzle must also be rectangular. Nor is it so, by the way, that structure-independent properties *can* be transferred in every case.

A relative term indicates a property that cannot simply be transferred to the parts of the whole, whereas, in principle, this is possible with an absolute term. But again, not always:

14. a. Sodium and chlorine are toxic.
    b. *Therefore:* Sodium chloride is toxic.

Sodium chloride is of course the chemical name of ordinary salt, which is not toxic at all but edible, even though it is composed of two highly toxic elements.

The difference between (14) and the example of the green peas is the very fact that the term *toxic* indicates a structure-dependent property and the term *green* a structure-independent property. Thus, the term *green* indicates a property that is both absolute and structure-independent, whereas a term such as *small* indicates

[5]Cf. Hamblin's distinction between physical and functional collections (1970).

a property which, although structure-independent, is not absolute, and the term *toxic* indicates a property that is absolute but not structure-independent. *Only an absolute property that is also structure-independent* is transferable from the parts to the whole or vice versa. All other properties are not automatically transferable in every case.

The relation between the absolute or relative character of a property and its structure-dependent or structure-independent character on the one hand and the transferability of that property between parts and wholes on the other hand is illustrated here:

| | structure-independent properties (2a) | structure-dependent properties (2b) |
|---|---|---|
| absolute properties (1a) | red, white, blue, glass, iron, wood (+) | round, square, edible, toxic (−) |
| relative properties (1b) | heavy, small, light, large, thick, thin (−) | good, expensive, strong, poor (−) |

Only in the combination of 1a-2a is there a transferable property capable of producing a correct argument.[6] In combination 1a-2b, 1b-2a and 1b-2b there is a violation of the rule that the arguments used in an argumentation must in principle be logically valid. The result is the fallacy of *incorrect transfer of properties between parts and wholes*. This fallacy has two variants: (a) the incorrect transfer of a property from the parts of a whole to the whole and (b) the incorrect transfer of a property from a whole to parts of the whole.

In variant (a), a property of the individual parts of a whole is incorrectly turned into a property of the whole. That is why this mistake is sometimes called the fallacy of *composition*. In variant (b), a property of the whole is incorrectly divided among the parts, which is why this mistake is sometimes known as the fallacy of *division*.[7]

A nice example of the fallacy of composition occurs when the novelist Gerard Reve argued that there is a generally anti Catholic feeling in the Netherlands:

[6]If the twofold condition is indeed fulfilled that the property is absolute and structure-independent, the symptomatic argumentation scheme of a part-whole argumentation is, at least in this respect, sound. In predicate logic, this state of affairs can be formalized as *a* $(x)(y)[(P_{xy}.R_x) \rightarrow R_y]$ (*composition*), or *b* $(x)(y)[(P_{xy}.R_y) \rightarrow R_x]$ (*division*). (P then refers to "is part of" and R to "property.") These formulas represent premises that validate the argument, but they are not necessarily true: their truth is dependent on the nature of the property and on the nature of the relation between the property and the structure of the whole. Because the conditions for R have so far not been satisfactorily formalized, in the classical division of the fallacies, the fallacies of composition and division are to be situated somewhere between the so-called *formal* and the so-called *informal* fallacies.

[7]Cf. Bar-Hillel (1964), Broyles (1975), Pole (1981), Rowe (1962), Woods and Walton (1989).

> The present accusations against the R.C. Church are every bit as nonsensical as those that used to be levelled against the Jews. You will be familiar with them: The Church does nothing. Or: The Church meddles in politics too much. Or: The Church is rolling in money. (Observation in passing: It isn't. It is extremely poor, because it is chiefly a Church of the poor. Rich people don't need a God.)

In the argumentation in brackets, there is an argument that can be reconstructed as follows:

15. a. The Church is a Church of the poor.
    b. *Therefore:* The Church is extremely poor.

In (15) no account has been given of the fact that the property of *poorness* is not only relative but also structure-dependent. In the first place, different yardsticks for wealth must be applied to people than to churches: The wealth of people is measured by comparing their income and possessions with those of other people, whereas the wealth of the church must be compared with that of other churches or similar institutions. Second, there is no direct link between the wealth of individual members of a church and the wealth of the church as such. Apart from the prosperity of its members, the wealth of the church also depends on other factors such as the proportion of their income and possessions that the members donate to the church.

Similar analyses can be carried out for the fallacy of division. A brief example suffices:

16. a. The government is indecisive.
    b. *Therefore:* Government ministers are indecisive.

In (16), no account is given of the fact that the (absolute) property of "indecisiveness" is structure-dependent. A government can only take decisions if its members are able to reach them. It is perfectly possible that all the members of the government are extremely resolute, but all happen to want different things. The government as a whole thus has difficulty in arriving at a single decision and is "indecisive."

## COMPLICATIONS REGARDING LOGICAL ARGUMENT FORMS

The property of whiteness is both absolute and structure-independent and hence transferable from a whole to its parts or vice versa. However, there is a complication in that the transfer of this property from a whole to its parts can look different from a transfer from the parts to the whole. Compare the following examples:

1. a. This chair is white.
   b. *Therefore:* The feet of this chair are white.
2. a. The feet of this chair are white.
   b. *Therefore:* This chair is white.

In (1) and (2) the wholes and the parts between which the transfer takes place are the same, but (1) is more likely to be correct than (2). (2) would have been correct if (2a) had read "All the parts of this chair are white," which is an unexpressed premise in (1):

1. a. This chair is white.
   (*Therefore:* All the parts of this chair are white.)
   (The feet of this chair are parts of this chair.)
   b. *Therefore:* The feet of this chair are white.

The step from "All parts of this chair" to "The feet of this chair" is justified here, but it is not, of course, justified in the opposite direction: What is true of the feet need not be true of all parts of the chair. This explains the asymmetry between (1) and (2).

There may also be subtler differences between a whole/part argumentation and a part/whole argumentation. Whereas the use of a relative term always produces an invalid argument, in some cases the division variant seems to produce a more serious defect than the composition variant, and in other cases it seems to be the other way round. Compare:

2. a. The bicycle is expensive, so all the parts of the bicycle are expensive.
   b. All the parts of the bicycle are expensive, so the bicycle is expensive.
3. a. The bicycle is cheap, so all the parts of the bicycle are cheap.
   b. All the parts of the bicycle are cheap, so the bicycle is cheap.

The fallacy of division in (2a) appears to be more serious than the fallacy of composition in (2b), whereas the fallacy of composition in (3b) appears to be more serious than the fallacy of division in (3a). If this observation is correct, this must surely be due to the difference in the "composition behavior" and "division behavior" of the properties of expensiveness and cheapness, but exactly what it is that causes the difference is not quite clear.

One problem when identifying the fallacy of composition or the fallacy of division is that the terms used to identify the transferred properties are, in principle, equally applicable to both the whole and the parts. If this were not the case, it would always be possible to spot the fallacies immediately, as in the following examples:

4. a. This house is comfortable.
   b. *Therefore:* The door knobs in this house are comfortable.
5. a. Jan is nice.
   b. *Therefore:* Jan's liver is nice.

A further complication is that it is not always clear from the terms used whether they are absolute or relative, structure-dependent or structure-independent. Nor can we immediately see exactly what implications a relative or structure-dependent character of the term would have on the transfer of the property concerned from the whole to the parts or vice versa.

Sometimes, there is a danger of overlooking the differences and confusing the properties of parts and wholes, as in the following caricatural example:

6. a. An elephant eats more than a mouse.
   b. *Therefore:* Elephants eat more than mice.

At first sight, (6) might appear correct. It becomes clear that the fallacy of composition has been committed when it is realized that the property of "eating more than" is relative and should thus be tested against different criteria in (6a) than in (6b). Moreover, in (6b), the total number of elephants and mice that is included in the comparison plays a part: In (6a), the individual consumption is at issue, in (6b), the collective consumption.

Although the fallacies of composition and division are not fallacies of ambiguity, they can, confusingly, occur in combination with ambiguous terms. Here is an example:

7. a. All Japanese soldiers are small.
   b. *Therefore:* The Japanese army is small.

The composite nature of (7) becomes clear when it is realized that Japanese soldiers are members of the Japanese army. In combination with the relative term *small*, this is enough to recognize the fallacy of composition. But the word *small* also has different meanings in (7a) and (7b). In (7a), it refers to the body length of the Japanese soldiers, in (7b), to the size of the Japanese army in terms of numbers of men. The first meaning cannot possibly be operative in the conclusion, and the second cannot possibly be operative in the premise.

A typical complication in determining whether an argument is logically valid, is that argumentative indicators are not always reliable clues for the reconstruction of underlying arguments. In the case of progressive presentation—which comes nearest to a logical pattern of reasoning—"so" or "therefore," in principle, precede a speech act expressing the conclusion of a logical argument. In ordinary usage, however, the presence of colloquial words such as "so" or "therefore" does not necessarily point to an argument. "So," in particular, is often used rather loosely. Sometimes, it is nothing more than a filler; sometimes, it merely suggests an otherwise unspecified logical connection between different utterances. In an amusing reply to a letter from a colleague about Pope John Paul II's visit to the Netherlands Gerard Reve provided a good example:

> As I say: I am very pleased to read your letter, but I shall still go to Mass in the usual way and will then light two or three fifty-cent candles before the image of the Mother of Sorrows. What you say in your letter is true, or it is not true, so I can't go wrong.

In this case, there is no need to apply the reasoning procedure to realize that there is no question of a logically valid argument. But in some other cases it may be more difficult to see that the word "so," or "therefore," is misplaced or, at least, impractical for a logical reconstruction.

The differences between ordinary discourse and the way in which terms are used in a logical context are considerable. That the antecedent in an "If . . . , then . . ." sentence represents a sufficient, not a necessary, condition, is, for instance, only true in a logical interpretation in which every conditional sentence is treated as a "material implication." In ordinary discourse, completely explicit and fully equivalent instantiations of logically valid argument forms such as *modus ponens* and *modus tollens* can seldom be found and certain variants of *modus ponens* and *modus tollens* are sometimes also found acceptable. Then, the starting point does not seem to be a deductive-logical principle of validity but some looser, intuitive, and pragmatically oriented notion of validity or soundness. Here are two examples:

8. a. If it snows, then the roofs turn white.
   b. The roofs are white.
   c. *Therefore:* It has snowed.
9. a. *Mother to small son:* "If you don't tidy up your room this instant, you can't go to the cinema."
   b. *Son:* "I'll do it now."
   (Son tidies up his room.)
   c. *Son:* "So now I can go to the cinema."
   *Mother:* "Not a bit of it, all I said was that if you *didn't* do it you *couldn't* go."

In (8), although we cannot conclude with certainty that it has snowed (to do so would be committing the fallacy of affirming the consequent), it is, in the absence of other plausible explanations, all the same very likely. Although the argument is not deductively valid, it is (inductively) plausible. In colloquial speech (and elsewhere), this kind of argument is sometimes called "valid" or "sound."

In (9), the son's conclusion is strictly logically speaking, again, not justified (he is guilty of the fallacy of denying the antecedent), but pragmatically speaking it is. In ordinary circumstances, the son is entitled to assume that in (9a) his mother has provided him with *all* the information that he needs to be able to obtain her permission to go to the cinema. Going by this starting point, the antecedent of (9a) is both a sufficient and a necessary condition for being allowed to go to the cinema. In (9b), this condition is fulfilled, hence the conclusion is justified. The mother's reaction in (9c) may be legitimatized if the laws of logic are taken to the letter, but it is unquestionably highly pedantic—and from the viewpoint of dispute resolution by critical discussion also most discouraging.

Another complication in identifying the fallacy of affirming the consequent or the fallacy of denying the antecedent is that the "If . . . , then . . ." premise is not always explicitly formulated as such. If it remains implicit, it will be practically impossible to catch the protagonist committing either of these fallacies. After all, one of the prerequisites for the explicitization of an unexpressed premise is that the invalid argument be complemented in such a way that it becomes valid. If the argument is made valid in such a way that a premise is added that produces an invalid argument of one of these two types, the protagonist can hardly be blamed for committing a fallacy because the fallacy was only inserted into the argument when the unexpressed premise was made explicit.

Sometimes, the "If . . . , then . . ." premise may not be entirely left out, but merely cast in a slightly (or more than slightly) different formulation. In such cases, one must be extremely careful and cautious, when interpreting the text, not to "build in" a fallacy that is then imputed to the protagonist.

A clear, although differently worded, case of the fallacy of affirming the consequent is:

10. a. *Son to father:* "Some Mr. van Heerwaarden called, Dad."
    b. *Father:* "What did he want? Was it important?"
    c. *Son:* "He didn't tell me. He would call again next year."
    d. *Father:* "Then, it must be bloody important. Important things take their time."

Even though there is no explicit "If . . . , then . . ." premise, the father in (10d) is guilty of the fallacy of affirming the consequent. In this case, an "If . . . , then . . ." premise can be inferred from the utterance "Important things take their time": "If something is important, then it will take time." From his son's statement "He would call again next year" (10c), the father concludes that Mr. van Heerwaarden's telephone call will take time and is thus "bloody important."

The father's argument can be reconstructed as follows:

11. a. If something is important, then it will take time.
    b. Mr. van Heerwaarden's telephone call will take time.
    c. *Therefore:* Mr. van Heerwaarden's telephone call is important.

According to (11a), important things take their time. In (11c) the father concludes that Mr. van Heerwaardens's call must be important, thereby assuming that something that takes time must be important, which is the reverse of (11a). Thus, the father's conclusion is based on the fallacy of affirming the consequent. Moreover, he rather naively assumes that a telephone call that may be a year in coming "takes time"—as if the caller needs all this time to be well-prepared for his call.

CHAPTER 17

# Fallacies in Concluding the Discussion

## ESTABLISHING THE RESULT OF A DISCUSSION

In the concluding stage of the discussion the final balance sheet must be drawn up. Has the dispute been resolved? If so, in favor of which party?

Where the dispute has been resolved in favor of the protagonist, he has succeeded in producing a conclusive defense of his standpoint, where it is resolved in favor of the antagonist, the protagonist has not. The protagonist has conclusively defended his standpoint if, and only if, all the evaluation procedures have been completed and neither the identification procedure nor the testing procedure nor the reasoning procedure has produced a negative result.

Even if the application of these procedures at the argumentation stage has presented no problems, and the protagonist and the antagonist have at all stages of the discussion observed all the other rules, at the final concluding stage the resolution of the dispute can still be obstructed. A resolution of the dispute demands that, in principle, the protagonist and the antagonist jointly establish which of them has won the discussion so that there is no uncertainty, let alone disagreement, about the outcome.

The interpretation of the results of the discussion relates to the question of whether the protagonist has succeeded in conclusively defending his standpoint. It is possible that he himself is perfectly convinced that he has indeed succeeded in this endeavor, but that the antagonist maintains that this is not so. If they cannot agree on this, the dispute continues. As an unbiased third party will often be in a better position to decide who has won, to an outsider it may, meanwhile, be perfectly clear what the outcome is, but this does not really solve the problem.

A joint decision by protagonist and antagonist as to who has won the discussion is usually impossible if the discussion is implicit, as is the case with many written texts. Of necessity, it is then up to the reader to decide for himself whether the protagonist has provided a conclusive defense of his standpoint. Trespassing upon the reader's preserves, some writers try to make out unilaterally that they have won the discussion. Often, the impression this creates is comical rather than serious. In the following example, the whole thing is turned into a caricature:

> A discussion about the relationship between parliament and public opinion might be fascinating, but not with Piet Grijs. I therefore do solemnly declare that I have won the discussion and proceed to the order of the day.

If the protagonist and the antagonist *can* agree on the outcome of the discussion, the dispute can really be resolved. With respect to each point at issue there are then two possibilities: The protagonist and the antagonist agree that the protagonist has succeeded in conclusively defending his standpoint, or the protagonist and the antagonist agree that the protagonist has not so succeeded. In the first case, the antagonist must withdraw his original doubt about the standpoint and the protagonist may continue to maintain his standpoint; in the second case, the protagonist must retract his original standpoint and the antagonist may continue to maintain his doubt. These consequences of a successful or failed defense of a standpoint are laid down in Rule 9 for a critical discussion: *A failed defense of a standpoint must result in the party that put forward the standpoint retracting it and a conclusive defense in the other party retracting his doubt about the standpoint.*

If the antagonist refuses to retract his doubt about the protagonist's standpoint even though he concedes that the protagonist has conclusively defended it, he is guilty of a violation of Rule 9. The same applies to a protagonist who refuses to retract a standpoint while at the same time admitting that he has not succeeded in defending it conclusively. In practice, this combination of conceding something and yet still refusing to draw the consequences will not occur explicitly all that often. What is more likely is that a recalcitrant antagonist will still attempt to dispute that the protagonist's defense has been successful, whereas a recalcitrant protagonist is more likely not to admit in so many words that his defense has not been successful.

Even if the protagonist and the antagonist do seem to observe Rule 9, things can still go wrong at the concluding stage. One party, for example, may exaggerate the consequences that the other according to Rule 9 is obliged to draw. There is a chance that the party doing the exaggerating will then allow his enthusiasm to get the better of him and try to link these consequences to other consequences which do not follow from them at all and which give the outcome of the discussion a completely different twist.

If the protagonist has succeeded in conclusively defending his standpoint, Rule 9 says that the antagonist must, in consequence, retract his doubt about the standpoint. That is the only obligation resting on the antagonist and the only thing the protagonist may require of him. The protagonist attaches exaggerated consequences to his successful defense if he concludes that he has now proved that his standpoint is true, and demands that the antagonist concede this.

If the protagonist has not succeeded in conclusively defending his standpoint, Rule 9 says that he must, in consequence, retract it. That is his only obligation and the only thing the antagonist can require of him. The antagonist is clearly attaching exaggerated consequences to the protagonist's failed defense if he concludes that it has now been proved that the opposite of the protagonist's standpoint is true and demands that the protagonist concede this.

## MAKING AN ABSOLUTE OF THE SUCCESS OF THE DEFENSE

If the protagonist violates Rule 9 by automatically attaching to a successful defense of his standpoint the consequence that he has proved that the standpoint is true, he makes, in principle, a double mistake.[1] In the first place, he ascribes an unjustified status to the common starting points on which his defense is based: He acts as if they were true a priori, whereas there is in fact no guarantee whatever that they are indeed true. In the second place, in doing so, he erroneously invests his successful defense with an objective rather than (inter)subjective status.

As a successful defense of a standpoint can only be achieved against a particular antagonist in a particular communicative situation where the protagonist can appeal to a particular set of common starting points, and not to others, generally, such a defense is relative in character. The antagonist in question, on his part, may not suddenly start denying the acceptability of these common starting points and start questioning them, for then he would be violating Rule 6. The starting points that can be used by the protagonist in his defense of his standpoint may thus be regarded as concessions by the antagonist: In the interest of resolving the dispute, the antagonist is prepared, if only for the sake of argument, to concede that these propositions are acceptable. In chapter 14, this dependence of a successful defense on the starting points of the argumentation has been terminologically expressed by saying that such a defense is always *ex concessu*.[2]

For a proposition, having the status of concession means that it is not at issue. One of the antagonist's reasons for including a proposition among the concessions is precisely that he does not think it necessary that its acceptability should first be proved or become an issue during the course of the discussion. If the proposition concerned is used in defense of a standpoint, it will be accepted just

[1]The exceptional case, of course, is the protagonist's conclusive defense of a standpoint that is a so-called *logical truth*.

[2]Cf. Schopenhauer (1970), Barth and Martens (1977).

like that. However, this is by no means to say that the protagonist and the antagonist may be deemed to believe that such a proposition is true or acceptable in a universal sense. It is very well possible that they are not quite sure about this, or indeed that they even assume that the proposition is *not* true: They may deliberately start their discussion on the basis of hypothetical or even patently false starting points.

The protagonist violates Rule 9 if, on the grounds of a successful defense achieved with the help of a concession by the antagonist, he claims that he has proved that his standpoint is true. All he has, in fact, done is show that with the help of the concessions made by the antagonist it is possible to produce a successful defense of the standpoint. In infringing Rule 9, the protagonist conflicts in two ways with the *ex concessu* nature of a successful defense: He acts as if the outcome of his defense did not depend on the concessions made by the antagonist and he acts as if this outcome could lay claim to universal acceptance. The protagonist's violation of Rule 9 in which this unwarranted denial of the relativity of the outcome of the defense occurs can be termed the fallacy of *making an absolute of the success of the defense.*

## MAKING AN ABSOLUTE OF THE FAILURE OF THE DEFENSE

If the antagonist violates Rule 9 by automatically attaching to the failure of the protagonist's defense of his standpoint the consequence that it has now been proved that the opposite standpoint is true, he makes two mistakes. In the first place, he confuses his role as antagonist with that of a protagonist; in the second place, he erroneously assumes that a discussion must always end in a victory for either a positive or a negative standpoint, so that not having the positive standpoint automatically means having the negative standpoint and the other way round. The first mistake is the result of an incorrect understanding of the way the burden of proof in mixed and nonmixed discussions is divided, the second results from ignoring the possibility of having a zero standpoint. The combination of these two mistakes leads to the mistaken conclusion that the fact that it has not been proved that something *is* the case proves that it is *not* the case, or that the fact that something has not been proved *not* to be the case proves that it *is* the case.

In this way, the antagonist exaggerates the consequences of a failed defense by the protagonist in an unacceptable way. The antagonist now claims that the standpoint that is the opposite of the protagonist's standpoint has been successfully defended, whereas his victory only entitles him to maintain his doubt about the protagonist's standpoint. That is why this violation of Rule 9 can be termed the fallacy of *making an absolute of the failure of the defense*. Traditionally, this fallacy is known as *argumentum ad ignorantiam*, a term that expresses the fact that the person making the mistake gives evidence of ignorance.[3]

The following dialogue contains a clear example of an *argumentum ad ignorantiam*:

1. *Hans:* "I'm giving up smoking, because it gives you cancer."
   *Bert:* "That has yet to be proved, so you can carry on smoking with complete peace of mind."
   *Hans:* "You're right, I'll light up straight away."

Suppose this dialogue is part of a discussion aimed at resolving a nonmixed single dispute in which Hans adopts a positive standpoint with respect to the proposition *Smoking causes cancer* and Bert questions this standpoint:

2. *Hans:* +/p
   *Bert:* ?/(+/p)

After Hans and Bert have established that they are having a dispute (confrontation stage), they decide to attempt to resolve the dispute by means of a critical discussion in which Hans takes the role of protagonist and Bert that of antagonist (opening stage). Then Hans advances certain arguments that Bert looks at critically (argumentation stage). In the concluding stage of the discussion (1), Hans is initially convinced that he has succeeded in defending his standpoint that smoking causes cancer conclusively, but in the second instance he somewhat unexpectedly concedes that his defense has failed. This means that the dispute has still been resolved, but this time in favor of Bert instead of Hans. Judging by his final words, Hans has failed to notice that Bert has committed an *argumentum ad ignorantiam*: From the (joint) observation that Hans has been unable to prove that smoking causes cancer, Bert has implicitly drawn the conclusion that it has now been proved that smoking does *not* cause cancer:

3. *Bert:* −/p

By drawing this conclusion from Hans' defeat, Bert confuses the roles of protagonist and antagonist. In the original dispute (2) Hans is the only one who has advanced a standpoint, so that he is the only one obliged to carry out a defense. Bert has only cast doubt on Hans' standpoint. This state of affairs is reflected by the division of roles: Hans takes the role of protagonist and Bert that of antagonist. Because the dispute is nonmixed, neither Hans nor Bert has any other role to play.

---

[3]Cf. Robinson (1971a), Woods and Walton (1989).

It follows from the division of roles that there are no options open to Hans other than to maintain his standpoint if his defense is successful or to have to retract it if his defense has failed). Bert's options are maintaining his doubt if the defense has failed or retracting it if the defense has succeeded. Bert has no standpoint of his own to defend, so that at the end of the discussion he has no standpoint to maintain or retract. When attaching the consequence that the negative standpoint has been successfully defended to Hans' failed defense of his standpoint, Bert confuses his role as antagonist of this standpoint with that of protagonist of the negative standpoint.

Even if the dispute had been mixed from the outset, Bert would still have been unable to attach to Hans' failure to defend his standpoint the consequence that the negative standpoint had been successfully defended. The initial situation would then have been as follows:

4. *Hans:* +/p, ?/(−/p)
*Bert:* ?/(+/p), −/p

Hans and Bert are both the protagonist of their own standpoint and the antagonist of each other's standpoint. If Hans fails to defend his positive standpoint, then Bert, in his role as antagonist, wins the discussion relating to Hans' positive standpoint. Because Bert himself has not yet put forward a defense for his negative standpoint, he still has the burden of proof for the negative standpoint. By claiming that the negative standpoint has been successfully defended, Bert confuses his victory in the role of antagonist of the positive standpoint with victory in the role of protagonist of the negative standpoint. Although Hans is according to Rule 9 obliged to retract his positive standpoint because he has failed to defend it, this does not at all mean that he is obliged to withdraw his doubt about Bert's negative standpoint. That only becomes necessary if Bert has successfully defended his own standpoint.

Bert also makes the second *ad ignorantiam* mistake of erroneously assuming that it is always necessary to adopt either a positive or a negative standpoint with respect to a proposition. Because the positive standpoint that smoking causes cancer has not been successfully defended, he automatically assumes that the negative standpoint that smoking does not cause cancer must then be proved right, thus overlooking the possibility that *no* standpoint is adopted with respect to the proposition that smoking causes cancer. If one has to abandon the positive standpoint that smoking causes cancer one could very well end up with the feeling that one is really not quite sure anymore whether smoking causes cancer or not without going from one extreme to the other. By pretending that there is only one alternative, in an *argumentum ad ignorantiam* the arguer ignores the possibility of taking the middle course of not having a standpoint at all or, to put it another way, adopting the zero standpoint.

An *argumentum ad ignorantiam* is often put forward in combination with a *false dilemma* in which a contrary opposition is presented as a contradiction.[4] It is then suggested that there are only two options and if one of them cannot be proved to be the case, it is concluded that this is *not* the case (the "ordinary" *argumentum ad ignorantiam*) and hence that the other option *is* the case. All other possibilities are then glossed over:

5. *Hans:* "I'm giving up running, because it's said to be bad for your health."
   *Bert:* "In all these years that's never been proved, so it must be very good for you."
   *Hans:* "In that case I'd better stick to my old habits."

In this example, *good* and *bad* are treated as contradictory, whereas the statements "Running is bad for you" and "Running is good for you," although they cannot both be true, can both be false. In principle, it is possible that smoking has no effect whatsoever, so that it is neither good nor bad for you, that is that it is "neutral." The terms *good* and *bad* are, in fact, the extremes on a scale on which there are all sorts of intermediate gradations which may apply to different cases in different ways. Acting as if there is just one absolute opposition is a denial of this variety of possibilities.

Here are some more examples of oppositions that are often wrongfully treated as contradictions:

6. a. intelligent/stupid
   b. beautiful/ugly
   c. strong/weak
   d. large/small
   e. rich/poor

Thinking in terms of black and white has several variants. One is to reduce three or more possibilities to two, where there is no question of there being two extremes on any scale. A coat, for example, can be any number of colors, so to conclude from the knowledge that a coat is not black that it is green is to ignore the possibility of its being brown or red, and so forth. The same black and white trick can be played with any other contrary pair:

7. a. copper/iron
   b. round/square
   c. sweet/sour
   d. Roman Catholic/Protestant
   e. homosexual/heterosexual

---

[4]Cf. Copi (1982) on false dilemma.

Sometimes, a party will allow himself to be tempted into conceding straight away that there are only two possibilities. This will make it difficult for him to conduct his defense: If he fails to defend the one option it will be a simple matter for the other party to conclude by way of an *argumentum ad ignorantiam* that the only remaining alternative has now been proved.[5] As early as the opening stage, the protagonist must allow for the possibility that this conclusion will be drawn. He must ensure that no false dilemmas are forced upon him. Particularly when facing a large and unexpert audience, the combination of an *argumentum ad ignorantiam* and a false dilemma can be extremely effective. If the protagonist fails to protest against the false dilemma right from the outset, the audience will be easily swayed into accepting the opposing party's conclusion.

A still more sophisticated way of using a false dilemma is when one of the two available alternatives is already acknowledged to be false or undesirable. This naturally leaves only the other alternative. Even without any actual defense it can at once be presented as having been conclusively defended: a false dilemma of the most serious kind which not only ignores other alternatives but also assumes that the alternative that does exist has been effectively ruled out. This is going a step further than the *argumentum ad ignorantiam*, for no attempt is made to defend anything at all:

8. a. Eat what's on your plate, or do you want to be small and weak all your life?
   b. I can't understand what you've got against the exact sciences, what is there in all that woolly philosophizing?
   c. I think we'd better go now, or would you prefer to miss the train?
   d. In my opinion you've got to have rules, you can't just let everyone muddle along on their own.
   e. Better dead than red.

In practice, such false dilemmas do not always go unnoticed, they are sometimes duly spotted and unmasked:

> The conservative leader said he would have been happy to take part with his entire political following in a demonstration against nuclear weapons if it had been acceptable to his party. The slogans carried on Saturday were not acceptable, he said, particularly "Jobs not Bombs," which he regarded as a false dilemma. "It's like offering a choice between Hitler and Moscow," he said.

---

[5]Even if there *were* only two possibilities, this would still be a mistake. If one knew that either X or Y were true and failed to prove X, then the possibility that one might later prove X would remain open. A failure to prove X shows that one does not know yet, whether the dichotomy is exhaustive or not.

## COMPLICATIONS REGARDING THE CONCLUSION OF THE DISCUSSION

The protagonist's fallacy of making an absolute of the success of the defense implies a failure to acknowledge the role of concessions. By denying that the defense of a standpoint can only succeed thanks to concessions made by the antagonist, the protagonist denies the relative nature of every successful defense. In principle, a dispute can only be resolved precisely because the antagonist is prepared to make certain concessions which the protagonist can utilize in his defense of his standpoint. That is why the fallacy of making an absolute of the success of the defense is also regarded by some as a special variant of the *argumentum ad hominem*: It can only come about by the grace of the persons who fulfill the roles of protagonist and antagonist.

Instead of saying that a resolution of a dispute is always *ex concessu*, we might also say that it is always *ad hominem*. There are three differences, however, between this variant of the *argumentum ad hominem* and the variants discussed in chapter 9: There, a direct (negative) correlation was seen between a standpoint and the person advancing it or calling it into question, whereas here there is a denial of any connection with persons; there, the violation was at the confrontation stage, whereas here it is in the concluding phase; there, the violation could be committed by either the protagonist or the antagonist, whereas here it can only be a violation by the protagonist.

It is sometimes pointed out that the *argumentum ad ignorantiam* is used in law, but that there it is not a fallacy. What is meant then is the principle of the presumption of innocence in criminal law, that is that a person is considered innocent of the charge against him until or unless his guilt is proved. The implication of this principle is that an accused is acquitted if his guilt cannot be proved to the satisfaction of the court.

Although at first sight there appear to be similarities with the *argumentum ad ignorantiam*, it is not that fallacy that we see here. The accused is acquitted "for lack of evidence," not because his innocence is deemed to have been proved. So an acquittal does not mean that the court believes the accused to be innocent. The purpose of the principle is to protect the legal security of the accused, who is naturally the party most at risk. Application of the principle is a consequence of the burden of proof in a criminal trial: The accused does not have to prove that he is innocent, but it must be proved that he is guilty. Thus in a trial the accused's innocence has the status of a *presumption*.

In science and scholarship, too, there is a common situation that bears a superficial similarity to the *argumentum ad ignorantiam*. The failure of an attempt to falsify a hypothesis is regarded as support for the rightness of the hypothesis. Indeed, following the lead given by the philosopher Karl Popper, the systematic performance of serious attempts at falsification is regarded by many as the only way of arriving at reliable scientific knowledge. Falsification is the alternative to the sinful path of verification.

Here again, the similarities with the *argumentum ad ignorantiam* must not be taken as a sign that falsification is a fallacy. After all, the failure of an attempt to refute a hypothesis is not regarded as grounds for concluding that the hypothesis is true, merely that it has not been proved that it is false. Every failed attempt to refute it makes it more reasonable to suppose that the hypothesis might actually be right. That is why it is sometimes said that the more carefully calculated attempts at refutation have failed, the stronger the hypothesis becomes. On the other hand, however many attempts to refute the hypothesis may fail, the conclusion can never be that its truth has been proved, only that it may be reasonable to assume for the time being that it is true.

The fallacy of the false dilemma must not be confused with the logically valid argument form of the *disjunctive syllogism*:

1. a. A v B
   b. not A (or: not B)
   c. *Therefore:* B (or: A)

In arguments taking the form of (1) there is a *disjunction* of two utterances which cannot both be false. If one of them is false, it may therefore be concluded that the other is true. Here is an example of an argument which has the form of the disjunctive syllogism:

2. a. Bert's in the Fox or the Rose and Crown.
   b. He is not in the Rose and Crown.
   c. *Therefore:* He is in the Fox.

The fallacy of the false dilemma arises if the disjunction embraces only two utterances when in fact there are three or more possibilities. In that case premise *a* of (1) is certainly incomplete and possibly even misleading. In the case of (2) this would mean that the impression is given that there are only two eligible pubs, whereas in fact Bert might, for example, also be in the Goat and Feathers. Then, the fact that he is not in the Rose and Crown does not necessarily mean that he is in the Fox.

An *argumentum ad ignorantiam* also arises if it is not so that *a* has been established *not* to be the case, but only that it is not certain that *a is* the case. In that case premise *b* of (1) is certainly premature and possibly even downright false. In the case of (2) this means that the fact that it cannot be said with certainty that Bert is at the Rose and Crown is taken as meaning that he is *not* at the Rose and Crown. To go running to the Fox because he must be there is to run the risk of wasting time and effort.

There is nothing wrong, in itself, with using the argument form of the disjunctive syllogism. The *argumentum ad ignorantiam*, whether or not in combination with a false dilemma, arises only when there is something wrong with one or both of the premises of the argument. In practice, this is not always apparent, so that distinguishing between a correct and an incorrect use of the logically valid argument form of the disjunctive syllogism may present certain difficulties.

CHAPTER 18

# Fallacies in Usage

## PRESENTING AND INTERPRETING ARGUMENTATIVE DISCOURSE

Unclear language can have direct negative consequences for the resolution of a dispute. If the protagonist fails to word his standpoint clearly and unequivocally at the confrontation stage, the antagonist may question it when there is no real need for him to question it, or he may not question it when he ought to question it. And if the wording used by the antagonist fails to make it understood that he is casting doubt on the protagonist's standpoint, the protagonist may erroneously believe there to be no dispute. On the other hand the protagonist might also have the impression that there *was* a dispute when in fact there was none or that the dispute is mixed when in fact it is nonmixed. These misunderstandings may give rise to spurious agreements or disputes.[1] In the case of a pseudo-agreement a discussion that is necessary may never take place, in the case of a pseudo-dispute there is a good chance that an unnecessary discussion will be conducted.

Lack of clarity and univocality at the confrontation stage continue to have an effect through the other stages of the discussion, and of course they may be joined by other unclearnesses and ambiguities at the other stages. As the protagonist and the antagonist take turns during the discussion in playing the parts of speaker and listener (or writer and reader), they effectively have a double responsibility for usage in the discussion: They must put what they mean into words as clearly and unequivocally as possible, so that the other party is enabled to determine

[1] Cf. Naess on pseudo-agreement (1966).

their intention, and they must do their best to determine the intended meaning of what the other party is saying. In order to do justice to these usage requirements, Rule 10 for a critical discussion runs as follows: *A party must not use formulations that are insufficiently clear or confusingly ambiguous and he must interpret the other party's formulations as carefully and accurately as possible.*

The two discussants are jointly responsible for achieving mutual understanding. This means that the wording of their speech acts must fulfill the requirement of clarity that is part of the Principle of Communication. For the interpretation, it implies that each party must assume that the other party is observing the Principle of Communication and has formulated everything he means as clearly as he can.[2] This does not necessarily mean that all intentions have to be formulated with complete explicitness and directness, nor that all speech acts are to be interpreted literally. It is perfectly possible for the communicative function of a speech act only to be made known indirectly and for all sorts of other things to remain implicit, as in the case of an unexpressed premise.

In practice, implicit and indirect speech acts do not, generally speaking, present much of a problem. Usually, the listener or reader can, using his background knowledge, see from the context and situation what is meant and what the unexpressed elements are. In most cases the speaker or writer will indeed assume the listener or reader to be able to do so and choose his wordings accordingly. If both the language users adapt their handling of the verbal information in such a way to each other's background that no problems of understanding do arise, we may speak of an *optimal formulation* and an *optimal interpretation*.

The communicative success or failure of verbal exchanges is not a matter of absolutes. As a rule, the formulation of the message is not inherently comprehensible, but it is comprehensible (or incomprehensible) to certain interpreters. Comprehensibility is a *relative* concept. Comprehensibility is also a *gradual* concept: It is not something that a formulation simply possesses or not, but something that a formulation may exhibit to a greater or lesser extent. Even formulations that seem particularly transparent may yet not be fully comprehensible to everybody, and even in the most opaque formulations there may be things that certain listeners or readers can understand.

The extent to which the communication is a success or a failure, cannot be

---

[2] In practice, it seems sometimes more important to the language users to do justice to social considerations than to conduct a critical discussion in accordance with the Principle of Communication. According to Leech, besides the Principle of Communication (or the Gricean Co-operative Principle), which regulates our language use in such a way that it contributes to some assumed communicative goal, a Politeness Principle should be postulated that serves "to maintain the social equilibrium and the friendly relations which enable us to assume that our interlocutors are being cooperative in the first place" (1983, p. 82). In Leech's opinion, it could be argued that the Politeness Principle of minimizing the expression of impolite beliefs has a higher regulative role than the Co-operative Principle. This agrees with Lakoff's observation that in a conversation it is often considered more important "to avoid offense than to achieve clarity" (1973, pp. 297-298).

completely determined by merely establishing whether the speaker's or writer's words are understood by the listener or reader. As it happens, it may for one purpose or context be necessary to achieve a higher degree or level of understanding than for another.[3] A surgeon explaining the precise details of an operation to a colleague will set higher standards for comprehension than the same man explaining the same thing to his small nephew. In the first instance it is up to the language users themselves to determine what level of understanding is required in order to bring a dispute to a satisfactory resolution.

In an explicit discussion it will be easier to tell whether the required level of understanding has been reached than in an implicit one. In the former, the speaker will be able to tell from the verbal and nonverbal reactions or the uncomprehending look of the listener that he has not been fully understood as he wants to be understood. The listener for his part can ask the speaker to amplify or explain his words if he thinks this necessary. Such amplifications or explanations of formulations are given by means of *usage declaratives.*

In order to be able to fulfill the requirements formulated in Rule 10 that the formulations must not be insufficiently clear or confusingly ambiguous, speakers and writers are always entitled to clarify their words with a usage declarative and listeners and readers are entitled to ask them for such a usage declarative. In principle, it is always an obligation for the speaker or writer to accede to such a request, because otherwise the Principle of Communication would be violated. With regard to contributions to implicit discussions, such as an address, a pleading or an editorial, there is usually no possibility of letting the speaker or writer through a direct response know that his words require clarification. In such circumstances it is up to the speaker or writer who wants to resolve the dispute to judge for himself whether he needs to give something like an amplification. When in doubt, he is best advised to be follow the maxim "If it doesn't help, at least it doesn't hinder." This, we call the strategy of *optimally clear and unequivocal presentation.*

## MISUSING UNCLEARNESS

If a discussant makes use of some unclearness in his wording to improve his own position in the discussion, he is guilty of a violation of Rule 10 that can be described as the *fallacy of unclearness.* Various sorts of unclearness can occur. If they result from the structuring of the text, they are cases of structural unclearness at the textual level: obscure structure, "illogical" order, lack of coherence, and so on. Various sorts of elements can also become mixed up in the text. Goudsblom, a sociologist, described its effect on discussions about politics and morals (*Folia,* October 17, 1981):

---

[3]Cf. Naess on "depth of intended meaning" (1966).

> In many discussions and discursive texts . . . a capricious intermingling takes place of descriptive, interpretative, declarative and valuational elements, the result of which is the creation of a combination of "sense" and "nonsense" that is difficult to grasp but which can perhaps best be termed "unsense."
>
> We notice that many discussions about politics and morals—that is, about society—are conducted by the grace of unsense. The starting points, the terms, the conclusions, often even the whole statement of the problem itself, together constitute an indissoluble tangle of description, interpretation, explanation and valuation. To take part in this discussion is to poke about in a rhetorical hornet's nest. The realization of this renders us powerless and speechless. . . .

Unclearness can also arise at the sentence level, in the performance of elementary speech acts. One of the first problems is sometimes that it is not clear what the communicative function is of a speech act. As a rule, this function is not explicitly indicated. Usually, this does not lead to any problems of interpretation, but sometimes the context and situation will leave too many possibilities open and the function of the implicit speech act will be obscure.

Another difficulty with elementary speech acts relates to the propositional content. The reference may be unclear, but so may the predication. In the first case it is not plain whom or what the speaker is actually talking about, in the second we have difficulty in understanding what he wishes to say about him or it. Suppose someone says "Charles is a kleptomaniac." If it is unclear which Charles is meant, the listener can ask "Who do you mean, your neighbor or your brother-in-law?" If he is unsure what a kleptomaniac is, he can ask "What's that?" In this example the communicative function of the speech act is also not explicitly indicated. It may be an assertion or a simple statement of fact, but it could also be a warning. Because the communicative function remains implicit, it is possible for the listener to draw the wrong conclusion and react in an inappropriate way.

Suppose the example has the function of an assertion with which the listener is supposed either to agree or disagree. Suppose also that he knows which Charles is meant and that he also knows what a kleptomaniac is. It is then conceivable that he still does not agree with the assertion, even if he has no quarrel with the "facts" as they relate to Charles. This discrepancy may be the result of a difference in the criteria being applied by him and the speaker in assessing whether or not someone is a kleptomaniac. It is perfectly possible that the speaker is one of those people who call someone a kleptomaniac as soon as they first steal a biscuit from the kitchen cupboard. The crucial question here is how often and how regularly someone has to steal things before we are entitled to label them a kleptomaniac. There will always be borderline cases, and this automatically makes the term *kleptomaniac* in some measure vague. In the example it is the vagueness of the word "kleptomaniac" that makes the assertion somewhat unclear.[4]

---

[4]Cf. for different types of vagueness, Olson (1970).

Another interesting example of how a term that, at first sight, seems clear enough can be exploited because of its unexpected vagueness, is discussed by Neil Lyndon in a newspaper article on "Bad mouthing" (*The Sunday Times*, December 9, 1990):

> Germaine Greer wrote an essay about rape in which she said: "Nevertheless, men do go to jail for rape, mostly black men, nearly all of them poor, and neither the judges nor the prosecuting attorneys are hampered in their dealings by the awareness that they are rapists too, only they have more sophisticated methods of compulsion." [. . .] Germaine Greer explained that "Probably the commonest form of noncriminal rape is rape by fraud—by phony tenderness or false promises of an enduring relationship, for example." By those criteria, there can't be many sexually active adults of either sex alive who have not been the victims of "noncriminal rape."

Corresponding to the four factors contributing most to a lack of clarity in the formulation of speech acts, we can now distinguish four main types of unclearness: (a) *implicitness* (of the communicative function), (b) *unfamiliarity* (of words and expressions), (c) (referential) *indefiniteness*, and (d) *vagueness*. Taking each of the four types individually, we can identify ways of removing the unclearness.

(a) Unclearness as the result of implicitness can be resolved by using usage declaratives to *make explicit* the nature and strength of the communicative function of the speech act and the scope of its propositional content. Thus the implicit speech act "Dogs are more sensitive than cats" can be further explicitized as "I have the impression that dogs might well be more sensitive than cats," or by adding "I am not talking about all dogs and cats, but about the average mongrel."

The strength of an assertive, for example, can vary from a firm assertion to a cautious supposition. This difference can be expressed (with a decreasing measure of certainty) by means of words and expressions such as "unquestionably," "certainly," "almost certainly," "doubtless," "probably," "possibly," and "conceivably." The greater the degree of certainty with which a standpoint is advanced, the higher the standards that may be expected to apply to the defense. If there is no explicit indication of the strength of the assertive, there is a danger that it will be wrongly assessed by the listener.

The scope of propositions can vary from one thing or individual to everything or everyone. This variation has certain implications for the defense of the standpoint. A standpoint with a particular proposition is, in principle, easier to defend than one with a universal proposition. If the scope of the proposition is not explicitly indicated, it is unclear what is required of the defense. In "Dogs are more sensitive than cats," for example, neither the strength nor the scope is clear. Hence the precizations given earlier.

A nice illustration of what can go wrong when the scope of a proposition is not clearly indicated can be given on the basis of a statement by Germaine Greer in her book *The Female Eunuch*:

> It always amazes me that women don't understand how much men hate them.

Neil Lyndon retorts in an article in *The Sunday Times*:

> What [. . .] would cause or allow a world-famous writer to speak so idiotically as to say that men hate women (as if *all* men hate *all* women); as if all men belonged by birth to a kind of natural Ku Klux Klan of woman-burners; as if—in opposition to the evidence of what they say and do, write, sing and dream—men *only* hate women and do not love them, do not want to love them?

(b) The example of unfamiliarity discussed earlier led to unclearness because the listener was not acquainted with the term *kleptomaniac*. This unclearness can easily be removed by giving a *definition* of the word: "A kleptomaniac is someone with a compelling urge to steal."

It is also possible that the unfamiliarity relates to the thing to which the word refers, in which case a nominal definition often does not resolve the unclearness so easily. It is unlikely that someone who does not know what inflation is and has no economic training will derive much benefit from a definition. What he needs is some *explanation* or *amplification*. And that will almost always require more than one sentence.

It is not always clear to what extent something is a question of vocabulary or specialist knowledge. Both of these are in many cases a matter of degree. There will often be some familiarity with a word or subject which may nevertheless be insufficient for a precise grasp of the thrust of the standpoint. Generally, the degree of familiarity can be increased by usage declaratives with which the word or thing is defined, explained, or amplified.

(c) The example of referential indefiniteness led to unclearness because the listener did not know to which person the word "Charles" referred. As a rule, the context and the situation in which an utterance occurs will provide sufficient information to avoid misunderstandings due to referential indefiniteness. Misunderstandings that might arise despite this can be avoided or resolved by asking for or giving a *precization*. This is a usage declarative by which it is indicated which interpretation among the possible interpretations that can be identified must be considered as the intended interpretation.

(d) The example of vagueness discussed earlier led to unclearness because one discussant called a person a kleptomaniac as soon as they had stolen one thing, whereas the other discussant only found the term appropriate where the person concerned was guilty of persistent theft. Both agreed that theft was involved: The difference was in the question of how often it must take place.

This form of vagueness is called *linear vagueness* because it is caused by possible differences in the degree to which something or someone has to fulfill a given criterion before a given description is regarded as appropriate. Obvious examples of linearly vague words are relative terms such as "bald," "rich," and "fat," but absolute terms like "red," "green," and other color descriptions can also be vague. How much money does a person have to have to be called rich? How much yellow can there be in red before it becomes orange?[5]

Another form of vagueness has to do with *family resemblance*.[6] Words in which this vagueness can occur include "nice," "intelligent," "poem," or "slum." What is common to these examples is that different people can apply different criteria to describe someone as nice or intelligent, to call a piece of writing a poem, or a part of a city a slum. The salient feature here is that there is no *single* criterion that applies to each word, but that two or more criteria from a longer list must be fulfilled before the word becomes appropriate. The unclearness is, for instance, caused by one language user placing the greatest emphasis on Criterion 1, 3, and 4 while another attaches most importance to Criterion 3, 4, and 5 and yet another regards Criterion 2, 3, and 4 as the most important. Because there are so many overlaps, it is not always immediately apparent that there are differences in the meaning different people give to the same word. This can lead to misunderstandings that may be difficult to clear up. If one person thinks that Bill is nice because he is honest, personal, and warm, whereas another likes him for being honest, helpful, and friendly, a dispute can easily arise about whether Bill is nice or not, without there being any actual disagreement about the traits attributed to him.

Vagueness relating to family likeness is caused by differences in meaning that have to do with the application of criteria which differ in a qualitative sense; with linear vagueness the differences are quantitative and relate to one and the same criterion. Besides prototypical cases, both types of vagueness also have borderline cases where the differences are less pronounced. A common characteristic that they both share is that they provide a good illustration of the relative and gradual nature of clarity and comprehensibility.

Unclearness because of vagueness, too, can be resolved by *precization*.[7] In this case the use of this usage declarative implies indicating which criteria are regarded as being applicable in the case in question, and the extent to which they must be fulfilled:

> I call someone intelligent if they are capable of understanding new things quickly and can think of adequate solutions to new problems fast.
>
> I call a place a slum if the houses are all in a state of disrepair, if there's rubbish all over the road, and if the place smells.
>
> Someone is rich if he's got a million in the bank.

All the types and forms of unclearness that are mentioned here can occur at all stages of the discussion and they can all be obstacles to the resolution of a dispute.

---

[5]In a *sorites*, linear vagueness can give rise to a special variant of the slippery slope.

[6]Cf. Wittgenstein (1953).

[7]Cf. Naess (1966).

If indeed they happen to hinder the conduct of a critical discussion, they must be regarded as variants of the fallacy of unclearness.

## MISUSING AMBIGUITY

It is only when unclearness is misused in a discourse to frustrate the resolution of a dispute that Rule 10 has been broken. The same effect can result from ambiguous language. Then we have the fallacy of *misusing ambiguity*, which is also (less precisely but more briefly) referred to as *equivocation*, *amphiboly*, or the *ambiguity fallacy*.[8] Misuse of ambiguity is closely related to the fallacy of unclearness and it can occur on its own but also in combination with other fallacies (such as the fallacy of *composition* or the fallacy of *division*). In this section we look at some of the subspecies.

Some examples of ambiguous language are really more like puns than anything else but they are still of the kind that are often cited as examples of the ambiguity fallacy. They are not especially likely to help resolve a dispute, even though they sometimes appear to be meant to be taken seriously. The first example is from Cees Nooteboom's novel *Rituals*:

> "What's it like," Arnold Taads asked, "not having a father?"
>
> This was a man who only asked things to which there was no answer. So he did not answer. Not having a father was *not* having something. So nothing could be said about it.

The following example, from an interview by Ilse Bulhof with the French philosopher Luce Irigaray (*NRC/Handelsblad*, November 25, 1982) appears to be intended perfectly seriously:

> Irigaray is not the only one to remark that women are "nowhere" in philosophical and other nonliterary writing. It is something proved by the well-intended footnotes at the beginning of many recent publications, where we are told that it speaks for itself that "he," where it refers to the reader, also means "she." But is it not highly questionable whether what does not speak can ever speak "for itself"? Before something speaks for itself it must already have been spoken many times—and that "he" also means "she" is something, on the contrary, that has never been said—how then could a man remain a man?
>
> It is questions of this kind which Irigaray puzzles her head about, and her originality lies in her conviction that the persistent absence of women from philosophy is not the fault of bad men but a consequence of language.

Referential indefiniteness as discussed in the previous section could also be termed

---

[8]Cf. for the fallacy of equivocation, Woods and Walton (1989). For the different types of ambiguity (equivocation, amphiboly, accent), see Rescher (1964), Copi (1982), and Olson (1969).

*referential ambiguity*. Apart from this type of ambiguity, there is also such a thing as *semantic ambiguity*, in which a word has more than one meaning, for instance "to affect" (influence/pretend) and "leaf" (part of a plant/piece of paper/part of a table). This type of ambiguity is probably the most familiar to us from everyday discourse. Here is an example of a semantic ambiguity fallacy:

*Mr. Fisher:* "I admit . . . this suit is a bit tight . . . but I do like it so much. . . ."

*Mr. Wenzel:* "Couldn't it be let out?"

*Mr. Fisher:* "Some things cannot be let out . . . nobody wants to hire them."

In this little dialogue the expression "let out" is first used (by Mr. Wenzel) in the sense of make larger, after which it is used (by Mr. Fisher) to mean rent out.

As referential and semantic ambiguity both have to do with the fact that words can have more than one meaning, they are referred to collectively as *lexical ambiguity*. There is also *syntactic ambiguity*, in which it is the structure of the utterance that is responsible for the ambiguity. Consider this example: "This is Herman's portrait." This might mean (a) that it is the portrait that Herman painted, (b) that it is a portrait owned by Herman, or (c) that it is a portrait of Herman.

Questions too may be syntactically ambiguous:

1. Who's Tony?

This question may be answered in the following ways (among others):

1. a. That man at the bar with a bourbon in his hand.
1. b. I am.
1. c. Me, if I'm lucky; it depends on the director.
1. d. A Canadian philosopher.
1. e. A very nice man with a heart of gold.

In argumentation, syntactic ambiguity can also occur:

2. I'm not going with you because it's raining.

This sentence can be paraphrased in at least two ways:

2. a. I'm not going with you and the reason is that it's raining.
2. b. I'm going with you, but for some other reason than that it's raining (e.g., because you are going to see someone I have also long wished to speak to).

Relative clauses may give rise to syntactic ambiguity if it is unclear whether they must be interpreted in a restrictive (informative) sense or a nonrestrictive (uninformative) sense:

4. a. You are best not to have anything to do with Dutchmen, who have no sense of morality.
4. b. You are best not to have anything to do with Dutchmen who have no sense of morality.

As indicated by the comma after "Dutchmen," in (4a) the relative clause "who have no sense of morality" is used nonrestrictively to separate nonessential or parenthetical material from the rest, in (4b) this relative clause is used in a restrictive way. Sentence (4a) means that you must have nothing to do with Dutchmen; the subordinate clause gives the reason for this viewpoint. Sentence (4b) means that you had better have nothing to do with a particular group of Dutchmen, namely those who have no sense of morality; there is a suggestion that you may, if you wish, have dealings with other Dutchmen.

Syntactic ambiguity is sometimes caused by referential words being able to refer to different words in a sentence:

3. Carla gave Sandra the post; it was her last day.

Here it is unclear whether "her" refers to Carla or Sandra.

Referential ambiguity is often caused by unclearness as to what a referential word refers to in the reality to which the sentence relates (the world we live in, the setting of a novel, and so on). Among these referential words are personal pronouns (I, you, he, she, we, you, they), demonstrative pronouns (this, that, these, those), and adverbs of place (here, there); they also include proper nouns (Charles, Diana, James Bond), and other definite descriptions (page 30, *op. cit.*, the undersigned). Here is a funny misuse of referential ambiguity:

*Peter:* "Are you going to Charlie's birthday party?"
*Sally:* "Who are the people that are going to be there?"
*Peter:* "The same people as last year."
*Sally:* "In that case, I can't stay away."

Even if lexical and syntactic ambiguity are combined with semantic ambiguity, the context and situation in which the sentence occurs will usually contain enough information to prevent any misunderstandings due to ambiguity. If not, the fallacy of misusing ambiguity might occur.

## COMPLICATIONS REGARDING USAGE

The various types of fallacious unclearness and fallacious ambiguity can occur separately or in combination. The standpoint "The Royal Library in The Hague is large," for instance, is ambiguous because it could be the size of the building that is at issue or the number of books contained in it. It is also vague, because it is unclear what criteria must be met before either the building or the number of books can be considered large.

A further complication is that the fallacies of unclearness and ambiguity can occur either as independent violations of Rule 10 or combined with violations of one or more other rules for critical discussion. Sometimes, unclearness or ambiguity are primarily instrumental in bringing about an occurrence of other fallacies. In particular, various sorts of implicitness may play a significant role here. The identification of fallacies, difficult as it already is, can then even be more troublesome.

Take, to begin with, the *argumentum ad baculum* and the *argumentum ad hominem* (violations of Rule 1). Such threats and personal attacks are often more effective if they are issued in veiled terms or made indirectly. Sometimes, indeed, the indirectness goes so far as to fake an emphatic denial of any intention to put pressure on the opposing party or attack him personally. The threat or attack is then presented as helpful information with which the listener or reader may do whatever he likes ("I wouldn't want you to be influenced by the fact that I happen to be the chairman of the committee that has to evaluate your work").

In the fallacy of *evading the burden of proof* (violation of Rule 2) implicitness is a means much used by the protagonist to suggest that there is no need to defend his standpoint or to render it immune to criticism. In the first case the standpoint character of an utterance is played down, in the second case the standpoint is exempted from discussion. These effects are achieved by leaving the communicative function of the standpoint undefined and omitting all specific quantifiers from the propositional content.

In the fallacy of the *straw man* (violation of Rule 3) implicitness can play a part both in the communicative function and in the propositional content of the standpoint at issue. An implicitness in the communicative function can be exploited by ascribing an excessively sure standpoint to the protagonist. If too general a standpoint is imputed to him, an implicitness in the propositional content is exploited. Because more often than not the protagonist neither indicates what the strength is of the communicative function nor what the scope is of the propositional content, the antagonist can do so without it being immediately conspicuous.

In the fallacies of using *irrelevant argumentation* and using *nonargumentative means of persuasion* (violations of Rule 4), implicitness is crucial with regard to both the communicative function and the propositional content. The protagonist, for example, is hardly likely to concede in so many words that his argumentation pertains to a standpoint other than the one being discussed (*ignoratio elenchi*) or that, instead of advancing arguments, he is merely playing on the emotions of the audience (*argumentum ad populum*) or parading his own qualities (*argumentum ad verecundiam*). Otherwise nobody would take the slightest notice of what he said.

In the case of *magnifying an unexpressed premise* and *denying an unexpressed premise* (violations of Rule 5) implicitness is a *sine qua non*. The antagonist can only magnify an argument thanks to the fact that it has not been formulated explicitly, and the same applies to the denial of an argument by the protagonist. Only due to the implicitness the antagonist can always maintain that something was really concealed in the protagonist's words, and the protagonist can always protest that he really never said what the antagonist says he said.

*Circular arguments* (violations of Rule 6) are generally based on differences in formulations, so that it is only on closer inspection that it becomes clear that the formulations amount to the same thing. Because the similarity between premise and standpoint is not expressed explicitly but remains implicit, the circularity of the argument is not immediately obvious.

In the *argumentum ad consequentiam* and the fallacies of the *slippery slope*, *post hoc ergo propter hoc* and *overhasty generalization* (violations of Rule 7), either an inappropriate argumentation scheme has been chosen or the argumentation scheme that has been chosen is used in an incorrect way. The right choice of an argumentation scheme and the way in which it is to be used generally depends on the type and scope of the proposition that is to be tested. In ordinary discourse however, it is neither always immediately clear whether a proposition is descriptive, evaluative, or inciting, nor whether its scope is singular, particular, or universal. The type of a proposition is often unclear because it is a part of a speech act whose communicative function is often implicit; its scope is often in doubt because it has not been explicitly indicated.

In the case of the fallacies of *denying the antecedent* and *affirming the consequent* and those of *composition* and *division* (violations of Rule 8) it is not immediately obvious to some that the argument is invalid. To establish its invalidity, it must be translated from ordinary speech into the language of a logical system, say that of propositional logic. However, the wording in ordinary speech will not usually point to one particular translation. In the composition and division fallacies there is the extra problem that the transferability of a property cannot be read off directly from the terms used. Whether a property is absolute or relative, and whether it is structure-dependent or structure-independent, can generally only be established after a thorough analysis of the terms used.

In the fallacy of *making an absolute of the failure of the defense* or *argumentum ad ignorantiam* (violation of Rule 9) the antagonist is often also guilty of the fallacy of the *false dilemma*. However, the confusion of contrary propositions with contradictory propositions which accompanies this fallacy is, again, not always immediately apparent from the terms that are used. The terms "open" and "closed," for example, are contradictory whereas "hot" and "cold" are contrary, but there is no way of seeing this just by looking at the words. Here again, a correct analysis of the terms is indispensable.

This short survey shows that usage, notably implicit use of language, plays an important role in fallacies in which the true fault lies elsewhere. The implicitness involved may relate to the communicative function of the speech act concerned (*argumentum ad baculum* or *ad hominem*), the propositional content (*circular* or *invalid argument*), or both (*straw man* or *argumentum ad ignorantiam*). The significance that usage characteristics such as implicitness can have for the production of fallacies may vary considerably. Sometimes implicitness is a phenomenon that conveniently accompanies the occurrence of the fallacy (*straw man*), sometimes it is more like a helpful tool for bringing about the fallacy (*argumentum ad baculum*), and sometimes it is a prerequisite for the fallacy to be possible at all (*magnifying an unexpressed premise*).

# Conclusion

## RULES FOR CRITICAL DISCUSSION

In order to be able to wind up our discussion of the fallacies in argumentative discourse with a final comparison between the pragma-dialectical approach and the more traditional approaches, it might be useful to start with bringing together the points made so far by summarizing our main findings. We first list the 10 rules for critical discussion that have been introduced in the previous chapters. Next, we give an overview of violations of the rules that hinder the resolution of a dispute at the various stages of the discussion. Finally, we show for a great many of the traditional fallacies how they can be more systematically accounted for by considering them as violations of rules for critical discussion.

These are the rules for critical discussion that we have formulated in the preceding chapters:

Rule 1: *Parties must not prevent each other from advancing standpoints or casting doubt on standpoints.*

Rule 2: *A party that advances a standpoint is obliged to defend it if the other party asks him to do so.*

Rule 3: *A party's attack on a standpoint must relate to the standpoint that has indeed been advanced by the other party.*

Rule 4: *A party may defend his standpoint only by advancing argumentation relating to that standpoint.*

Rule 5: *A party may not falsely present something as a premise that has been left unexpressed by the other party or deny a premise that he himself has left implicit.*

Rule 6: *A party may not falsely present a premise as an accepted starting point nor deny a premise representing an accepted starting point.*

Rule 7: *A party may not regard a standpoint as conclusively defended if the defense does not take place by means of an appropriate argumentation scheme that is correctly applied.*

Rule 8: *In his argumentation a party may only use arguments that are logically valid or capable of being validated by making explicit one or more unexpressed premisses.*

Rule 9: *A failed defense of a standpoint must result in the party that put forward the standpoint retracting it and a conclusive defense in the other party retracting his doubt about the standpoint.*

Rule 10: *A party must not use formulations that are insufficiently clear or confusingly ambiguous and he must interpret the other party's formulations as carefully and accurately as possible.*

## VIOLATIONS OF RULES FOR CRITICAL DISCUSSION

There are, of course, a lot of things that can go wrong in argumentative discourse aimed at resolving a dispute. Some of the most important violations of the rules for critical discussion are listed here. Although this list is by no means complete, it gives a good impression of the fallacious moves that can erroneously be made at the various stages of the discussion.

*Violations of Rule 1 by the protagonist or antagonist at the confrontation stage:*

1. *With reference to standpoints:*
   - ban standpoints
   - declare standpoints sacrosanct
2. *With reference to opponent:*
   - put pressure on the other party by playing on his feelings of compassion or threatening him with sanctions
   - make personal attack on the other party by
     - depicting him as stupid, bad, unreliable, and so forth
     - casting suspicion on his motives
     - pointing out an inconsistency between his ideas and deeds in past and/or present

*Violations of Rule 2 by the protagonist at the opening stage:*

1. *Evading the burden of proof*
   - presenting the standpoint as self-evident

- giving a personal guarantee of the rightness of the standpoint
- immunizing the standpoint against criticism

2. *Shifting the burden of proof*
   - *in a nonmixed dispute:*
     The antagonist must show that the standpoint is wrong
   - *in a mixed dispute:*
     Only the other party must defend his standpoint as a result of the principle of presumption or the criterion of fairness

*Violations of Rule 3 by the protagonist or antagonist at all the discussion stages of mixed discussions:*

1. *Imputing a fictitious standpoint to the other party*
   - emphatically advancing the opposite as one's own standpoint
   - referring to the views of the group to which someone belongs
   - creating an imaginary opponent
2. *Distorting the other party's standpoint*
   - taking utterances out of context
   - oversimplification (ignoring nuances or qualifications)
   - exaggeration (absolutization or generalization)

*Violations of Rule 4 by the protagonist at the argumentation stage:*

1. *The argumentation does not refer to the standpoint under discussion*
   - irrelevant argumentation
2. *The standpoint is defended not by argumentation, but by nonargumentative means of persuasion*
   - playing on the emotions of the audience
   - parading one's own qualities

*Violations of Rule 5 by the protagonist or the antagonist at the argumentation stage:*

1. *Denying an unexpressed premise* (by the protagonist)
2. *Magnifying an unexpressed premise* (by the antagonist)

*Violations of Rule 6 by the protagonist or the antagonist at the argumentation stage:*

1. *Falsely presenting something as a common starting point* (by the protagonist):
   - falsely presenting a premise as self-evident
   - wrapping up a proposition in a presupposition
   - hiding away a premise in an unexpressed premise
   - advancing argumentation that amounts to the same thing as the standpoint
2. *Denying a premise representing a common starting point* (by the antagonist):
   - casting doubt on an accepted starting point

*Violations of Rule 7 by the protagonist at the argumentation stage:*

1. *Relying on an inappropriate argumentation scheme*
   - inappropriate choice of symptomatic argumentation
   - inappropriate choice of similarity argumentation
   - inappropriate choice of instrumental argumentation
2. *Using an appropriate argumentation scheme incorrectly*
   - incorrect use of symptomatic argumentation
   - incorrect use of similarity argumentation
   - incorrect use of instrumental argumentation

*Violations of Rule 8 by the protagonist at the argumentation stage:*

1. *Confusing necessary and sufficient conditions*
   - a necessary condition is treated as a sufficient condition
   - a sufficient condition is treated as a necessary condition
2. *Confusing the properties of parts and wholes*
   - a relative or structure-dependent property of a whole is ascribed to a part of the whole
   - a relative or structure-dependent property of a part of the whole is ascribed to the whole

*Violations of Rule 9 by the protagonist or antagonist at the closing stage:*

1. *Making an absolute of the success of the defense* (by the protagonist):
   - conclude that a standpoint is true just because it has been successfully defended
2. *Making an absolute of the failure of the defense* (by the antagonist):
   - conclude that a standpoint is true just because the opposite has not been successfully defended

*Violations of Rule 10 by protagonist or antagonist at all stages of the discussion:*

1. *Misusing unclearness*
   - structural unclearness
   - implicitness
   - indefiniteness
   - unfamiliarity
   - vagueness
2. *Misusing ambiguity*
   - referential ambiguity
   - syntactic ambiguity
   - semantic ambiguity

## TRADITIONAL FALLACIES AS VIOLATIONS OF RULES FOR CRITICAL DISCUSSION

The fallacies that are traditionally listed as such can be more systematically accounted for by considering them as violations of rules for critical discussion. This can be shown on the basis of a pragma-dialectical analysis of a number of the most well-known traditional fallacies.

| FALLACY | RULE | STAGE | PARTY |
|---|---|---|---|
| 1. *Affirming the consequent*<br>Confusing necessary and sufficient conditions by treating a necessary condition as a sufficient condition | 8 | 3 | P |
| 2. *Ambiguity (fallacy of)*<br>Misusing referential, syntactic, or semantic ambiguity | 10 | 1–4 | P/A |
| 3. *Argumentum ad baculum*<br>Putting pressure on the other party by threatening him with sanctions | 1 | 1 | P/A |
| 4. *Argumentum ad consequentiam*<br>Using an inappropriate (causal) argumentation scheme by rejecting a descriptive standpoint because of its undesired consequences | 7 | 3 | P |
| 5. *Argumentum ad hominem (direct personal attack, abusive)*<br>Doubting the expertise, intelligence, or good faith of the other party | 1 | 1 | P/A |
| 6. *Argumentum ad hominem (indirect personal attack, circumstantial)*<br>Casting suspicion on the other party's motives | 1 | 1 | P/A |
| 7. *Argumentum ad hominem (tu quoque)*<br>Pointing out an inconsistency between the other party's ideas and deeds in past and/or present | 1 | 1 | P/A |
| 8. *Argumentum ad ignorantiam*$_1$<br>Shifting the burden of proof in a nonmixed dispute by requiring the antagonist to show that the protagonist's standpoint is wrong | 2 | 2 | P |

| FALLACY | RULE | STAGE | PARTY |
|---|---|---|---|
| 9. *Argumentum ad ignorantiam*$_2$ Making an absolute of the failure of the defense by concluding that a standpoint is true just because the opposite has not been successfully defended | 9 | 4 | A |
| 10. *Argumentum ad misericordiam* Putting pressure on the other party by playing on his feelings of compassion | 1 | 1 | P |
| 11. *Argumentum ad populum (populistic fallacy)* (variant of *argumentum ad verecundiam*)$_1$ Using an inappropriate (symptomatic) argumentation scheme by presenting the standpoint as right because everybody thinks it is right | 7 | 3 | P |
| 12. *Argumentum ad populum*$_2$ Defending a standpoint by using nonargumentative means of persuasion and playing on the emotions of the audience | 4 | 3 | P |
| 13. *Argumentum ad verecundiam*$_1$ Using an inappropriate (symptomatic) argumentation scheme by presenting the standpoint as right because an authority says it is right | 7 | 3 | P |
| 14. *Composition (fallacy of)* Confusing the properties of parts and wholes by ascribing a relative or structure-dependent property of a part of the whole to the whole | 8 | 3 | P |
| 15. *Denying the antecedent* Confusing necessary and sufficient conditions by treating a sufficient condition as a necessary condition | 8 | 3 | P |
| 16. *Division (fallacy of)* Confusing the properties of parts and wholes by ascribing a relative or structure-dependent property of a whole to a part of the whole | 8 | 3 | P |

| FALLACY | RULE | STAGE | PARTY |
|---|---|---|---|
| 17. *False analogy*<br>Using the appropriate argumentation scheme of analogy incorrectly by not fulfilling the conditions for a correct comparison | 7 | 3 | P |
| 18. *Ignoratio elenchi (irrelevant argumentation)*<br>Putting forward argumentation which does not refer to the standpoint under discussion | 4 | 3 | P |
| 19. *Many questions (fallacy of)*<br>Falsely presenting something as a common starting point by wrapping up a standpoint in the presupposition of a question | 6 | 3 | P |
| 20. *Petitio principii (begging the question, circular reasoning)*<br>Falsely presenting something as a common starting point by advancing argumentation that amounts to the same thing as the standpoint | 6 | 3 | P |
| 21. *Post hoc ergo propter hoc*<br>Using the appropriate argumentation scheme of causality incorrectly by inferring a cause-effect relation from the mere observation that two events take place one after the other | 7 | 3 | P |
| 22. *Secundum quid (hasty generalization)*<br>Using the appropriate argumentation scheme of concomitance incorrectly by making generalizations based upon observations that are not representative or not sufficient | 7 | 3 | P |
| 23. *Shifting the burden of proof$_1$ (argumentum ad ignorantiam)*<br>Requiring the antagonist in a nonmixed dispute to show that the protagonist's standpoint is wrong | 2 | 2 | P |

| FALLACY | RULE | STAGE | PARTY |
|---|---|---|---|
| 24. *Shifting the burden of proof$_2$* Requiring only the other party in a mixed dispute to defend his standpoint due to the Principle of Presumption or the Criterion of Fairness | 2 | 2 | P |
| 25. *Slippery slope* Using the appropriate argumentation scheme of causality (argument from consequence) incorrectly by erroneously suggesting that by taking the proposed course of action one will be going from bad to worse | 7 | 3 | P |
| 26. *Straw man$_1$* Imputing a fictitious standpoint to the other party or distorting the other party's standpoint | 3 | 1-4 | P/A |

## ADVANTAGES OF THE PRAGMA-DIALECTICAL APPROACH

A simple comparison between the overview of violations of the rules for critical discussion and the overview of traditional fallacies makes clear that a more systematic account of the fallacies can be given if the fallacies are considered as violations of the rules for critical discussion. Even more importantly, this comparison also shows that they are treated in a subtler way, so that the analysis of fallacies becomes more refined. Fallacies that were only nominally lumped together are now clearly distinguished, and genuinely related fallacies that were separated are brought together. Thus analyzing the two variants of *argumentum ad populum* as violations of different rules (4 and 7) makes, for instance, clear that they are, in fact, *not* one of a kind and analyzing one particular variant of *argumentum ad verecundiam* and one particular variant of *argumentum ad populum* as a violation of the *same* rule (7) makes clear that seen from the perspective of resolving a dispute, these variants *are* one of a kind. Here are a few more examples of some further distinctions that easily escape attention in the traditional approach:

| | | | |
|---|---|---|---|
| 10a. *Argumentum ad misericordiam (as an ethical fallacy)* Swaying the audience in one's own favor by very modestly presenting oneself as a layman | 4 | 3 | P |

| | | | |
|---|---|---|---|
| 13a. *Argumentum ad verecundiam*$_2$ Evading the burden of proof by giving a personal guarantee of the rightness of the standpoint | 2 | 2 | P |
| 13b. *Argumentum ad verecundiam*$_3$ *(as an ethical fallacy)* The standpoint is defended by nonargumentative means of persuasion and parading one's own qualities | 4 | 3 | P |
| 26a. *Straw man*$_2$ Magnifying an unexpressed premise | 5 | 3 | A |

It is an extra asset of the violations of rules for critical discussion approach that even so far unrecognized "new" categories of obstacles for resolving disputes do emerge that should be considered as fallacies. Here are some examples:

| | | | |
|---|---|---|---|
| 27. *Declaring a standpoint sacrosanct* | 1 | 1 | P |
| 28. *Evading the burden of proof*$_1$ Immunizing the standpoint against criticism | 2 | 2 | P |
| 29. *Denying an unexpressed premise* | 5 | 3 | P |
| 30. *Denying an accepted starting-point* | 6 | 3 | A |
| 31. *Falsely presenting something as a common starting point* | 6 | 3 | P |
| 32. *Evading the burden of proof*$_2$ Falsely presenting a premise as self-evident | 6 | 3 | P |
| 33. *Making an absolute of the success of the defense* | 9 | 4 | P |
| 34. *Structural unclearness, implicitness, indefiniteness, unfamiliarity, vagueness* | 10 | 1-4 | P/A |

Rather than considering the fallacies to belong, just like that, to an unstructured list of nominal categories, which happen to have come down to us from the past, as occurs in the Standard Treatment, or considering all fallacies to be violations of one and the same (validity) norm, as occurs in the logico-centric approaches, in the pragma-dialectical approach to fallacies a functional variety of norms is differentiated. Instead of restricting the norm for fallaciousness to formal validity, a whole series of other norms than just the logical one is taken into account.

In resolving a dispute by way of a critical discussion, there are, after all, various stages to be distinguished and in each of them certain fallacies can occur if the rules are not observed. In this perspective, the logical norm of validity gets its proper (and limited) place in the argumentation stage.

The pragma-dialectical ideal model specifies the rules for reasonable argumentative discourse as rules for the performance of speech acts in a critical discussion aimed at resolving a dispute. For each stage of the discussion, the rules indicate when participants intending to resolve the dispute should carry out a particular move. Fallacies are analyzed as incorrect moves that violate one or more of the discussion rules. This explains why not only logical mistakes are included among the fallacies but also many other things that can go wrong in argumentative discourse.

# Epilogue

Our general aim with *Argumentation, Communication, and Fallacies* was to elucidate the pragma-dialectical perspective on the analysis and evaluation of argumentative discourse. How have we proceeded in attempting to achieve this goal? And where has this led us?

The book consists of two parts. Part I, "Argumentation and Communication" lays the theoretical foundation for Part II, "Communication and Fallacies." The main purpose of Part II is to show that the pragma-dialectical approach to fallacies leads to a much clearer outcome than the logico-centric approaches, whether they be traditional or modern. It is the communicative perspective in which the fallacies are looked at that accounts for the gains. Fallacies are no longer, one-sidedly, considered as exclusively flaws of reasoning, but are put in the context of a critical discussion consisting of a diversity of speech acts distributed over the various stages of the discussion. Thus analyzing the fallacies as obstacles for resolving a dispute by way of argumentative discourse, the problem of the fallacies is seen as an integral part of the problem language users have in adequately realizing their communicative and interactional goals in a specific speech event that takes place in a specific context and a specific situation.

It is worth remembering that in real-life settings it is only in conjunction with the fulfillment of higher order conditions concerning attitudes and circumstances that observance of the rules can constitute a sufficient condition for resolving a dispute. Furthermore, of course, not all discourse is argumentative. However, there hardly ever is any discourse without, at least, some argumentative aspects. In a pragma-dialectical analysis, a reconstruction of the discourse should be given that does justice to these aspects. This can be achieved by using the strategies of maximally dialectical analysis and maximally argumentative interpretation.

Finally, even argumentative discourse that is presented monologically, such as a parliamentary address or a leading article in a newspaper, can be reconstructed as (part of) a critical discussion. Implicitly, there is always another party that the arguer is trying to convince.

The main purpose of Part I is to provide the theoretical background for an appropriate communicative analysis of argumentative discourse. Such an analysis is necessary for several reasons. If it is unclear which standpoint is being defended, there is no way of telling whether the argumentation is conclusive. In case more than one standpoint is being defended, it must be clear which language user is acting as the protagonist of which standpoint; otherwise it would be impossible to tell whether the various arguments for a standpoint constitute a coherent whole. Where crucial unexpressed premises are overlooked or the argumentation structure is misrepresented, an adequate evaluation is impossible. In an analytic overview of the argumentative discourse all these factors affecting the outcome of the critical discussion must be incorporated.

Among the elements that are relevant to the resolution of the dispute and therefore to the analytic overview are the points at issue in the dispute, the type of dispute, the positions that the parties adopt and their discussion roles, the stages in the discussion, the explicit and implicit arguments that are put forward, and the argumentation structure. In order to get a firm and coherent conceptual grasp on these matters, a theoretically-motivated terminological apparatus has been presented. The pragma-dialectical terminology includes, among other things, mixed and nonmixed dispute, protagonist and antagonist, confrontation, opening, argumentation and concluding stage, unexpressed premise, and simple and complex argumentation. As is shown by the aforementioned overviews, these terminological distinctions prove to be very useful in describing the various fallacies.

Due to the amended theory of speech acts and the formulated communication rules, a pragmatic explanation could be given of indirect speech acts and unexpressed premises, which adds considerably to the findings of the purely logical approaches. In making unexpressed premises explicit, relying on pragmatic knowledge of the verbal and nonverbal context, the logical minimum can be replaced by a pragmatic optimum. As speakers and writers know that in many respects they have undertaken more than the words they have used literally mean, they may be held liable for implicit commitments such as those formulated in the pragmatic optimum. This pragmatic optimum is, by the way, usually also a useful pointer to the argumentation scheme that is being used in the argumentation.

In this two-part study we have attempted to give shape to a critical rationalist ideal of reasonableness by explaining our pragma-dialectical views concerning the analysis of argumentative discourse and the identification of fallacies. The dialectical aspect of our approach consists, basically, in postulating two parties who attempt to resolve a difference of opinion by means of a methodical exchange of moves in a critical discussion, the pragmatic aspect in describing their moves in the discussion as exchanges of speech acts. In treating argumentative discourse pragma-dialectically, we have externalized, functionalized, socialized, and dialectified the subject-matter of the study of argumentation. Along these lines we think to have achieved the combination of normative and descriptive insight which is a prerequisite for dealing adequately with argumentative discourse in a consistent research program.

# References

Albert, H. (1967). *Marktsoziologie und Entscheidungslogik* [Sociology of the market and decision logic]. Berlijn: Herman Luchterhand Verlag.
Albert, H. (1975). *Traktat über kritische Vernunft* [Treatise on critical reason] (3rd rev. ed.). Tübingen: Mohr. (Original work published 1968).
Albert, H. (1985). *Treatise on critical reason*. Princeton: Princeton University Press. Translation of: Hans Albert, *Traktat über kritische Vernunft*, Tübingen: Mohr, 1975.
Austin, J.L. (1962). *How to do things with words*. Cambridge, MA: Harvard University Press.
Austin, J.L. (1970). Other minds. In *Philosophical papers* (2nd ed., pp. 76–116). London: Oxford University Press.
Ballmer, Th., & Brennenstuhl, W. (1981). *Speech act classification. A study in the lexical analysis of English speech activity verbs*. Berlin: Springer.
Bar-Hillel, Y. (1964). More on the fallacy of composition. *Mind, 73*, 125–126.
Barth, E.M., & Krabbe, E.C.W. (1982). *From axiom to dialogue. A philosophical study of logics and argumentation*. Berlin, New York: De Gruyter.
Barth, E.M., & Martens, J.L. (1977). Argumentum ad hominem: From chaos to formal dialectic. *Logique et Analyse, 77/78*, 76–96.
Barth, E.M., & Martens, J.L. (Eds.). (1982). *Argumentation. Approaches to theory formation. Containing the contributions to the Groningen Conference on the theory of argumentation, October 1978*. Amsterdam: John Benjamins.
Beardsley, M.C. (1975). *Thinking straight. Principles of reasoning for readers and writers* (4th ed.). Englewood Cliffs, NJ: Prentice-Hall.
Belnap, N.D., Jr. (1969). Questions: Their presuppositions, and how they can fail to arise. In K. Lambert (Ed.), *The logical way of doing things*. New Haven and London: Yale University Press.
Billig, M. (1988). The notion of "prejudice": Some rhetorical and ideological aspects. *Text, 8*(1/2), pp. 91–110.
Biro, J., & Siegel, H. (1991). Normativity, argumentation and an epistemic theory of fallacies. In F.H. van Eemeren, R. Grootendorst, J.A. Blair, & Ch. Willard (Eds.), *Proceedings of the Second ISSA Conference on Argumentation 1990*. Amsterdam: SICSAT.
Blair, J.A., & Johnson, R.H. (Eds.). (1980). *Informal logic: The first international symposium*. Inverness, CA: Edgepress.

Braet, A.C. (in press). Ethos, pathos and logos in Aristotle's Rhetoric: A re-examination. *Argumentation*.

Broyles, J.E. (1975). The fallacies of composition and division. *Dialogue, 15*, 241–255.

Bühler, K. (1934). *Sprachtheorie* [Speech theory]. Jena: Fischer.

Burke, M. (1985). Unstated premises. *Informal Logic, 7*(2/3), 107–118.

Copi, I.M. (1982). *Introduction to logic* (6th ed.). New York: MacMillan.

Crawshay-Williams, R. (1957). *Methods and criteria of reasoning. An inquiry into the structure of controversy*. London: Routledge & Kegan Paul.

Damer, T.E. (1980). *Attacking faulty reasoning*. Belmont, CA: Wadsworth.

Dascal, M. (1977). Conversational relevance. *Journal of Pragmatics, 1*, 309–328.

Dijk, Teun A. van. (1983). Cognitive and conversational strategies in the expression of ethnic prejudice. *Text, 3*(4), 375–404.

Dijk, Teun A. van. (1984). *Prejudice in discourse*. Amsterdam: John Benjamins.

Dijk, Teun A. van. (1988). Social cognition, social power and social discourse. *Text, 8*(1/2), 129–157.

Edmondson, W. (1981). *Spoken discourse. A model for analysis*. London/New York: Longman.

Eemeren, F.H. van. (1987). Argumentation studies' five estates. In J.W. Wenzel (Ed.), *Argument and critical practice. Proceedings of the Fifth SCA/AFA Conference on Argumentation* (pp. 9–24). Annandale, VA: Speech Comunication Association.

Eemeren, F.H. van, & Grootendorst, R. (1984). *Speech acts in argumentative discussions. A theoretical model for the analysis of discussions directed towards solving conflicts of opinion*. Dordrecht, Cinnaminson: Foris/Berlin: Mouton de Gruyter. PDA1.

Eemeren, F.H. van, & Grootendorst, R. (1988). Rationale for a pragma-dialectical perspective. *Argumentation, 2*(2), 271–291.

Eemeren, F.H. van, Grootendorst, R., & Kruiger, T. (1987). *Handbook of argumentation theory*. Dordrecht-Providence: Foris/Berlin: Mouton de Gruyter. PDA7.

Eemeren, F.H. van, Grootendorst, R., & Meuffels, B. (1989). The skill of identifying argumentation. *Argumentation and Advocacy, 25*(4), 239–345.

Eemeren, F.H. van, Grootendorst, R., Jackson, S.A., & Jacobs, C.S. (in press). *Reconstructing Argumentative Discourse*.

Ennis, R.H. (1982). Identifying implicit assumptions. *Synthese, 51*(1), 61–86.

Ennis, R.H. (1987). A taxonomy of critical thinking dispositions and abilities. In J. Baron & R. Sternberg (Eds.), *Teaching for thinking* (pp. 9–26). New York: W.H. Freeman.

Evans, J.St.B.T. (1982). *The psychology of deductive reasoning*. London/Boston: Routledge.

Fair, F. (1973). The fallacy of many questions: Or, how to stop beating your wife. *Southwestern Journal of Philosophy, 4*, 89–92.

Feteris, E.T. (1987). The dialectical role of the judge in a legal process. In J.W. Wenzel (Ed.), *Argument and critical practice. Proceedings of the Fifth SCA/AFA Conference on Argumentation* (pp. 335–339). Annandale, VA: Speech Communication Association.

Feyerabend, P. (1970). Consolations for the specialist. In I. Lakatos & A. Musgrave (Eds.), *Criticism and the growth of knowledge* (pp. 197–230). London/New York: Cambridge University Press.

Finocchiaro, M.A. (1974). The concept of ad hominem argument in Galileo and Locke. *The Philosophical Forum, 5*.

Finocchiaro, M.A. (1980). *Galileo and the art of reasoning. Rhetorical foundations of logic and scientific method*. Dordrecht: Reidel.

Finocchiaro, M.A. (1981). Fallacies and the evaluation of reasoning. *American Philosophical Quarterly, 18*, 13–22.

Finocchiaro, M.A. (1987a). Six types of fallaciousness: Toward a realistic theory of logical criticism. *Argumentation, 1*(3), 263–282.

Finocchiaro, M.A. (1987b). An historical approach to the study of argumentation. In F.H. van Eemeren, R. Grootendorst, J.A. Blair, & C. Willard (Eds.), *Argumentation. Across the lines of discipline* (pp. 81–91). Proceedings of the Conference on Argumentation 1986. Dordrecht/Providence: Foris/Berlin: Mouton de Gruyter. PDA 3.

Fisher, A. (1988). *The logic of real arguments*. Cambridge: Cambridge University Press.

Fogelin, R.J. (1978). *Understanding argument. An introduction to informal logic.* New York: Harcourt Brace Jovanovich.

Freeman, J.B. (1988). *Thinking logically. Basic concepts for reasoning.* New York: McGraw-Hill.

Gerber, D. (1974). On argumentum ad hominem. *Personalist, 55,* 23–29.

Gill, C. (1984). The ethos/pathos distinction in rhetorical and literary criticism. *Classical Quarterly, 34,* 149–166.

Goodnight, G.T. (1980). The liberal and the conservative presumptions: On political philosopy and the foundation of public argument. In J. Rhodes & S. Newell (Eds.), *Proceedings of the Summer Conference on Argumentation* (pp. 304–337). Annandale, VA: Speech Communication Association.

Goodwin, P.D., & Wenzel, J.W. (1979). Proverbs and practical reasoning: A study in socio-logic. *The Quarterly Journal of Speech, 65,* 289–302.

Govier, T. (1981). Worries about *tu quoque* as a fallacy. *Informal Logic Newsletter, 3,* 2–4.

Govier, T. (1982). What's wrong with slippery slope arguments? *Canadian Journal of Philosophy, 12,* 303–316.

Govier, T. (1985). *A practical study of argument.* Belmont, CA: Wadsworth.

Govier, T. (1987). *Problems in argument analysis and evaluation.* Dordrecht: Foris/Berlin: Mouton de Gruyter. PDA 5.

Govier, T. (1988). *A practical study of argument* (2nd ed.). Belmont, CA: Wadsworth.

Grice, H.P. (1975). Logic and conversation. In P. Cole & J.L. Morgan (Eds.), *Syntax and semantics 3: Speech acts* (pp. 45–38). New York: Academic Press.

Grice, H.P. (1989). *Studies in the way of words.* Cambridge, MA/London: Harvard University Press.

Grize, J-B. (1982). *De la logique à l'argumentation* [About the logic of argumentation]. Genève: Droz.

Haack, S. (1978). *Philosophy of logics.* Cambridge: Cambridge University Press.

Hamblin, C.L. (1970). *Fallacies.* London: Methuen.

Hare, R.M. (1963). *Freedom and reason.* Oxford: Clarendon.

Hare, R.M. (1981). *Moral thinking: Its levels, method and point.* Oxford: Clarendon.

Harman, G. (1986). *Change in view. Principles of reasoning.* Cambridge, MA: MIT.

Hastings, A.C. (1962). *A reformulation of the modes of reasoning in argumentation.* Unpublished doctoral dissertation, Northwestern University, Evanston, IL.

Hintikka, J. (1976). *The semantics of questions and the questions of semantics.* Amsterdam: North-Holland.

Hintikka, J. (1981). The logic of information-seeking dialogues: A model. In W. Becker & W.K. Essler (Eds.), *Konzepte der Dialektik* (pp 212–231). Frankfurt: Vittorio Klostermann.

Hintikka, J. (1987). The fallacy of fallacies. In *Argumentation, 1*(3), 211–238.

Hitchcock, D. (1987). Enthymematic arguments. In F.H. van Eemeren, R. Grootendorst, J.A. Blair, & Ch. Willard (Eds.), *Argumentation. Across the lines of discipline* (pp. 289–298). Proceedings of the Conference on Argumentation 1986. Dordrecht/Providence: Foris/Berlin: Mouton de Gruyter. PDA 3.

Hoaglund, J. (1982). Argumentum ad hominem: aut bonum aut malum? *Informal Logic Newsletter, 4*(3), 7–9.

Iseminger, G. (1986). Relatedness logic and entailment. *Journal of Non-Classical Logic, 3,* 5–23.

Jackson, S. (1985). What can speech acts do for argumentation? In J.R. Cox, M.O. Sillars, & G.B. Walker (Eds.), *Arguments and social practice. Proceedings of the Fourth SCA/AFA Conference on Argumentation* (pp. 127–138). Annandale, VA: Speech Communication Association.

Jackson, S., & Jacobs, S. (1980). Structure of conversational argument: Pragmatic bases for the enthymeme. *Quarterly Journal of Speech, 66,* 251–265.

Jackson, S., & Jacobs, S. (1981). Argument as a natural category: The routine grounds for arguing in conversation. *Western Journal of Speech Communication, 45,* 118–132.

Jacobs, S., & Jackson, S. (1982). Conversational argument: A discourse analytic approach. In J.R. Cox & C.A. Willard (Eds.), *Advances in argumentation theory and research* (pp. 205–237). Carbondale/Edwardsville: Southern Illinois University Press.

Jacobs, S., & Jackson, S. (1983). Strategy and structure in conversational influence attempts. *Communication Monographs, 50*, 285–304.

Jason, G. (1987). The nature of the *argumentum ad baculum*. *Philosophia, 17*, 491–499.

Johnson-Laird, P.N. (1983). Thinking as a skill. In J.St.B.T. Evans (Ed.), *Thinking and reasoning: Psychological approaches* (pp. 164–196). London/Boston: Routledge.

Johnson, R.H., & Blair, J.A. (1983). *Logical self-defense*. Toronto: McGraw-Hill.

Johnstone, H.W., Jr. (1952). Philosophy and argumentum ad hominem. *Journal of Philosophy, 49*, 489–498.

Johnstone, H.W., Jr. (1970). "Philosophy and argumentum ad hominem" revisited. *Revue Internationale de Philosophie, 24*, 107–116.

Kamlah, W., & Lorenzen, P. (1984). *Logical propaedeutic. Pre-school of reasonable discourse*. Lanham, NY: University Press of America.

Kasher, A. (1982). Gricean inference revisited. *Philosophica, 29*, 25–44.

Kempson, R.M. (1975). *Presuppositions and the delimitation of semantics*. Cambridge: Cambridge University Press.

Kennedy, G.A. (1963). *The art of persuasion in Greece*. Princeton, NJ: Princeton University Press.

Kennedy, G.A. (1972). *The art of rhetoric in the Roman world*. Princeton, NJ: Princeton University Press.

Kennedy, G.A. (1980). *Classical rhetoric and its christian and secular tradition from ancient to modern times*. London: Croom Helm.

Kielkopf, C.F. (1980). Relevant appeals to force, pity and popular pieties. *Informal Logic Newsletter, 2*(2), 2–5.

Krabbe, E.C.W. (1982). Theory of argumentation and the dialectical garb of formal logic. In E.M. Barth & J.L. Martens (Eds.), *Argumentation. Approaches to theory formation. Containing the contributions the Groningen Conference on the theory of argumentation, October 1978* (pp. 123–132). Amsterdam: John Benjamins.

Kreckel, M. (1981). *Shared knowledge and communicative acts in natural discourse*. London: Academic Press.

Kuhn, T.S. (1970). *The structure of scientific revolutions* (2nd ed.). Chicago: University of Chicago Press.

Kuhn, T.S. (1974). Reflections on my critics. In I. Lakatos & A. Musgrave (Eds.), *Criticism and the growth of knowledge* (pp. 231–278). London/New York: Cambridge University Press.

Lakoff, R. (1973). The logic of politeness; or, minding your p's and q's. In *Papers from the Ninth Regional Meeting of the Chicago Linguistic Society* (pp. 292–305). Chicago: Chicago Linguistic Society.

Lambert, K., & Ulrich, W. (1980). *The nature of argument*. New York: MacMillan.

Leddy, T. (1986). Is there a fallacy of small sample? *Informal Logic, 8*(1), 53–56.

Leech, G.N. (1983). *Principles of pragmatics*. London/New York: Longman.

Leisi, E. (1952). *Der Wortinhalt: seine Struktur im Deutschen und Englischen* [The content of words: its structure in German and English]. Heidelberg: Quelle & Meyer.

Levinson, S.C. (1983). *Pragmatics*. Cambridge: Cambridge University Press.

Locke, J. (1961). Of reason. In *An essay concerning human understanding* (Book IV, Chapter XVII, 1690). Dent, London: J.W. Yolton.

Lyons, J. (1971). *Introduction to theoretical linguistics*. Cambridge: Cambridge University Press.

MacKenzie, J.D. (1979). Question-begging in non-cumulative systems. *Journal of Philosophical Logic, 8*, 117–133.

MacKenzie, P.T. (1981). Ad hominem and ad verecundiam. *Informal Logic Newsletter, 3*(3), 9–11.

Meyer, M. (1986a). *De la problématologie*. Bruxelles: Mardaga.

Meyer, M. (1986b). *From logic to rhetoric*. Amsterdam: John Benjamins.

Minot, W.S. (1981). A rhetorical view of fallacies: *ad hominem* and *ad populum*. *The Rhetoric Society Quarterly, 11*, 222–235.

Naess, A. (1966). *Communication and argument. Elements of applied semantics*. London: Allen & Unwin.

Nolt, J.E. (1984). *Informal logic: Possible worlds and imagination*. New York: McGraw-Hill.

O'Keefe, D.J. (1990). *Persuasion. Theory and research*. Newbury Park, CA: Sage.

Olson, R.G. (1969). *Meaning and argument. Elements of logic*. New York: Harcourt, Brace and World.

Parker, R.A. (1984). *Tu quoque* arguments: A rhetorical perspective. *Journal of the American Forensic Association, 20*, 123–132.

Peirce, C.S. (1955). What is a leading principle. In J. Buchler (Ed.), *Philosophical writings of Peirce* (pp. 129–134). New York: Dover Publications.

Paul, R.W. (1982). Teaching critical thinking in the "strong" sense: A focus on self-deception, world views, and a dialectical mode of analysis. *Informal Logic Newsletter, 4*(2), 2–7.

Perelman, C., & Olbrechts-Tyteca, L. (1958). *La nouvelle rhétorique; traité de l'argumentation* [The new rhetoric: A treatise on argumentation]. Bruxelles: l'Université de Bruxelles.

Perelman, C., & Olbrechts-Tyteca, L. (1969). *The new rhetoric: A treatise on argumentation*. Notre Dame/London: University of Notre Dame Press.

Petty, R.E., & Cacioppo, J.T. (1981). *Attitudes and persuasion: Classic and contemporary approaches*. Dubuque, IA: Wm. C Brown.

Petty, R.E., & Cacioppo, J.T. (1986). *Communication and persuasion: Central and peripheral routes to attitude change*. New York: Springer.

Pole, N. (1981). Part/whole fallacies. *Informal Logic Newsletter, 3*(3), 11–13.

Popper, K.R. (1972). *Objective knowledge: An evolutionary approach*. Oxford: Clarendon Press.

Popper, K.R. (1974). *Conjectures and refutations. The growth of scientific knowledge* (5th ed.). London: Routledge & Kegan Paul.

Rescher, N. (1961). On the logic of presupposition. *Philosophy and Phenomenological Research, 21*, 521–527.

Rescher, N. (1964). *Introduction to logic*. New York: St Martin's Press.

Rescher, N. (1977). *Dialectics: A controversy-oriented approach to the theory of knowledge*. Albany: State University of New York Press.

Rescher, N. (1980). *Induction. An essay on the justification of inductive reasoning*. Oxford: Blackwell.

Robinson, R. (1971a). Arguing from ignorance. *The Philosophical Quarterly, 21*, 97–108.

Robinson, R. (1971b). Begging the question. *Analysis, 31*, 113–117.

Rowe, W.L. (1962). The fallacy of composition. *Mind, 71*, 87–92.

Sadock, J.M. (1974). *Toward a linguistic theory of speech-acts*. New York: Academic Press.

Sanders, R.E. (1980). Principles of relevance: A theory of the relationship between language and communication. *Communication and Cognition, 13*(1), 77–97.

Sanford, D.H. (1972). Begging the question. *Analysis, 32*, 197–199.

Schopenhauer, A. (1970). Eristische Dialektik [Eristic Dialectics]. In *Der Handschriftliche Nachlass* (Vol. 3). Frankfurt a.M.: Waldemar Kramer.

Scriven, M. (1976). *Reasoning*. New York: McGraw-Hill.

Searle, J.R. (1969). *Speech acts. An essay in the philosophy of language*. Cambridge: Cambridge University Press.

Searle, J.R. (1979). *Expression and meaning. Studies in the theory of speech acts*. Cambridge: Cambridge University Press.

Siegel, H. (1987). *Relativism refuted. A critique of contemporary epistemological relativism*. Dordrecht: Reidel.

Siegel, H. (1988). *Educating reason. Rationality, critical thinking and education*. New York: Routledge.

Simons, H.W. (1976). *Persuasion: Understanding, practice and analysis*. Reading, MA: Addison-Wesley.

Sperber, D., & Wilson, D. (1986). *Relevance: Communication and cognition*. Cambridge, MA: Harvard University Press.

Sproule, J.M. (1980). *Argument. Language and its influence*. New York: McGraw-Hill.

Stalnaker, R.C. (1977). Pragmatic presuppositions. In A. Rogers, B. Wall, & J.P. Murphy (Eds.), *Proceedings of the Texas conference on performatives, presuppositions and implicatures*. Arlington, VA: Center for Applied Linguistics.

Sykes, M. (1985). Discrimination in discourse. In T.A. van Dijk (Ed.), *Handbook of discourse analysis* (Vol. 4, pp. 83–101). London: Academic Press.

Thomas, S.N. (1986). *Practical reasoning in natural language* (3rd ed.). Englewood Cliffs, NJ: Prentice-Hall.

Toulmin, S.E. (1958). *The uses of argument*. Cambridge: Cambridge University Press.

Toulmin, S.E. (1976). *Knowing and acting. An invitation to philosophy*. New York: MacMillan.

Tracy, K. (1982). On getting point: Distinguishing "issues" from "events," an aspect of conversational coherence. *Communication Yearbook, 5*, 219–301.

Walton, D.N. (1984). *Logical dialogue-games and fallacies*. Lanham: University Press of America.

Walton, D.N. (1985a). Are circular arguments necessarily vicious? *American Philosophical Quarterly, 22*, 263–274.

Walton, D.N. (1985b). *Arguer's position. A pragmatic study of ad hominem attack, criticism, refutation and fallacy*. Westport, CT: Greenwood Press.

Walton, D.N. (1987a). The ad hominem argument as an informal fallacy. *Argumentation, 1*, 317–331.

Walton, D.N. (1987b). *Informal fallacies*. Amsterdam/Philadelphia: John Benjamins.

Walton, D.N. (1988a). Burden of proof. *Argumentation, 2*, 233–254.

Walton, D.N. (1988b). Question-asking fallacies. In M. Meyer (Ed.), *Questions and questioning* (pp. 195–221). Berlin: Walter de Gruyter.

Walton, D.N. (1989a). *Informal logic. A handbook for critical argumentation*. Cambridge: Cambridge University Press.

Walton, D.N. (1989b). *Question-reply argumentation*. New York: Greenwood.

Walton, D.N. (1989c). Reasoned use of expertise in argumentation. *Argumentation, 3*(1), 59–73.

Walton, D.N., & Batten, L.M. (1984). Games, graphs, and circular arguments. *Logique et Analyse, 106*, 133–164.

Wenzel, J.W. (1980). Perspectives on argument. In J. Rhodes & S. Newell (Eds.), *Proceedings on the Summer Conference on Argumentation* (pp. 112–133). Annandale, VA: SCA.

Wenzel, J.W. (1987). *Argument and critical practices*. Unpublished contribution to the Fifth SCA/AFA Conference on Argumentation.

Wenzel, J.W. (1989). Reflections on the revolution in Willard's theory of argument. In B.E. Gronbeck (Ed.), *Spheres of argument. Proceedings of the Sixth SCA/AFA Conference on Argumentation* (pp. 303–308). Annandale, VA: Speech Communication Association.

Wenzel, J.W. (1990). Three perspectives on argument. Rhetoric, dialectic, logic. In R. Trapp & J. Schuetz (Eds.), *Perspectives on argumentation. Essays in honor of Wayne Brockriede* (pp. 9–26). Prospect Heights, IL: Waveland.

Willard, C.A. (1983). *Argumentation and the social grounds of knowledge*. Tuscaloosa: The University of Alabama Press.

Willard, C.A. (1989). *A theory of argumentation*. Tuscaloosa: University of Alabama Press.

Windes, R.R., & Hastings, A.C. (1969). *Argumentation and advocacy*. New York: Random House.

Wisse, J. (1989). *Ethos and pathos from Aristotle to Cicero*. Amsterdam: Hakkert.

Wittgenstein, L. (1953). *Philosophical investigations*. (G.E.M. Anscombe, Trans.). New York: MacMillan.

Woods, J. (1988). Buttercups, GNP's and quarks: Are fallacies theoretical entities? *Informal Logic, 10*(2), 67–76.

Woods, J., & Hudak, B. (1991). Verdi is the Puccini of music: Analogical characterization. *Synthese*.

Woods, J., & Walton, D. (1982a). *Argument: The logic of the fallacies*. Toronto: McGraw-Hill Ryerson.

Woods, J., & Walton, D. (1982b). The *petitio*: Aristotle's five ways. *Canadian Journal of Philosophy, 12*, 77–100.

Woods, J., & Walton, D. (1989). *Fallacies. Selected papers 1972–1982*. Dordrecht/Providence: Foris/Berlin: Mouton de Gruyter. PDA 9.

# Author Index

## H



## I



## J



## K



## L



## M



## N



## O



## P



## R

## S



## T



## U



## V



## W

# Subject Index

## D



## E

## Q



## R



## S

## T



## U



## V



## W



## Z

CPSIA information can be obtained
at www.ICGtesting.com
Printed in the USA
FSOW02n2103050217
30447FS

9 780805 810691